THOMAS GRAY: HIS LIFE AND WORKS

Les Sources Françaises de Goldsmith
(Prix Bordin of the Académie Française)
The Early Life of J.-J. Rousseau
Earth of the Tarentines: A Novel
Animal Poetry in French and English Literature
The Italian Influence in English Poetry
The Paradise of Travellers
Oliver Goldsmith: His Life and Works

THOMAS GRAY
From a painting by Benjamin Wilson

THOMAS GRAY:
His Life and Works

by A. L. LYTTON SELLS

Assisted by IRIS LYTTON SELLS

> He is among poets what Cellini is among
> artists; ornament is less the accessory
> grace than the essential merit of his designs.
> Lord Lytton

London
GEORGE ALLEN & UNWIN
Boston   Sydney

First published in 1980

GEORGE ALLEN & UNWIN LTD
40 Museum Street, London WC1A 1LU

© Estate of A. L. Lytton Sells, 1980

British Library Cataloguing in Publication Data

Lytton Sells, Arthur Lytton
  Thomas Gray.
  1. Gray, Thomas, *b.1716* – Criticism and interpretation
  I. Lytton Sells, Iris
  821′.6   PR3503   79–41624

ISBN 0–04–928043–0

For Miccia

Typeset in 11 on 12 point Imprint by Bedford Typesetters Ltd
and printed in Great Britain
by William Clowes (Beccles) Ltd, Beccles and London

Author's Preface

It has been difficult to compose the present work, not, as in the case of *Oliver Goldsmith: His Life and Works* (1974), for want of information, but, on the contrary, because there is too much of it. There is the abundant correspondence of Gray and his friends, and the innumerable commentaries that have appeared on his poems. He wrote hundreds of letters, 'pour se désennuyer', as he explained; that is, as a means of occupying the unprofitable hours. He published only a small volume of fourteen poems, and nothing in prose. Successive editors have printed about twenty-three other poems in English, of which only three have any value; a few translations from Latin and Italian poets; and some twenty-five poems and fragments in Latin, of which perhaps six merit comparison with the verses in English. Even so, his total output occupies fewer than two hundred pages in the latest edition of his poems, and these include translations of the Latin verses, indications of the variants, and explanatory notes.

It is a paradox that a body of verse so slender should have excited from the outset a stream of comment so voluminous. Poets, essayists, and historians of literature have studied him. Johnson, Wordsworth, Coleridge, Hazlitt, Arnold, Newman, Leslie Stephen, Gosse, Saintsbury and very many others, have delivered judgements, often contradictory. There is a similar lack of unanimity among the papers read at the Thomas Gray Bicentenary Conference held some years ago at Carleton University. It is this state of critical uncertainty, and also the fact that no general study of Gray has appeared since Roger Martin published his *Essai* in 1934, that justify the present attempt at explanation and appraisal.

There are at least five questions which a critic of Gray should try to answer:

1 Why did Gray, while enjoying the advantage of an independent income, and the comfort and amenities of rooms in Cambridge

colleges, do so little in return? Why did he publish no more than a few verses?

2 What was Gray's character? Was he the delicate poet and fastidious scholar which he appeared to be to many contemporaries? Or, as Johnson asserted, 'dull in conversation . . . dull everywhere, dull in a new kind of way . . .', or, again, as Norton Nicholls declared, 'one of the greatest men who have ever existed'?

3 What is the value of his literary output?

4 Why has he remained well known *by name*? And why is the churchyard Elegy one of the most celebrated poems in the language and one of those most often quoted and parodied?

5 Why did Gray refuse the offer of being appointed Poet Laureate and decline that of an honorary doctorate from Aberdeen? Why, on the other hand, did he anxiously seek the chair of Modern History at Cambridge, and why, when he was appointed to it, did he not deliver a single lecture or publish a single article?

The answer to the second question would throw light on the first and the last. Gray's character emerges clearly from his correspondence. The poems enable one to guess at some of its aspects and the letters confirm and amplify the image which emerges from the poems.

A verdict on the merit of the poems will of course depend on the taste and knowledge of the critic. How – he will be asked – does the Elegy (granting that this poem is considered the best of Gray's verses) stand in relation to the best poems of, say, Wordsworth and Keats?

Gray's character, observed above, emerges from a study of his letters. *The Correspondence of Gray, Walpole, West and Ashton*, edited by Dr and Mrs Paget Toynbee (2 vols, 1915), and *The Correspondence of Thomas Gray*, edited by Paget Toynbee and Leonard Whibley (3 vols, 1935), are for this purpose indispensable. The late R. W. Ketton-Cremer's *Thomas Gray: a Biography* (1955) is a work of most scholarly and sensitive appreciation; in covering the same ground in Part One of the present work, I have thought fit to throw light on other aspects of his life and character.

The most recent edition of Gray's verses is *The Complete Poems* (Oxford, 1966), edited by H. W. Starr and J. R. Hendrickson. I have relied on this for the text and for some of the commentary.

It is not, however, an altogether satisfactory publication. The poems are divided between those which appeared in Gray's life-time and those which have been published subsequently. The notes are divided between footnotes to the text and explanatory notes at the end of the work. The editors, being American, are not perhaps the best qualified to comment on matters English – hence two or three minor errors of fact. Gray was not even well served by his first editor. William Mason seems to have discarded, if he ever possessed them, the letters which Gray received from his parents; although he published a few of those which he wrote to them, especially to his mother, from the Continent. In his *Memoirs of the Life and Writings of Mr Gray* (York, 1775) he included a bowdlerised version of the letter in which Gray had commented insultingly – indeed obscenely – on his, Mason's, intention of marrying; but he laid aside other letters to himself, presumably because he thought them too indecent. They have appeared in editions by the Rev. John Mitford and his successors. In respect of Gray's verses, Mason decided to publish 'The Candidate', while omitting the last couplet which Walpole thought unfit for young women to see; but he destroyed the 'Satire on the Duke of Newcastle going to Hanover' – which leaves one with the impression that this was equally unfit. Recent editors have printed the most trivial fragments, such as the 'Satire on the Heads of Houses', which is neither clever nor funny – and certainly a strange production for an aspirant to a professorship.

For the study of Gray's Latin poems I have been indebted to the learning and advice of Professor Gavin Townend, of the Department of Latin in Durham University. As Gray's favourite holiday resort was Dr Wharton's Durham home at Old Park, some knowledge of the social and economic life of eighteenth-century Durham has been called for, and in this matter I have been greatly assisted by Dr David Reid and Dr C. W. Gibby.

On the other hand, I have enjoyed the advantage of having lived for long periods both in Cambridge and Durham and so of having a first-hand acquaintance with both regions. Undertaking the present work with no great previous knowledge of Gray, and very little knowledge of his verse, I have been able to approach him with an open mind. My wife has helped to keep me informed of much critical comment on Gray and has pointed out many of his borrowings, not noted by previous annotators. She has read the manuscript and amended it where necessary. In certain cases of new material, she has collaborated to the point of contributing whole passages to the text. I should have missed much of the latest critical work on Gray if Dr Ian Jack, of Pembroke College, Cambridge, had not very kindly lent me the symposium of papers which were read at the Gray Conference at Carleton University and published in 1974. To the Library of Durham University, and in particular to the kindness of Mrs H. Guy, I have been indebted for many facilities; while the Cambridge University Library, where I was able to study for many weeks, has supplied me with books and illustrations which I could not have found elsewhere. It is a pleasure in this matter to acknowledge the courtesy of Mr J. C. T. Oates, the Rare Books Librarian, and the helpfulness of his assistants.

Contents

PART ONE

The Life

CHAPTER 1

Cornhill and Eton: 1716–1734[1]

When Thomas Gray was born in 1716, England had recently emerged from a period of revolutionary change which had been generally acceptable to public opinion. Accession to the Throne by the Elector of Hanover, whose indifference to his subjects was coolly reciprocated, had left the Whig oligarchy in effective possession of power. The County members were nearly all Whigs, while control of the House of Commons was consolidated by the purchase of boroughs and by winning the support of the mercantile classes through a policy of peace and free trade. The oligarchs used their power with wise moderation. They stood for religious tolerance. To mulct or torture Catholics was now to appear barbarous and absurd.

Anything akin to religious zeal was, however, discouraged. The memory of the Civil War, which had been as much a religious as a political conflict, was too terrible for a government to act otherwise. The national Church had lapsed into a state of easygoing quiescence which suited the needs of the age. The clergy in general, the episcopate in particular, felt that Christianity was better defended by reason than by 'enthusiasm'. 'Enthusiasm' indeed had become as abhorrent to the English as to the French. All this was very reasonable, very prosaic, well fitted to promote contentment, but not to inspire poetry.

However solid their majorities in Parliament, the Whigs could hardly have retained power for fifty years without – at the beginning – the political genius of Robert Walpole. In the first ministry (1714–16), ostensibly under Lord Stanhope, he shared actual power with Lord Townshend. In 1721 he returned to office as First Lord of the Treasury, and remained the virtual ruler of Britain until forced to resign in 1742. His success was due to the common sense which endeared him to all classes, except the irreconcilable country squires; but, above all, to a sound financial policy and encouragement of the export trade. He maintained peace with France. In 1716 Alberoni's aggressive Spanish policy had led Britain, France and the Netherlands to form a Triple Alliance which was soon, by the accession of the Emperor, to be transformed into a Quadruple.

Under Walpole the nation quickly became wealthy, comfortable and contented. Many of the great landowners built themselves mansions in the Italian style and had their parks and gardens laid out by Kent and Brown, nicknamed 'Capability'. These survived under private ownership until the days of heavy estate duties.

Population had begun to increase rapidly in the countryside and in the industrial cities of the Midlands and the north; but not in London, which was unhealthy in the extreme. The factories along the Thames and the Fleet Ditch poured waste and offal into the river, and filled the air with a pall of smog which obscured the sun for days on end. Small wonder if the death-rate exceeded the birth-rate.

Such was the England, and the London, into which Thomas Gray was born on 26 December 1716.

He was unfortunate in his father. Philip Gray was a scrivener, a sort of money-broker, and at this time a man of means. In 1709 he had married Dorothy Antrobus, a milliner, and she and her sister Mary had then moved into Gray's house in Cornhill. This contained a shop where they carried on their business, paying Dorothy's husband £40 a year for the privilege. Philip Gray was subject to intermittent fits of insanity when he would beat, kick and insult his wife – treatment which she endured for many years, mainly for the sake of her surviving child. Twelve children were born of this marriage and, of these, eleven children died soon after birth, apparently of 'suffocation'. Dorothy saved the life of her fifth child, the future poet, by opening one of his veins with her scissors.

In his *Essai sur Thomas Gray* Professor Roger Martin has subjected the poet to the most searching analysis so far attempted. He examined the Philip Gray 'case' and the Thomas Gray 'case' in the light of the best treatises on psychiatry available,[2] especially the works of Dr A. Hesnard. He consulted Dr Hesnard personally, and they concluded that Thomas Gray was the child of an alcoholic, irritable and jealous, and subject to gout and arthritis.

Hence a disastrous heredity, the effects of which appear to have pursued the poet throughout his life. There seems little doubt that they affected both his character and his work.

The portrait of Thomas Gray as a boy of about fourteen, now in the Fitzwilliam Museum at Cambridge, goes far to bear out Dr Hesnard's diagnosis.[3] The head is abnormally large by contrast with the emaciated body and slender legs. To the effects of heredity must be added the influence of environment. Few households can have been so unhappy. The child must at times have witnessed his father's treatment of his mother, and such scenes may partly explain the melancholy habitual with him and also, perhaps, his aversion for marriage. If, as seems likely, he witnessed the death of some of the younger children, this familiarity with the spectacle of death would account for his macabre imagination, and, on the other hand, for the hard-heartedness which he displayed on the occasion of the trial of the Scottish lords and, much later, at the time of Dr Long's unseemly burial.

Philip Gray clearly suffered from a sense of moral inferiority as regards his wife, whose gentleness enraged him; and from a sense of social inferiority, as regards her brothers, of whose influence he was violently jealous. Robert and William Antrobus were assistant masters at Eton College. In 1725 they offered to find a place for young Gray at Eton. Philip Gray refused to contribute to the expenses, but Dorothy agreed to pay the fees; and so in 1725 Thomas Gray moved from Cornhill to the pleasant riverside college. From this time until 1734 he experienced the happiest years of his life.

Eton then offered the best education in England for those boys who cared to take advantage of it. But it was a sort of Liberty Hall. Many of the boys amused themselves by fighting the townsfolk and river-men, and making amends by handing out largesse. Now and then the school intervened and offenders were flogged. There were no organised games. Eton was a school for initiative; a preparation for life in the world for young men who had enough character to adapt themselves to it.

Thomas Gray 'entered Eton as an Oppidan, and was placed low down in the Second Form'.[4] He was not apparently subject to any bullying.[5] R. W. Ketton-Cremer, in *Thomas Gray, A Biography*, thought that Robert Antrobus probably kept an eye on the boy. He taught him a certain amount of botany and expressed the hope that he would study for the medical profession; on condition of his doing so, he bequeathed him his books on the subject.[6] In 1726 William Antrobus had left Eton for a living in Northamptonshire, while Robert died in 1730. But in that year an event of importance for Gray took place.

By one of those happy chances that often occur at school or university, Gray fell in with three other boys whose tastes for reading and poetry were similar to his own: the Honourable Horatio Walpole, a younger son of Sir Robert; Richard West, son of a former Lord Chancellor of Ireland; and Thomas Ashton, whose father was a schoolmaster at Lancaster. These boys, whose ages ranged from about twelve to fourteen, felt no attraction for the rough sports to which most of the youngsters were addicted. They formed a 'quadruple alliance' in imitation of the European alliance of 1718, and devoted themselves to the study of Latin and the practice of composing Latin verses. In this last exercise Gray and West were to become proficient. Students were apparently encouraged to insert in their verses choice expressions from Virgil, Horace and others, and Gray later followed a similar practice with regard to English and other poets, in composing his English poems. Greek also was taught at Eton, and apparently a certain amount of French. Gray and his friends had some knowledge of the French romances of the seventeenth century. Nor was English poetry neglected.

As often among schoolboys, they adopted nicknames. Walpole, a good-looking boy, was Céladon, the hero of Honoré d'Urfé's *Astrée*; West was Favonius, the mild west wind; Orosmades (a variation of Oromasdes, the Persian deity) was Gray's nickname; while Ashton figured as Almanzor, a character in Dryden's *The Conquest of Granada*.[7]

Something is known of their characters and physique at this time. Walpole, who had nearly died when a child, is described as 'pale and fragile', but 'vivacious'. Gray's health, though never robust, had greatly improved; he gave no sign of the various maladies which were later to afflict him. West's father had died when the boy was only nine. His mother, a daughter of Bishop Burnet, was not sympathetic, and her son's home life was not a happy one. Gifted as a poet in Latin and English, West was said to versify in his sleep, and was so absent-minded that in the dormitory he would sometimes snuff a neighbour's candle by mistake for his own.[8] He was the gentlest and most lovable of the four.

The 'quadruple alliance' was not exclusive. Thanks to Horace Walpole, Gray met other Eton boys: George and Frederick Montagu, the Hon. Francis Seymour Conway and Henry Seymour Conway, cousins of Walpole; and William Cole, who later became Rector of Milton near Cambridge – a frequent correspondent of Gray's in later years. It is not known where Gray spent his holidays; sometimes perhaps in Cornhill. But here the situation was going from bad to worse. Philip Gray, who was neglecting his business, had been secretly building an expensive country house in Essex. One day he threatened his wife that he would 'ruin himself to undo her and his only son'. Finally he ordered her and her sister to leave his house by a specified date. In 1734 Dorothy was envisaging a legal separation and then, or in 1735, consulted Dr Audley, a lawyer, who had been at Peterhouse with her brother Robert. Audley could not hold out much hope: the judge might decide against her.[9] But the steps which Dorothy had taken seem to have scared Philip, and thereafter his behaviour improved. Dorothy and Mary remained in their Cornhill home.

In 1734, when he was seventeen, Thomas Gray went up to Cambridge. There was then, and still is, a close connexion between Eton and King's College. Henry VI, 'the murthered saint' as Gray called him, had founded King's College the year after his foundation of Eton. And, generally speaking, Eton boys tended to go to Cambridge, where the Eton Club foregathered at the Mitre. However, as Robert Antrobus had been a Fellow of Peterhouse, it was natural that his nephew should be entered at that college; while Ashton and Walpole went to King's. West entered Christ Church, Oxford, in the following year. Gray missed Eton sadly. At Eton,

> Where once my careless childhood stray'd,
> A stranger yet to pain!

he had been happy.

CHAPTER 2

Peterhouse: 1734–1737[1]

Gray's response to Cambridge was to take an immediate dislike to the place. After going into residence as a pensioner on 9 October 1734, he was awarded a Bible Clerkship of £10 a year and a Cosin Scholarship. In 1735 he received in exchange for the Clerkship a Hale Scholarship, which was worth a little more.

He thought nothing of the town, which was 'shaped like a spider'; he thought even less of the dons. Yet Peterhouse, the oldest of the colleges, had a handsome little court and chapel; while the Gibbs Building at King's and the fine Senate House had both been erected by 1730. The streets, however, were unpaved and, in consequence, very muddy in winter; the Cam had not yet been embanked and cleared of rushes. In a letter of 31 October to Walpole, who had not yet come up, he gives a minute description of the ceremony of admission, and explains that each college has its own customs:

> . . . what passes for Wit in one, would not be understood if it were carried to another: thus the Men of Peter-house, Pembroke and Clare-hall of course must be Tories; those of Trinity, Rakes; of King's, Scholars; of Sidney, Wigs; of St John's, Worthy men & so on . . . there are 5 ranks in the University, subordinate to the Vice-Chancellor, who is chose annually: there are Masters, Fellows, Fellow-Commoners, Pensioners, & Sizers; the Masters of Colleges are twelve grey-hair'd Gentlefolks, who are all mad with Pride; the Fellows are sleepy, drunken, dull, illiterate Things; the Sizers are Graziers Eldest Sons, who come to get good Learning, that they may be all Archbishops of Canterbury: these 2 last orders [Pensioners and Sizars] are qualified to take Scholarships, one of which your humble Serv.[t] has had given him.

Gray thus sums up the university after residing there for less than a month. The caricature contains a few grains of truth. He adds that Ashton had offered to introduce him to the Eton wits at the Mitre, but that he had no desire to 'go abroad', since his own room is so 'hugeous . . . that little i is quite lost in it'. To travel from the bed to the door was quite a journey, he writes.

Walpole responded by sending a prescription for 'spirit of ridicule' which the apothecary is to make up; and on 17 November Gray replied in a letter to 'Nurse Walpole':

With care   To mie Nuss att London   Present
                                                These

Carridge pade.

Honner'd Nurse
This comes to let you know, that I am in good health, but that I should not have been so, if it had not been for your kind promise of coming to tend me yourself . . .

He complains of a drinking party in which he had been 'pent up in a room' with thirty men 'below the meanest People you could even form an idea of', drinking and smoking, while Gray was 'deafened with their unmeaning roar'. He continues with allusions to Shakespeare and to Wycherley's *The Plain Dealer*; describes the impudence of the apothecary's apprentice who had been given the 'prescription'; and loads the apprentice with abuse as an 'ill-begotten, pocky, rascally, damned Son of a Bitch', and concludes from 'Your ever-dutiful & . . . most loving God-daughter – Pru: Orosmades'.

This mixture of childishness, learning and vulgarity betrays clearly enough the son of Philip Gray.

What Walpole thought of the letter is not known, except that he erased one word and cut out certain pieces of it. Orosmades wrote to Céladon, and continued to write, about once every week. Walpole certainly replied, at least twice in all. Gray was at this time, and for a few more years, infatuated with Walpole; while he neglected West who was in real need of diversion. Was there, in all this, an unconscious *arrière-pensée*? Through his friendship with Walpole, he may have hoped that Sir Robert would provide him with an agreeable sinecure. This was definitely Ashton's motive for courting Sir Robert's son. Ketton-Cremer observes that, after Gray's estrangement from the latter, he, Gray, 'could no longer hope that the Walpole influence . . . would now be exerted for his benefit'. West, on the other hand, though of a far higher social position than Gray, enjoyed no power of patronage. One observes that Horace Walpole invited West to Sir Robert's hunting-lodge in Richmond Park – as he was never to invite Gray, so far as is known – and that Sir Robert sat between the two young men and listened to them; and that Walpole kept in touch with West, who was neglected by Gray.

On 8 December Gray enclosed in a letter to Walpole some verses supposedly written by the ghost of John Dennis, the critic, who had died in the previous January. He has now returned 'from the Elysian Scene'.

> I reascend: in Atropos' despight
> Restored to Celadon, & upper light.

He describes his experiences in the nether-world, where people and places are ghostly replicas of those on earth:

> Here Spirit-Beaux flutter along the Mall,
> And shadows in disguise scale o'er ye Iced Canal

Gray, taking over the pen, concludes: 'There never was so faithful friend . . . as Orozmades to his Celadony.'

This letter suggests that Gray was obsessed with visions of death and mortality, and, in effect, the college adjoined the graveyard of Little St Mary's. The next letter to survive, which probably dates from 28 December and a part of which has been torn off, makes this a certainty. It is headed: 'From St Peter's Charnelhouse', and begins: 'Dear Dimidium meae'.[2] Gray is now dead; but Walpole's letter has so diverted him as to make every nail in his coffin

> start with laughing . . . On the 26th Instant at . . . midnight, being a hard frost; I had wrapped myself up in my Shroud very snugg and warm; when in comes your letter, which . . . made me stretch my skeleton-jaws in such a horse-laugh, that all the dead

pop'd up their heads . . . but to see the frowzy Countenances of
the Creatures especially one old Lady-Carcase, that . . . would
needs tell me, that I was a very uncivil Person to disturb a
Woman of her Quality, that did me the honour to live so near
me . . .

and more in a similar vein, and worse. To hear, towards New
Year's Day, that the more a corpse stirred, the more it would
stink, in a letter signed 'your friend the Defunct', would have led
most people to suppose the writer not quite sane. One wonders
what Gray had written on the leaf of the letter which has been
torn off; and also what Walpole thought of it.

In an earlier letter to Walpole, of uncertain date, but probably
written on 23 December, Gray writes: 'sure West is as much
improved as he says Plato is' – which suggests that Gray or
Walpole had heard from West. The news had probably come from
Walpole, because Gray had first written 'you say' and changed it
to 'he says'. If 'Plato' was the name they had adopted for William
Cole,[3] it is odd that Gray did not know about his 'improvement',
since Cole, an acquaintance of Eton days, was then at Clare Hall.

Gray's next letter, apparently written on 6 January 1735, is
addressed

To the faithful Miradolin
third son of the Vizier-azem.
Continuance of Health & long life.

It is full of allusions to G.-B. Marana's *Espion turc*, and is dated
at the end: 'The last day of the Ramadan, 6th of ye 1st Moon'.

On 12 January he has evidently heard that Walpole, who was
staying in Sir Robert's house in St James's Square, had been
seeing plays and operas. He feels envious, because in Cambridge
'everything is so tediously regular, so samish, that I expire for
want of a little variety'. Seven ensuing letters to Walpole are
written in a similar vein. Gray has been 'living' on Walpole's
letters '& a few mince-pyes'. But Walpole came up in March,
entering King's, which had been Sir Robert's college, as a fellow-
commoner. In this way three members of the 'quadruple alliance'
were reunited, together with the mysterious 'Plato', and their

gaiety did something to relieve Gray from the tedium of Peter-house. His subsequent letters contain much less incoherence and showing-off of miscellaneous knowledge.

Not that serious work was neglected. Gray and Walpole took lessons in Italian from Signor Piazza, and Gray was obliged to attend college lectures on logic and probably on mathematics, for which he had no bent.

It was in June 1735 that West went into residence at Christ Church. He felt his loneliness keenly and complained that his Cambridge friends neglected him; but on 9 November Walpole wrote to him: 'Orosmades and Almanzor are just the same . . . Plato improves every day . . .'. But he adds that there is now no quadruple alliance: '. . . that was a happiness which I only en-joyed when you was[4] at Eton'. In December Gray apologised to West for having written only once, alleging the monotony of his days. 'You need not doubt', he added, 'of having a first row in the front box of my little heart . . .'.

Gray had returned to Cornhill in July, and so had missed seeing West in London. He had not yet realised that he had more in common with West than with Walpole. In deference to his mother's wishes that he should study for the Bar, he had his name entered at the Inner Temple, with a view to the day when he would come down from Cambridge with a degree – as she fondly hoped. Back at Peterhouse late in October, he returned home in January 1736 when, as one may surmise, peace had been established at the house in Cornhill.[5] However that may be, Philip Gray received a shock in the spring when his sister, Sarah, died, leaving the bulk of her property, consisting of houses and tenements in London, to her nephew Thomas. The latter was of course elated. He could now supplement his commons with daintier dishes from the college kitchen; and, above all, he found himself in possession of an independent income. But may it not have been a misfortune in disguise? He had no desire to work for a degree or, as his mother wished, to adopt a profession. Inveigh as he might against the 'laziness' of Cambridge, it suited him down to the ground.

He spent the long vacation with an elder sister of his mother's, who was married to a Mr Jonathan Rogers and was living in a country house at Burnham. Rogers had been a great sportsman in his day, riding to hounds and living like a lord. But abundant food, wine and liquor had by now confined him to his chair with gout –

'th' inevitable end', as one might say. He had little patience with young Gray who was mooning about the fields when he ought to have been hunting on horseback. But Gray never had the courage, or possibly the stamina, to get on a horse. He preferred to wander about with a volume of Virgil in his hand, watching the birds and butterflies and absorbing the impressions of the countryside. He was always to be at heart a country man.

Walpole's heart, on the contrary, was in London. Life in the family mansion in Norfolk did not appeal to him. His vacations, and even part of the terms at Cambridge, were spent at Sir Robert's house in Arlington Street, and probably at times in Downing Street. He also saw his mother, who adored him. It is one of the most pleasing features of his character that he remained on excellent terms with his parents, although they were living estranged from each other. Sir Robert spent much of his time with his mistress, while Lady Walpole had a circle of her own. There were never any vulgar recriminations or public éclat.

Immersed though he was in the political activities of the Prime Minister, Horace Walpole found time to write to West, who had remained at Oxford in the summer, pacing along Addison's Walk at Magdalen and recalling the happy days of the 'quadruple alliance'. West replied in August: 'My dearest Walpole: Yesterday I received your lively – agreeable – gilt-epistolary – parallelogram . . .', and enclosed the manuscript of a poem he had composed, an 'Ode – To Mary Magdalene'.

From Cambridge, towards 10 October, Walpole wrote to Gray, who had lingered in Cornhill, a letter 'in the style of Addison's Travels' in Italy. It was an account of his own journey up to Cambridge in which he had substituted Latin names for all the towns or villages he passed through. Thus Littlebury is Parvulum; Bone Bridge, Pont Ossoria; Newmarket, 'Nuovo Foro [the Novum Forum of Jockius], where are held the greatest races in all Italy. The inhabitants are wonderfully fond of horses, and to this day tell you most surprising stories of one Looby, a Boltognian. I saw a book dedicated to the head of that family, intitled *A Discourse on the Magnanimity of Bucephalus*, and of the Duke of Boltogne's Horse Looby.' Looby, who belonged to the Duke of Bolton and had previously been a Newmarket winner, was on this occasion 'magnanimous' enough to let Mr Panton's Conqueror beat him and win 300 guineas for his master. After three days at 'Nuovo

Foro', Walpole stopped at the Palace of Delfini (Lord Godolphin's house) on a 'barren mountain' called Gog, opposite another called Magog – dangerous precipices which 'occasioned the famous verse, "Incidit in Gogum qui vult vitare Magogon" ' (from 'Incidit in Scyllam qui vult vitare Charibdim'). And so at last he reached Pavia and its University (Cambridge), called Pavia because of a circumstance which escaped the learned Addison, namely that its streets are not paved: *'Pavia a non pavendo*, as *Lucus a non lucendo'*.

Whether or not these undergraduate witticisms appeal to modern readers, they marked Horace Walpole as destined to become the wittiest letter writer of eighteenth-century England.

Gray, on his return to Cornhill from Burnham, wrote an unseemly letter to the Rev. George Birkett, his tutor at Peterhouse, requesting him to pay any of his bills that might have come in, such as Signor Piazza's. Birkett was justifiably annoyed. Unfortunately he was drunk at the time, and made two futile efforts to reply. At last, as the effects of liquor wore off, good humour prevailed; and when Gray returned for the Michaelmas Term he had nothing really worse to face than the need to reimburse his tutor.

In other respects, however, the prospect did not appeal to him. His interests still lay in classical studies, and these did not flourish at Cambridge. Freshmen were expected already to know Latin, and most of them did. Mathematics took precedence of other subjects, although there was as yet no mathematical tripos or any other, the word 'tripos' being used simply to designate the thirty-three or thirty-four best students in the final examinations. The course for an arts degree required attendance at lectures or tutorials in logic, philosophy and mathematics, and these subjects were displeasing to Gray. The college, however, was so far indulgent as not to insist on his continuing these studies in the New Year. In December he wrote to West:

> You must know that I do not take degrees and, after this term, shall have nothing more of college impertinences to undergo . . . Surely it was of this place, now Cambridge, but formerly known by the name of Babylon, that the prophet spoke when he said: 'the wild beasts of the desert shall dwell there . . .' You see here is a pretty collection of desolate animals, which is verified

in this town to a tittle, and perhaps it may also allude to your habitation.

Is it possible that Gray considered himself so superior that he ought not to be subjected to the usual disciplines? It is difficult, in other respects, to account for so strange a diatribe. He had made it clear that he did not wish to read for a degree, but pensioners were not obliged to do so, unless they wished to take holy orders or compete for a fellowship. Gray was allowed to remain in the large room which he had described to Walpole, and the college may have had more than one reason for indulgence. The undergraduate body of pensioners and sizars was very small; the fellows and fellow-commoners outnumbered them. None of the fellows had any particular talent. A little later, and especially in the nineteenth century and in our own, Peterhouse was to produce men of the highest distinction. Meanwhile, in 1736, Gray was becoming known as one of the more competent Latinists among Cambridge undergraduates, and no doubt it was thought desirable to keep him.

CHAPTER 3

Gray, West and Walpole: 1737–1739[1]

Gray, for his part, was not inclined to take academic life seriously. He had entered his name at the Inner Temple; and West, as the son of an eminent lawyer, was destined also for the Temple. They intended to study together there, but both felt that the evil hour could be deferred. Gray had acquired a harpsichord and was learning to play it. During the Lent and Easter terms he read a great deal, mainly in English and French poetry and novels. He and Walpole had learned enough French at Eton to browse in the *Astrée* – whence Walpole's nickname. They were also familiar with Mademoiselle de Scudéry's novel, *Clélie, histoire romaine*, a sort of handbook for the guidance of lovers. In the *Carte du Tendre* – a map of the land – one could study the various pitfalls which a lover must avoid, not the least dangerous being 'the Sea of Indifference'. In the eighteenth century all this had of course become *vieux jeu*, except for learned and curious schoolboys. One now read, and Gray was probably reading, Marivaux's *Vie de Marianne*, a masterpiece of its kind, in which the minutiae of psychological realism were pushed to their limit. He probably also read the younger Crébillon's novels: these were short and pointed, and of a propriety more than dubious. The study of 'love', at a safe distance, was far more agreeable than the study of law close at hand. He found it no hardship to take lessons in Italian and so to peruse Tasso's *Gerusalemme liberata*.

Richard West, on the contrary, enjoyed few such diversions and apparently had no friends in Oxford to stimulate him. On 27 February 1737 he wrote to remind Walpole that it was a long time since he had heard from Cambridge. Gray had disparaged the place, but Oxford was no better:

I could tell you strange things of . . . men whose heads do grow beneath their shoulders. I have seen learning drest in old

frippery . . . I have seen Stupidity in the habit of Sense, like a
footman in the master's clothes; I have seen the phantom mentioned in the Dunciad, with a brain of feathers and a heart of
lead: it walks here, and is called Wit . . . .

He has been wishing to visit his friends at Cambridge, but is
'unwillingly obliged to follow . . . less agreeable engagements'.

These are not specified, but he was evidently feeling lonelier
than usual. His mother, under the influence of a certain Williams,
who had been her late husband's secretary, seems to have changed
towards him and was no longer sympathetic; and his health,
affected by incipient consumption, was now precarious. In June
he became very ill. Writing to Gray on 4 July, he speaks of having
scarcely recovered. He is recalling a melancholy elegy by Tibullus
(Book IV, No. 5) and has composed 'a more melancholy epistle . . .
to you & my friends at Cambridge'.

AD AMICOS

> While you, where Camus rolls his sedgy tide,
> Feel every joy, that friendship can divide:
> Now, as each art and science you explore,
> And with the ancient blend the modern lore,
> Studious to learn alone whate'er may tend
> To raise the Genius or the heart to mend . . .
> At me meantime (while e'en devoid of art
> These lines give back the image of my heart)
> At me the power, that comes or soon or late,
> Or aims, or seems to aim the dart of fate.

He foresees only too clearly that he has not long to live; but
concludes, referring to his friends:

> To them may these fond lines my name endear,
> Not from the Author but the Friend Sincere.

Of the three others, he felt most sympathy with Gray; but he
probably felt more respect for Walpole. It was, one conjectures,
Walpole's tactful friendship that was holding the 'quadruple
alliance' together. Thus, West's next letter, dated 12 July 1737,
was to Walpole at King's College:

To thee my thoughts magnetically roll,
My heart the needle is, and thine the pole.
Since thou art gone, no Company can please,
They rather show my Want, than give me ease. . . .

Feeling better, he continues on the same light note and ends by enclosing a charming English version of Horace's ode 'Ad Pyrrham'.

Gray had done little to cheer West in the past seven or eight months. In the previous December he had written about his attacks of 'the hyp' – by which he meant hypochondria, or melancholy: 'We must all submit to that wayward Queen.' On 22 August 1737 he wrote: 'Low spirits are my true & faithful companions.' However, he and West took comfort in the thought that in the following year they would share rooms in the Temple.

All his talk of melancholy – his careful distinction between leucocholy (white melancholy), his usual state, which was pleasant enough to live with, and melancholy (the real thing) – was probably exaggerated. If he had had work like one of the sizars, to clean his rooms, wait on the fellows, and so on, he would have had less time to dwell on his neurosis. For the present generation, it is not very easy to sympathise with the victims of eighteenth-century *ennui*.

From the academic point of view, the university year was a successful one. The authorities had selected Gray to compose the so-called tripos-verses, which would be printed and issued with the class-lists in March; and they had proposed as the subject: 'Luna est habitabilis'. Gray produced a fairly long poem in hexameters, in which he speculated as to what the moon-dwellers with their telescopes were thinking about us, and envisaged the possibility of aerial communication, and colonisation of the moon. This poem was something of a *tour de force*.

But if the university and the college were impressed, the fellow-commoners and pensioners were not interested. Taking note of his short, mincing steps and slightly effeminate manners, they dubbed him Miss Gray; without, however, otherwise annoying him. It was only in the 1750s that their successors were to prove a thorn in the flesh. Meanwhile, in 1737, he was making more acquaintances. He already knew John Clerke, a Peterhouse undergraduate, and William Cole, of Clare. But his principal connections were with members of Pembroke Hall, on the far side of the road: Thomas Wharton, a son of the Mayor of Durham, who was studying medicine, and the Rev. James Brown, a Fellow of the College. These were destined to become two of his dearest friends.

In this year Walpole lost his mother, to whom he had been greatly attached; and then, to make matters worse, Sir Robert very soon married his mistress. Horace, who was never to marry, tried to divert his thoughts by indulging in a flirtation; however, it did not go very far. Gray seemed to understand Walpole's situation and, without *arrière-pensée*, wrote a sympathetic letter, adding that he would like to divert himself in the same way. Unfortunately, he had neither the money nor the charm to please any woman. He felt like an 'ours mal léché'. And he concluded: 'Your faithful creature, Bruin'.

West left Oxford early in the New Year of 1738. In June he received from Gray a letter in Latin, with a Latin ode, inspired by Horace's 'Septimi, Gades', on the dire prospect facing both of them of becoming a 'toga'd advocate' amid a crowd of wrangling barristers. To this he added an 'Alcaic Fragment', which has been much admired, though it is not easy to understand. It was time for Gray to go down; but he had grown used to Cambridge life, which was inexpensive and easygoing. 'Cambridge', he wrote on 20 March, 'is very ugly, she is very dirty, and very dull; but I'm like a cabbage.' To be uprooted was painful. He returned in September to the house in Cornhill and probably remained there for some months. In December he wrote an amusing letter to West, relating that he had heard a 'hubbub of tongues' in his room, arising from his books which were all quarrelling with each other, books modern and ancient: Madame de Sévigné being jostled by Aristotle, Boileau contradicting Euclid, and so on. In the end Gray laughed so much that the books stopped talking.

And now there occurred something which neither Gray nor West had expected, and which put a stop to their plans of study in the Temple. Sir Robert Walpole, who was certainly aware of Horace's distress, the more so as he was fonder of Horace than of his elder sons, suggested that he could take a friend for a prolonged stay in France, beginning in Paris and then travelling in the provinces. The Prime Minister's son would have entry into the best society; he would improve his knowledge of the language, and also of the world. Horace was apparently left free to choose his companion; and, in view of recent events, it may not be entirely surprising that he chose Gray.

The venture was hazardous. Gray was never more than a bourgeois; and for a bourgeois and an aristocrat to spend a year or two in close companionship, and mainly in the society of aristocrats, was likely to put a strain on them. Walpole would have done better to invite West; though it is likely that West was not now strong enough to face the hardships of travel.

CHAPTER 4

France and Savoy: 1739[1]

The first few months were delightful. Leaving Dover on 29 March, they reached Calais in five hours. The sea was a little rough and Gray was sick. 'Calais . . . surpriz'd us agreeably.'[2] It was a very pretty town, utterly different from anything they had seen in England. The fact that snow was falling did not damp their interest. On the morning of the 30th they attended high mass and met an English nun; in the afternoon they left by post-chaise – a large vehicle drawn by three horses – for Abbeville. The journey to Paris could have been achieved in two days, since a post-chaise could cover eighty miles a day; but Walpole preferred to travel in a leisurely way and see the country. They slept the first night at Boulogne, where the English colony seemed to outnumber the French; they started early next morning for Montreuil. Gray described the dinner here as 'execrable'; but they 'supped and lodged pretty well' at Abbeville. Both young men agreed that the roads were admirable and the country pleasant and well tilled. They had passed few travellers. The cathedral at Amiens seemed to Gray what Canterbury must have looked like before the Reformation – or at least before the Commonwealth. Thousands of little statues adorned it; the stained-glass windows were exquisite.

They reached Paris on the Saturday, after lingering for a short time at the Abbey of Saint-Denis, where 'a jolly old Benedictine' showed them the treasures, the monuments of the Kings of France, various relics and jewels, and an onyx vase over five inches in breadth. In Paris they put up at the Hôtel du Luxembourg in the rue des Petits-Augustins, as it was then called. It is now that part of the rue Bonaparte which lies between the river and the rue Jacob.[3] Walpole's cousins, Lord Conway and his brother, with Robert, Lord Holdernesse, came to welcome them, and after supper stayed talking until the small hours. The following days were full of excitement. On Sunday Lord Holdernesse invited them to a dinner at which they met a number of their countrymen, and also the famous Abbé Prévost, whom Gray described in a letter to West as 'author of the Cleveland, and several other pieces much esteemed'. Of *Manon Lescaut*, which had appeared in 1731, Gray seems to have had no knowledge. *Le Philosophe anglois, ou Histoire de Monsieur Cleveland, fils naturel de Cromwell*, which was to contain several volumes, had been begun about 1733, and the first volume or two had been translated. This, and the *Doyen de Killerine*, did more than any other novels to colour the popular French view of the Englishman as a being addicted to melancholy, and even finding pleasure in it. By 1739 Prévost had abandoned the amorous adventures and financial makeshifts which had involved him in so much trouble, including incarceration in the Gatehouse prison in London, and was leading the tranquil life of editor, or rather author, of *Le Pour et le Contre*, an important periodical.

After dinner Lord Holdernesse took his guests to a 'spectacle' called *Pandore* in the Palais des Tuileries, a show admirable only for the 'machinery'. On the following day they dined with the ambassador, Lord Waldegrave, and attended an opera, of which the scenes were unconnected, the singing bad, and everything absurd – according to Gray. He was however greatly impressed by the actors and actresses at the Théâtre Français, in the rue des Fossés-Saint-Germain, excellent both in tragedy and in comedy. In Destouches's *Le Philosophe marié* he especially admired F.-C. Grandval and Mademoiselle Quinault. But the splendid view along the Seine as seen from the Pont-Neuf, the swarms of people and carriages, and the churches and other monuments interested him as much. He does not appear to have met any French 'people of high quality' because one needed, in order to have the entrée of a fashionable house, to speak fluent French, and gamble for high stakes.

The two months of his and Walpole's stay in Paris were none the less very agreeable. Henry Conway acted everywhere as their guide. Towards 13 May they went to Versailles. The façade of the palace as approached from the town, which Gray called a 'front', he described as 'a huge heap of littleness'. The real, or 'garden', front was, however, 'magnificent'. He admired the marble 'basons' and the long 'bason of Apollo', flanked by forest trees and leading the eye away to the distant horizon. But everything was

too artificial for his taste, except the little palace of the Trianon,
which delighted him; as did Chantilly which they visited soon
afterwards.[4] On 17 May they paid a second visit to Versailles,
where they saw the royal family assembled, and they also saw nine
notables, including the Comte de Cambis, ambassador to the Court
of St James, invested with the Order of the Holy Spirit. In the
evening, Gray wrote, 'we walk by moonlight and hear the ladies
and the nightingales sing'.

On the 21st 'I saw Britannicus . . .; all the characters, particularly
Agrippina and Nero, done to perfection; to-morrow Phaedra and
Hippolytus'. Racine's *Britannicus*, in which Mademoiselle
Dumesnil played the role of Agrippina, left so strong an impression on Gray's mind that he afterwards attempted a sequel to it, in
blank verse. What he thought of *Phèdre*, a greater masterpiece, is
not recorded. He was probably more interested at this time in
Roman history than in the poetry of Greek mythology. They saw
L'Avare on 21 September, and *Le Cid* the next day, but Gray does
not mention them. It does not appear that he and Walpole met any
of the notable French writers of the time, apart from Prévost. He
tells West that they are making up for him a parcel of short plays
then on the stage, together with one of the younger Crébillon's
novels and the Abbé Bougeant's *Amusement philosophique sur le
langage des bêtes*.

Some ten days later they left for Rheims in the company of Henry
Conway, Walpole's favourite cousin. Both Walpole and Gray
corresponded with West and Ashton. West was to prove a model
of discretion; Ashton less so. Gray found Rheims far from unpleasant. Lord Conway being known there, the gentry received
them with great cordiality. Private homes and social assemblies
opened their doors; and one evening, in a private garden, they
enjoyed the gayest of parties, with an al fresco supper, followed by
singing, dancing and minuets which continued until four in the
morning. No one could have been more kindly and easygoing than
their hosts. Gray and Walpole worked hard at their French (one of
Sir Robert's main objects in arranging the tour), and conversation
with the natives did even more to improve their fluency. Gray was
anxious to see Provence, where he had probably heard of the
interesting Roman antiquities, but departure from Rheims was
delayed by the arrival of Selwyn and George Montagu, who were

close friends of Walpole. It is curious that neither Gray nor Walpole mentions the cathedral, one of the glories of Europe; nor did Gray, on many subsequent visits to Durham, appear to have been interested in its great cathedral and Norman castle.

The travellers left Rheims on 8 September and three days later reached Dijon, the ancient capital of the Dukes of Burgundy, 'one of the gayest and most agreeable little cities of France', as Gray later told his mother. From Dijon he wrote to his father, describing the splendour of the churches and palaces. Towards the 18th they reached Lyons with its pleasant suburbs and surrounding hills. Wishing to visit the Grande Chartreuse before they took leave of Conway in Geneva, they followed the route through Dauphiné, entering Sardinian territory at Pont Beauvoisin. After spending the night at Les Echelles, they set off early next morning for the steep ascent to the monastery, apparently on horseback. This must have been one of the rare occasions that Gray was on a horse; but where there's a will there's a way, and he was probably assisted. The Grande Chartreuse stands near the southern end of an isolated massif in the pre-Alps of Savoy. This excursion was to prove the highlight of Gray's experiences, and he described it three times, in a letter to his mother of 13 October; in his private journal; and in a letter to West, of 16 November, from Turin.

The way led up a narrow mule-track, cut out of the side of the precipice that overhangs the gorge of the Guier Mort, so-called because, after a rainless summer, it dries up. At this time it was in full spate, roaring over the boulders far below.

The best and most interesting description is inserted in a letter written by Walpole to West, begun probably at Les Echelles:

From a Hamlet among the Mountains of Savoy.

Sept. 28, 1739, N.S.

Precipices, mountains, torrents, wolves, rumblings, Salvator Rosa . . . I am to undergo many many transmigrations before I come to 'yours ever'. Yesterday I was a shepherd of Dauphiné; to-day an Alpine savage; tomorrow a Carthusian monk; and Friday a Swiss Calvinist. . . .

Resuming his letter on the 30th, from Aix-les-Bains, he mentions that an abbé has come to play chess with Conway, who had not accompanied them on their expedition:

We rode three leagues yesterday to see the Grande Chartreuse . . . The building is large and plain . . . they entertained us in the neatest manner, with eggs, pickled salmon, dried fish, conserves, cheese, butter, grapes and figs, and pressed us mightily to lie there . . . They desired us to set down our names in the list of strangers . . . But the road, West, the road! winding round a prodigious mountain, and surrounded with others, all shagged with hanging woods, obscured with pines or lost in clouds! Below, a torrent breaking through cliffs . . .! sheets of cascades forcing their silver speed down channelled precipices . . . Now and then an old foot-bridge, with a broken rail, a leaning cross, a cottage, or the ruin of an hermitage! This sounds too bombast and too romantic to one that had not seen it . . . Almost on the summit, upon a fine verdure, . . . stands the Chartreuse. We staid there two hours, rode back through this charming picture, wished for a painter, wished to be poets! Need I tell you we wished for you?[5]

Gray's description, written to West two months later, is more 'literary' and calculated.

On the following day they drove to Chambéry, spent the night at Aix-les-Bains and the following night at Annecy, reaching Geneva by noon on the morrow. Gray was impressed by the wealth, the military discipline and the cheerfulness of the inhabitants; and charmed by the beauty of the lake. He and the others took a boat round the shores, as far as Genevese territory extended, and at supper enjoyed part of an enormous trout, said to have weighed thirty-seven pounds. Taking leave on the morrow of Conway, who was staying on with friends, they returned to Lyons by a different route. Walpole here received a letter from his father, advising him to extend his tour to Italy instead of going to Provence. The prospect was more than pleasing. However, as bad weather had set in, and the passage of the Alps promised to be very wintry, they provided themselves 'with muffs, hoods . . . fur-boots and bear-skins'.

CHAPTER 5

Italy: 1739–1741[1]

On 18 November Gray sent West a disparaging picture of Turin and a brief account of the crossing of the Mont Cenis, which 'carries the permission mountains have of being frightful rather too far', he wrote, adapting a remark of Madame de Sévigné's.[2] The scene had scared him. He had been poring over his copy of Livy and had begun to read Silius Italicus. The visit to the Grande Chartreuse, on the other hand, had enchanted him, and his description of it, which will be cited later, has become famous. West, however, received full details of the Mont Cenis in a letter from Walpole of 11 November:

> So, as the song says, we are in fair Italy!... We were eight days in coming hither [to Turin] from Lyons; the four last in crossing the Alps... At the foot of Mont Cenis we were obliged to quit our chaise which was taken all to pieces and loaded on mules; and we were carried in low arm-chairs on poles... When we came to the top, behold the snows fallen!... We had twelve men and nine mules to carry us, our servants and baggage... the day before, I had a cruel accident... I had brought with me a little black spaniel, of King Charles's breed; but the prettiest, fattest, dearest creature! I had let it out of the chaise for the air, and it was waddling along close to the head of the horses, on the top of one of the highest Alps, by the side of a wood of firs. There darted out a young wolf, seized poor dear Tory by the throat, and, before we could possibly prevent it, sprung up the side of the rock and carried him off... the road was so narrow, that the servants that were behind could not get by the chaise to shoot him... it was but two o'clock, and broad sun-shine. It was shocking to see anything one loved run away with to so horrid a death...

We passed the Pas de Suze, where is a strong fortress on a

rock . . . and then, through a fine avenue of three leagues, we at
last discovered Turin . . .

'Tis by far one of the prettiest cities I have seen . . .

The death of Tory had taken place, not 'on the top of one of the
highest Alps' – for Walpole had not yet understood how high that
was – but on the road up the valley of the Arc to Lanslebourg,[3] at
the foot of the pass.

Gray and Walpole put up at the Auberge Royale and stayed for
about a week. Walpole paid his respects at Court; but both he and
Gray agreed that a comedy and a sort of tragedy entitled *Rappre-
sentazione d'un' anima dannata* were not worth seeing. A number
of Englishmen were in Turin, including Lord Lincoln and the
Rev. Joseph Spence, who was Professor of Poetry at Oxford. It is
curious that Gray does not mention the great Roman gate with its
high flanking walls. The onset of winter may partly account for his
jaundiced description of the city.[4]

Genoa, on the other hand, inspired him to such raptures as he
nowhere else expresses. His first sight of the Mediterranean; the
bay full of shipping; the tall palaces with their marble terraces
rising in tiers up the hillside; the cypresses, orange trees and lemon
trees – all this is described to West in one of the liveliest of his
letters:

We are fallen in love with the Mediterranean sea [he concludes],
and hold your lakes and your rivers in vast contempt. This is
'The happy country where huge lemons grow', as Waller says;
and I am sorry to think of leaving it in a week for Parma,
although it be
'The happy country where huge cheeses grow'.

A letter of 9 December to Mrs Gray, from Bologna, contains an
account of the journey from Genoa and an enthusiastic picture of
the Lombard plain, the broad, straight Via Emilia, the mulberry
and olive trees garlanded with trailing vines; and in Bologna the
streets lined with porticoes. From Gray's private journal, under
the date 28 November, one learns that the passage of the Trebbia
had especially interested the reader of Livy. On the west bank he
identified the place where the Roman general had encamped; on
the other bank, the site of the battle.[5] At Bologna Gray and

Walpole spent twelve days 'al Pelegrino'. Gray makes no mention of the Accademia di Belle Arti, which contains a fine collection of paintings by the seventeenth-century masters, the Caracci, Domenichino, Guido Reni and others, who were then more admired by English and French visitors than the great Venetians and Florentines of the cinquecento.

On the 15th they started to cross the Apennines. From the steep descent to the Val d'Arno the view of Florence delighted them. They were received by Horace Mann, the acting Resident, who lodged them in one of his houses and looked after them in every way. It is true that he had owed his appointment to Sir Robert Walpole, but he was himself a very kindly and agreeable person. He introduced them to the Prince de Craon, a good-natured old Frenchman who was acting as Regent in the Grand Duke's absence. He and the Princess invited them to supper and gave them to understand that they would be welcome any evening at the palace. They were also entertained by the Countess Suarez, who was the heart and soul of Florentine gaieties. Small wonder if they enjoyed themselves. Gray spent days in the Palazzo Pitti and the Uffizi, making detailed notes on the paintings and sculptures. He considered the Venus de' Medici 'a modern performance', and, as already observed, regarded the more recent painters as superior to Raphael, Andrea del Sarto and the Venetians.

Although Walpole in no way neglected the sights and the picture galleries, he wearied of spending so many hours in the latter: '. . . à force d'en avoir vu', he wrote to West, 'I have left off screaming Lord! this, and Lord! that . . .'. Most people can have a surfeit of picture galleries. A duel between a *cavaliere* and an Englishman offered a possible diversion, but they unfortunately missed seeing it. The real diversion was provided by the Carnival, to which Walpole abandoned himself whole-heartedly: '. . . all the morning one makes parties to the shops and coffee-houses, and all the evening to the operas and balls. Then I have danced, good Gods! how I have danced!' This joyful news is contained in one of the four letters which Walpole wrote to West between 24 January and 27 February 1740. On 15 January Gray had sent a few lines with some Latin verses; two letters, one of them in Italian, which Mason did not reprint; and on 12 March, to Wharton, a long, facetious account of the whole journey from Dover. On the 19th, in a letter to his mother, he announced the death of the Pope and added that he and Walpole were leaving in a few days' time for Rome. His letters contain no reference to the Carnival. He had been making minute catalogues of paintings and antiquities, covering scores of pages with his small handwriting. Walpole thought this rather too much of a good thing, while Gray evidently disapproved of Walpole's merrymaking.

They reached Rome, after a night at Sienna, on 26 March. In a long letter to his mother Gray relates how he had first seen the dome of St Peter's from thirty miles away and how they had entered the city by the Porta del Popolo. 'As high as my expectation was raised, I confess, the magnificence of this city infinitely surpasses it.' He had not yet seen 'his majesty of Great Britain', but had had a glimpse of his sons in the gardens of the Villa Borghese, little guessing that in a few years' time Charles Edward would make a daring attempt to regain the throne of his ancestors. The Cardinals were in conclave, but it was not expected that they would decide on a new pope until after Easter.

Walpole, for his part, was struck by the dire poverty of the Romans, a misery due to the mismanagement of the papal finances by Cardinal Corsini. The nobility were so impoverished that they had to live on the equivalent of eighteen pence a day. In an addition to the same joint letter, Gray described a visit to St Peter's and the spectacle of a man 'naked to the waist', lashing his back 'with a scourge filled with iron prickles'; Walpole 'fainted away' at the sight of it. This was in April. On 14 May they attended 'a great Assembly, at one of the Villas just out of the City'. All the English visitors were invited, as were 'Mr Stuard and his two sons', together with Lord Dunbar 'who wou'd be his Minister, if he had any Occasion for One. I meet him frequently', wrote Walpole '. . . & like him. He is very sensible, very agreeable and well bred.' A little later in the month they visited the Falls of the Anio at Tivoli, and the next day drove to Palestrina, returning to Rome by way of Lake Regillus. They also attended a reception at the Villa Patrizi, where La Diamantina, a famous virtuosa, 'played on the violin divinely, and sung [*sic*] angelically'. This was followed by a ball, while Gray 'sat in a corner, regaling [himself] with iced fruits, and other pleasant rinfrescatives', he told West.

His next letter to West, a day or two later, is full of references to Pompey, Lucullus, the Curatii, Tullus Hostilius and of course Livy. He and Walpole had just been to see the Alban Mount,

Frascati and Castelgandolfo. At Albano their meal, he says, had comprised 'a peacock, a dish of thrushes, a noble scarus (a sea-fish) and some conchylia of the Lake with garum sauce'. He had found the Appian Way 'somewhat tiresome' and considered 'Windsor, or Richmond Hill . . . infinitely preferable to Albano or Frescati [*sic*]'. Back in Rome, however, the view from his window made amends: 'There is a moon! there are stars for you! Do not you hear the fountain? Do not you smell the orange flowers?'

This letter had begun with a long poem in Alcaics, dedicated 'Ad C: Favonium Zephyrinum', in which he calls upon the 'Mother of Roses' to tell him under what shade Zephyrino loves to spend the day. He calls the pine forests to bear witness that 'lofty Tibur' and the surrounding hills have echoed the name of his dear friend. This is one of the pieces which suggest that Gray expressed himself more easily and more gracefully in Latin verse than in English. This joint letter contains some Roman inscriptions which Walpole had transcribed in the Vatican Library. One wonders, however, if Sir Robert's son was not beginning to tire a little of all these antiquities.

Towards 10 June they left for Naples, travelling by way of Velletri and Terracina, through 'the most beautiful part of the finest country in the world'. Gray describes it more fully in his Journal than in this letter to his mother, which he wrote from Naples on 14 June. In this he dwells on the wide, well-kept road, the corn-fields, the elms festooned with vines, the ancient fig trees and 'the oranges in full bloom'. The Neapolitans were 'a jolly, lively kind of animals, more industrious than Italians usually are'. The visitors saw Solfatara, the Lake of Avernus, the 'Grotta del Cane' and the Sibyl's cave at Cumae. What most impressed Gray were the excavations of Herculaneum and the many buildings and wall-paintings which had recently been uncovered.

On their return to Rome towards the end of June they found that the Cardinals had still not elected a new pope, and Walpole thought there was no reason for waiting longer. He had seen of Rome as much as he wanted, and he had heard that the climate in late summer was not merely unhealthy but dangerous, and that everyone who could afford it went to stay in the hills. He and Gray therefore left for Florence about 3 July. For Gray this was disappointing. He could have spent weeks exploring the vestiges of antiquity – unaware that he would probably have caught fever; whereas Florence had less to offer, except to one whose interests lay in medieval architecture, sculpture and painting. But he had little to complain of. Horace Mann lodged his guests in the Casa Ambrogi, a 'charming apartment', with a balcony overlooking the Arno. There was no lack of comfort, and the weather was temperate and 'serene'. Gray, meanwhile, had received from West a letter dated 5 June and written in a mood of deep despondency. Having left his chambers in the Temple for lodgings in Bond Street, he continued to pore over law-books and to speculate about his future. On 16 July Gray replied in a long letter full of reflexions and sage advice, very different in tone from his usual manner. In a joint letter of 31 July, Walpole wrote that they were expecting the arrival of Lady Pomfret, Lady Walpole (Horace's sister-in-law) and Lady Mary Wortley Montagu, bringing with them a 'rhapsody of mystic nonsense'. Gray described Florence as 'an excellent place to employ all one's animal sensations in, but utterly contrary to one's rational powers'. His motto was '*Nihilisimo*'. Their way of life was to rise at noon and go to bed at 2 a.m.

Despite its 'nothingness', the life suited him well enough. In Mann's house in the Via dello Spirito Santo the minister entertained both the Florentine gentry and travelling English people. It was probably here that Walpole met and courted the lovely young Marchesa Grifoni; exactly with what success is not known, but sufficiently to win her adoration. Gray disapproved of this and, generally, of what he considered Walpole's selfishness. He himself spent hours copying manuscript music and making nine volumes of it; composing for West a poem on Mount Gaurus (Monte Nuovo, near Naples) in Latin hexameters, and another on the philosophy of Locke: 'De Principiis Cogitandi'; and he continued to study Livy and Silius Italicus – all of which struck Walpole as pushing pedantry too far.

As they spent nearly nine months in Florence, it was natural that Gray should have wished to see Pisa, Pistoia and other cities. Walpole, who had had enough of sightseeing, offered to let him take the carriage and the servants and to meet the expenses; but Gray felt it beneath his dignity to accept such an offer. Relations between the two had been growing strained. Gray is reported to have told Walpole that his behaviour was that of 'a spoilt child'. One wonders if Gray's was not the same. It is impossible to know

the rights and wrongs of an estrangement which was to culminate
in a resounding quarrel; but in the light of the known facts, it
appears that Gray had begun to feel increasingly the dependence
of his position.

They had been joined in the autumn by John Chute, a Hampshire gentleman, and his cousin Francis Withed, who remained
with them through the winter. On 24 April 1741 they all set out
for Reggio in Emilia. When it had come to the point of departure,
Gray felt sorry to leave. In a letter to West he had enclosed a few
lines in hexameters, picturing the heights of Fiesole on which
Pallas had conferred the greatest beauty in the Tuscan Apennines:
henceforth he will see them no more from Arno's vale. The tone
of these Latin verses is in strange contrast with that of his plans for
the future – after Reggio: 'next to Venice by the 11th of May, there
to see the old Doge wed the Adriatic whore. Then to Verona, so
to Milan, so to Marseilles, so to Lyons, so to Paris, so to West,
&c, in saecula saeculorum. Amen.'

Walpole had decided to break the journey at Reggio because the
fair being held there was enlivened by operas and masquerades.
But any enjoyment he had expected was ruined by the open
quarrel which now broke out with Gray. It is clear that Gray
considered himself Walpole's equal, if not his superior; while
Walpole thought that he had the right to decide on their plans of
action, that it was for him to decide where they should go and how
long they should stay, in Rome, in Naples and especially in
Florence. But it was not agreeable to a young man of Gray's
character and sense of importance to play second fiddle to this
lively aristocrat. He did not seem able to accept the fact that,
since he was enjoying a free tour, with every luxury, acquiescence
in his host's arrangements was clearly indicated. The cause of the
final explosion appears to have been a letter which Gray had previously written to Ashton in which he seems to have criticised
Walpole; Ashton had passed on his remarks to the latter. The facts
of the case have never been clarified, but all that is known supports
this explanation. Gray, who was evidently extremely angry, went
on to Venice with Chute and Withed; while Horace Mann, who
had heard all about the quarrel, wrote to Walpole 'to assure him'
that Gray, 'except writing that letter . . . was not so much to blame
as on the sight of it you might imagine'. Mann 'took the greatest

part of the fault on' himself – inexplicably. He wrote again, a little later, to say that Gray was in despair and to entreat Walpole 'to forget and forgive'.[6]

When, years later, Mason was composing his *Memoirs of Gray*, he received a letter from Walpole, who took the blame for the quarrel mostly on himself:

> I am conscious that, in the beginning of the differences between Gray and me, the fault was mine. I was too young, too fond of my own diversions, nay . . . too much intoxicated by indulgence, vanity, and the insolence of my situation . . . not to have been inattentive . . . to the feelings of one I thought below me . . . I have since felt my infinite inferiority to him. I treated him insolently; he loved me, and I did not think he did . . . Forgive me, if I say that his temper was not conciliating; at the same time that . . . he acted a more friendly part, had I had the sense to take advantage of it – he freely told me of my faults . . . .

and so on. An impartial critic might regard this as a very one-sided account of the affair, inspired by his good nature. Walpole was probably vain, rather high-handed and self-indulgent. But it is an overstatement for him to speak of his 'infinite inferiority' to Gray. Gray, in youth, had probably still to learn tolerance. The sense of his obligation to Walpole had been a burden that he finally could not accept.

Walpole, in the meantime, had been taken ill with a severe attack of quinsy; and it was only the chance arrival of Lord Lincoln and Joseph Spence – whom they had met in Turin – and their calling in a good physician, which saved his life. On his recovery, Walpole wrote to Venice, asking Gray to come back and make it up. Gray did return; Mann wrote to Walpole that what he had heard of the interview had 'destroyed all the hopes of a reconciliation'. Had Walpole not offered apologies sufficiently humble to one who 'loved' him? One conjectures that Gray was aware that he himself had been partly to blame, and was too proud to admit it. 'Quarrels would not last for long', says La Roche-foucauld, 'if the fault were only on one side.' It is known that Gray returned to Venice, apparently angry at heart, and with nothing in his pocket. He wrote home for a remittance, and probably borrowed from Chute. Walpole, however, very generously asked Mann to instruct the British Consul in Venice to supply Gray with what funds he needed, but without letting him know the source of the supply. In acknowledging this letter on 1 July, Mann added that he had also written to Gray to offer him money and that Gray had drawn forty zecchini from the Consul, seemingly under the impression that the Consul was providing them.

Walpole had proceeded to Venice, according to plan, and was staying with Chute; but there is no record of his seeing Gray, who must have taken other lodgings. On receiving a letter of credit from his people, he drew what he needed for the journey and left for home, attended only by a *laquais de voyage* (which seems to have been considered a hardship!). He made short stays in the principal cities of northern Italy, recrossed the Mont Cenis and once again visited the Grande Chartreuse. In 1739 he had seen the place in October; this time it must have been about 20 August, and the scenery would be less austere. He stayed a short while with the hospitable monks. The stillness of the forests soothed his troubled mind, and in the visitors' book he wrote an ode in Alcaics, addressing the holy spirit of the place ('O Tu, severi relligio loci'), whom he felt nearer to him among these crags and sombre groves than in the most splendid temple of the plains. He begs the Deity to grant repose to his weary head; and, if he is to be drawn roughly back into a worldly life, then he prays that at least in old age he may live in freedom, and that God will deliver him from the tumult of the crowd and the cares of mankind ('Tutumque vulgari tumultu/Surripias hominumque curis) – far from the madding crowd, as Sir Sydney Roberts has commented.[7]

These lines are generally regarded as beautiful and moving; perhaps, for a man of twenty-five, they are slightly morbid. The breach with Walpole had upset him, and he does not seem to have been willing to accept any responsibility for it. It is amusing to compare the grandiloquent style of the Latin ode with the laconic account of the experience which he sent to Wharton.

CHAPTER 6

The death of West and the
return to Cambridge: 1741–1742[1]

In about another fortnight he was back in Cornhill. There was nothing here to cheer him. The English had wanted a war with Spain; the country had gone to war against the advice of Sir Robert; and it was going badly. The London crowds were rough and mannerless. London did not feel like home. Gray's wig and accoutrements provoked laughter from the crowds.

A letter from Chute and Mann filled him with nostalgia for Florence and gave him an opportunity to pour out his troubles:

> I am as an alien in my native land . . . It rains, every body is discontented and so am I . . . would I might be with you again . . . As it is, my prospects can not well be more unpleasing; but why do I trouble your Goodnature with such considerations? Be assured, that when I am happy (if that can ever be) your esteem will greatly add to that happiness.

Philip Gray's condition, mental and physical, had been worsening, and his death in November revealed the fact that he had depleted his fortune by building the mansion at Wanstead. Gray was obliged to spend some time in seeing what money could be salvaged. The family did not sell the Wanstead house, which was ultimately let to a tenant; it was at any rate a piece of real estate. But the situation at the time was bad enough to depress anyone, particularly a young man who had no profession and no desire for one.

Early in September Conway had written a kind letter, which has not been preserved; and he must have told Walpole about Gray's situation. Walpole had returned home soon after Gray, and on 14 September he replied to Conway: 'Before I thank you for myself, I must thank you for that excessive good nature you showed in writing to poor Gray . . .'. But Gray made no advances to Walpole, and the latter, apart from writing to West and possibly seeing him, was too much immersed in politics to think of much else. He had been elected MP for a Cornish borough and was busy defending Sir Robert against the faction which was trying to oust him from power.

It is supposed that Gray and West saw a fair amount of each other during the winter of 1741–2, but West's health was giving way as consumption undermined it. His late father's secretary had poisoned Mrs West's mind against her son; and, according to Gray, her indifference was a contributory cause of his depression. In March he was so ill that, feeling the need for country air, he went to lodge with a Mr David Mitchell at Popes, near Hatfield. From here, where he sat 'purring by the fire-side' (he had once signed himself 'Grimalkin'), he wrote to ask Gray to write to him. Gray replied sympathetically, explained the merits of Tacitus and appraised Book IV of the *Dunciad*, which had just appeared. He added a speech by Agrippina from the tragedy he had begun, and sought West's opinion of it. West wrote in reply that the speech was too long and the style 'too antiquated'. As Racine had not used the language of Ronsard, so it would be more fitting for an English tragedian to use Otway's language rather than Shakespeare's. In his letter West seems to anticipate Matthew Arnold's remark that a writer is conditioned by the age into which he is born. West wrote that he himself was now 'tossing and coughing' in bed, 'and all unable to sleep'.[2]

Gray seems not to have realised how serious was his friend's condition, though he tried to cheer him by discussing books and questions of style. He had been reading *Joseph Andrews*, at West's suggestion. He considered the incidents in the novel 'ill-laid', but some of the characters very true to life. As the Mohammedan heaven was full of houris, 'be mine to read eternal new romances of Marivaux and Crébillon'. He was thinking of *La Vie de Marianne*, then much in demand by English readers; and probably also of Crébillon's *Le Sopha* (1740). Gray evidently considered the French writers superior to Fielding; but Fielding was attempting a new and more ambitious kind of novel. Gray went on to discuss poetic style, to praise Shakespeare's language as 'one of his principal beauties', but to admit that in 'Agrippina' he himself had gone a little too far in imitating that language.

He had already started to compile the first of his Commonplace Books, into which he copied extracts from his reading. He spent most of April in studying the Peloponnesian War in Thucydides, and reading Anacreon, Theocritus, Pliny, Martial and Plutarch. 'From this time forward', writes Edmund Gosse, 'we find that his ailments, his melancholy, his reserve, and his habit of drowning consciousness in perpetual study, have taken firm hold upon him, and he begins to plunge into an excess of reading, treating the acquisition of knowledge as a narcotic.'[3] This was so. Having no settled profession, it was Gray's misfortune that he enjoyed an income sufficient for his needs. Had he been compelled to earn his living, he could still have found time to write all that he did manage, while the discipline of regular work might have encouraged in him a greater facility and inventiveness.

The very literary correspondence between the two friends continued until the end of May. Gray submitted for West's approval a neat version of an elegy which Propertius had dedicated to Maecenas, turning the Latin poet's elegiacs into rhymed couplets. West sent a cheerful little ode –

> . . . O join with mine thy tuneful lay
> And invocate the tardy May

– which Gray thought very good. Other letters appear to have been lost. On 27 May Gray wrote that often-quoted description of his 'white Melancholy, or rather Leucocholy, . . . which though it seldom laughs or dances . . . yet is a good easy sort of state . . . the only fault of it is insipidity . . . But there is another sort, black indeed, which I have now and then felt . . .'. He is planning to go into the country, evidently to Stoke, for a few weeks. He encloses an imaginary 'Sophonisba Massinissae Epistola', in Latin elegiacs, based on Livy, and with phrases taken from Ovid.

Quite unconscious that West's last hour was near, he was surprised when another letter was returned to him unopened; and when, on 17 June, he happened to see in a newspaper some verses, unsigned but by Ashton, 'To the Memory of Richard West, Esq.; who died at Popes in Hertfordshire, June 1, 1742, after a tedious and painful indisposition, in the 26th year of his Age', he was deeply shocked.

He wrote the same day to Ashton, reflecting bitterly on the

behaviour of the Mitchells, West's hosts, in not informing him of
West's demise: 'I am a fool indeed to be surpriz'd at meeting with
Brutishness or want of Thought among Mankind.' He congratulated Ashton on his 'new Happiness', which was an appointment
to a Crown living which Walpole had obtained for him. At the foot
of the manuscript of 'Noontide', the ode which he had written at
West's urging, he wrote: 'At Stoke, at the beginning of June 1742,
to Fav. not knowing he was then dead'. At the end of June he added
twenty-nine lines to the still unfinished 'De Principiis Cogitandi',
and this is the best and sincerest of his tributes to his friend.

Returning to London in July, he heard from Chute and Horace
Mann, the latter having now been formally appointed as Minister
to the Grand Duchy. In a facetious reply, of which the first part is
to Chute and the second to Mann, who had asked for a number of
books, he mentions those which he is dispatching. They were
mainly historical works, and State papers; but for Chute he sent
Crébillon's *Le Sopha* and three parts of *La Vie de Marianne*. To
Chute he had written: I am just going into the Country for an
easy fortnight, & then in earnest intend to go to Cambridge to
Trinity Hall. My sole Reason (as you know) is to look as if . . .' –
that is, as if he really intended to study for the Bar.

It was discovered about this time that what remained of Philip
Gray's property amounted to less than the family had hoped,
although the rent of the house in Cornhill, if they vacated it, and
the rent of the Essex mansion would be enough to support
Dorothy Gray and her sister in the country. As the husband of
Mrs Rogers had died in the autumn, the two ladies went to live
with his widow at Stoke Poges. Although Gray had a small income
of his own, prudence would have suggested some regular employment. A doctorate in civil law at Oxford or Cambridge qualified its
holder to plead in the Ecclesiastical and Admiralty Courts.[4] The
plan of entering Trinity Hall shows that he had nerved himself to
the prospect of taking at least a bachelor's degree.

In the event, he did not enter Trinity Hall, but obtained the
assent of the governing body of Peterhouse to return to his old
college, this time as a fellow-commoner. He expressed his chagrin
and detestation of Cambridge in his 'Hymn to Ignorance':

> Hail, Horrors, hail! ye ever gloomy bowers,
> Ye gothic fanes, and antiquated towers,

Where rushy Camus' slowly-winding flood
Perpetual draws his humid train of mud;
Glad I revisit thy neglected reign.
Oh take me to thy peaceful shade again.
　But chiefly thee, whose influence breath'd from high
Augments the native darkness of the sky,
Ah Ignorance! soft salutary Power!
Prostrate with filial reverence I adore . . .

The irony has a heavy touch, and it is difficult to account for his attitude. He apparently is asserting that the intellectual darkness of Cambridge 'augments the native darkness' of its sky, and this, though Cambridge skies are admittedly clearer and sunnier than in many other parts of the country. His animadversions, though hardly playful, must be taken with a grain of salt. The university was neither as indolent nor as ignorant as he complained. Very different indeed had Cambridge appeared to Nicholas Ridley, Master of Pembroke in 1540, who thanked his 'loving mother and tender nurse, Cambridge, for all her kindness', in his farewell letter. The late Dr D. A. Winstanley's careful researches[5] have put the picture in its true focus.

The colleges were indeed no longer producing great scholars comparable with those of earlier days; but there were some good colleges, not always the biggest. Clare gave great attention to its undergraduates, as did Trinity Hall. St John's and Trinity had the largest student bodies, and the former had excellent tutors; though Trinity took the lead in later years. Jesus and Peterhouse were very small colleges at this time. More senior wranglers were produced by Pembroke and Caius than by any other college; and here it may be recalled that mathematics was the main subject of study at Cambridge. Pembroke men also distinguished themselves in classics; Christopher Smart was regarded by many people as the great ornament of the university in this field.

As for the fellows, their interests often lay mainly in eating, drinking and lewd conversation; yet even here there were notable exceptions. The tutors, however, worked hard and sometimes deserved the gratitude of their students. Parkinson, of Christ's, was a first-rate tutor. They all lectured regularly, which, as Dr Winstanley observes, afforded the professors a pretext for ignoring their duties. The rule that all fellows were required to take holy orders[6] was not invariably observed; but a fellow who married was always obliged to vacate his office.

Heads of Houses, on the contrary, were allowed to marry. They had usually been tutors before they were elected, and their quality as scholars sometimes left much to be desired. But they were very badly paid, and most of them regarded a mastership as a stepping-stone to a bishopric. Who would refuse a see, at even £400 a year like Oxford, in exchange for a mastership at £120? Most bishop-rics were worth far more than the Oxford see. From the point of view of amenities, Ely was very desirable; but to be appointed to Durham (£50,000 a year) was like being given a front seat in heaven – except that the country and the climate were far from heavenly (the bishops resided outside Durham city in various palaces).

After the five Regius Professorships founded by Henry VIII, eight or nine more had been founded, mostly by private benefac-tors after the Restoration. These included the Lucasian Chair of Mathematics (1663) and the Plumian Chair of Astronomy (1704). In 1724 chairs of modern history, associated with modern lan-guages, were established by George I at both universities. The stipend was £400 a year. Incumbents were required to give one lecture each term, and to pay a Frenchman and an Italian to teach their respective languages.

There was variety among the stipends and statutory duties of the professorships; the chairs of chemistry and botany had no stipend at all. During Gray's years in Cambridge, standards had gone down further, and most of the professors did not even trouble to lecture. The first Lucasian Professors of Mathematics, Barrow and Newton, had been men of great eminence; not so their successors. Bentley, titular Professor of Divinity, had been one of the greatest of classical scholars. Joshua Barnes, Regius Professor of Greek, had published admirable editions of Homer; but after his death, little work of value was done before the election of Richard Porson in 1792. Medical research amounted to nothing. On the other hand, Dr Dickins, Professor of Civil Law from 1714 to 1755, not only possessed great learning, but was an admirable teacher. John Mickleborough, who held the unpaid chair of chemistry, con-tinued to make ends meet out of his income as vicar of St Andrews, and by running a pharmacy! Richard Watson, a theologian who succeeded him, set about learning his subject and, in less than two years, acquired enough knowledge to give regular lectures, and to publish a respectable book on the subject. Dr Roger Long of Pembroke was an inventive genius and a man of real and varied talents. Thomas Martyn, a Fellow of Sidney, held the title of Professor of Botany from 1738 to 1793, and maintained himself on fees from his students, who averaged about fifty a year. Towards 1740, Trinity College had conveyed to the university sufficient ground for a botanic garden, which Martyn used for his demonstrations. One of the most industrious of the professors, he lectured regularly, using the Linnaean system as the basis of his teaching.

There was little to be said in favour of the professors of modern history. Shallet Turner, appointed in 1732, 'did absolutely nothing', writes Winstanley. In 1762 he was succeeded by Laurence Brockett, an ignorant and drunken cleric. In 1768 Thomas Gray, who had long hankered after the post, was appointed. His qualifications were admirable; but he could never bring himself to deliver a lecture. It is evident from the above that, during the middle years of the century, few professors were either scholars or conscientious teachers.

College lecturers generally neglected Greek, Latin and history; they did, however, teach mathematics, logic and philosophy. The system of Locke, ignored by his own university, had been taken up with enthusiasm by Cambridge.

Undergraduate work consisted in writing, every week, an essay on a philosophical proposition and in defending it against an opponent of the same aptitude. This was followed by an annual examination, apparently in philosophy and mathematics, with the latter gradually taking precedence. The best seventeen candidates were classified under the heading of First Tripos, the next sixteen, of Second Tripos. In 1753 they were classified as wranglers, senior and junior optimes, and those qualified for a degree. The extension of the term 'tripos' to examinations in other subjects came later. Undergraduates were expected to keep ten terms of residence. They often missed part of a term, but most of them took the degree of BA, and some, afterwards, of BCL. It was usual for a nobleman to spend a few terms at the university, but often without proceeding to a degree. Most of the undergraduates came from middle-class families, and were called pensioners. Pensioners and fellow-commoners, some of the latter being very rich young men, were often riotous and, in the later years of the century, gave a great deal of trouble.

The habits and routine of a student's life were markedly different from what they are today. A student gave a great deal of attention to his dress and donned a clean shirt daily. In the morning any interval between lectures and tutorials was spent at the hairdresser's. Dinner in Hall was served towards 2 p.m. Supper was often taken in one's own room, or in a friend's; and, as it was specially ordered from the kitchen, it was better than dinner.

Social life was catered for by the coffee-houses. These were numerous and adapted to every taste and pocket. The Mitre Coffee-House was frequented by old Etonians; the Greeks', by professors and other senior persons. There was a coffee-house opposite Pembroke, probably on the site now occupied by the Presbyterian church. Taken all in all, life was neither dull nor monotonous. The studious could study, the frivolous amuse themselves. Thus, Gray's criticisms seem to be, in a large measure, unfounded and biased.

CHAPTER 7

'The Power of Laziness': 1742–1747[1]

Although the Master and Fellows of Peterhouse must have been aware of Gray's aversion for undergraduate work, they none the less received him back as a fellow-commoner, with the privilege of dining at High Table and consorting with them in the Combination-Room. He was given a very agreeable set in the Burroughs Building, which had just been completed. The bedroom window looked across Little St Mary's churchyard to Pembroke Hall and King's College Chapel; the window of the sitting-room gave a view along the Trumpington Road, which here ran into open country. Such privileges may be explained by his ability as a Latinist and by the small number of undergraduates; of these there were fewer than twelve, as against fourteen fellows. The Master, Dr Whalley, who had just been elected Regius Professor of Divinity, seems to have been as indolent as the fellows. But Peterhouse was not then typical of Cambridge colleges.

Gray followed the course of lectures given by Professor Dickins of Trinity Hall, who has already been mentioned. He sedulously took notes throughout the academic year, and at the end of the Michaelmas Term of 1743 passed the examination for the degree of Bachelor of Civil Law, the only degree which he was ever to take. This had represented an exceptional effort on his part, and had clearly exhausted his patience. He did not attempt to proceed to the doctorate, but relapsed into the state of indolence with which he reproached the university – 'that ineffable Octogrammaton the Power of LAZINESS', which he attributes to it in writing to Wharton on 26 April 1744.

Social life was pleasant. While the Master may not have been sympathetic, Gray must have been treated in a friendly way, or he would hardly have remained in Peterhouse for another fourteen years. Meanwhile his friends at Pembroke, Dr James Brown, Thomas Wharton and William Trollope, were delighted to see

him, and one supposes that they often entertained him to tea or
supper, and that all of them foregathered in the coffee-houses.
Brown lent him books from the college library. And Gray made
other friends, though when exactly he met them is not known.
Indeed, the principal events of his life between 1742 and 1750,
apart from his reconciliation with Walpole, cannot be dated with
certainty.

William Antrobus, one of his uncles, had become rector of a
Northamptonshire parish in 1726. He had married the daughter of
Thomas Nutting, a Cambridge merchant and sometime Mayor,
and they had had a son and two daughters. But as Antrobus died
towards 1743, his widow brought the children to live in her father's
house, probably later in the year, and so made a second home for
Gray. In the years to come, the two girls, Dorothy and Mary,
made and laundered his linen and generally ministered to his
comfort.

It appears also from the correspondence that by 1747 he was
frequenting the home of Conyers Middleton, who lived at the far
end of the High Street, now King's Parade, on the site of a more
recent addition to Caius. Gray described this house as 'the only
easy Place one could find to converse in at Cambridge'. Middleton,
who was University Librarian, was a lively and unorthodox
controversialist, and there is evidence to show that, under his
influence, Gray's religious views leaned distinctly to deism.

Gray had probably written the 'Epitaph' which forms the conclusion of the so-called 'Elegy', in 1742, and it is uncertain whether
he began to compose the first stanzas of the poem before 1746,
when he seems to have shown them to Walpole. Meanwhile he had
consented to a reconciliation in November 1745. Some lady, whose
identity is unknown,[2] had suggested to Walpole that he should
make the first advances. Sir Robert had died early in that year, and
Horace, now very well-to-do, was living in the house which his
father had left him in Arlington Street. In response to Walpole's
overture, Gray came up to London, in a mood somewhat sus-
picious, but willing to hear what the Honourable Horatio had to
say.

I wrote a Note the Night I came [he confided to Wharton in a
letter of 14 November] and immediately received a very civil
Answer. I went the following Evening to see *the Party* (as

Mrs Foible[3] says) was something abash'd at his Confidence: he came to meet me, kiss'd me on both Sides with all the Ease of one, who receives an Acquaintance just come out of the Country, squatted me into a Fauteuil, begun to talk of the Town & this & that & t'other, & continued with little Interruption for three Hours, when I took my Leave very indifferently pleased, but treated with wondrous Good-breeding . . .

Walpole entertained him to supper the following evening; he found Ashton there; and, on their leaving together, Ashton made some kind of excuse which led to 'a sort of reconciliation'. Gray 'breakfasted alone with Mr W.' next morning, and the misunderstanding was pretty well cleared up – 'when I return I shall see him again'.

One can well imagine these scenes, with Gray standing on his dignity, and Walpole ready to let bygones be bygones. It was surely better to treat the matter as lightly as possible. Ashton's presence makes it clear that, as D. C. Tovey suggested, Gray had written to Ashton complaining of Walpole, that Ashton had promptly passed on Gray's remarks to Walpole, and this had been the cause of the rupture. It would have been natural for Walpole to resent being criticised behind his back.

In response to the kindness he was receiving, Gray gradually thawed. On 3 February 1746 he wrote, commenting on the Scottish army's recent defeat of General Hawley, and remarked that the Duke of Cumberland 'is gone, it seems . . . to undefeat us again'. On 28 March he sent a hurried note about an election at Peterhouse, and on 7 July apologised for his 'long Interval of Silence . . . don't imagine it Neglect, or Want of Sensibility to the many expressions of Kindness . . . in your last Letter'. He is now as anxious to retain Walpole's good opinion as he had previously been indifferent to it; though he did not fully realise that he had more need of this generous friend than the latter, with his multifarious duties and activities, had of him. He had an inkling of it, however, as appears from the fact that he now began to confide his poems one by one to Walpole, who persuaded him to publish them. Three of them appeared as by 'Mr ——' in Dodsley's *Miscellany*, and it seems that for many years Gray objected to signing any of them. He agreed to do so, with reluctance, in 1753, and more readily in respect of the Pindaric odes. He desired only the approval of the cultured few. There is no evidence that Gray would ever have published his verses if Walpole had not given one or two manuscript copies of the Elegy to friends, and urged him to continue his writing. And, in that event, he would never have been recognised as the leading poet of the day; and if his poems had come to light in a later age they would not have made the same impact.

He had passed the summer of 1746 partly at Stoke, partly in London. In a letter of 10 August to Wharton he wrote: 'My Evenings have been chiefly spent at Ranelagh & Vaux-Hall, several of my Mornings, or rather Noons, in Arlington Street, & the rest at the Tryal of the Lords' – that is, of the Earls of Kilmarnock and Cromarty, and of Lord Balmerinoch. He describes in a curiously indifferent way their appearance and demeanour, as well as the efforts made by Lady Cromarty, with her four children, to obtain a reprieve for her husband. There is no sign of any sympathy for men whose offence was to take up arms for a prince whom they regarded as their legitimate sovereign. Gray clearly now disliked Ashton ('an ungrateful toady') as much as Walpole had previously disliked him. He adds: 'the Muse, I doubt, is gone, and has left me in far worse Company: if she returns, you will hear of her'.

Meanwhile, he had posted a copy of the Eton ode to Walpole, and continued to send him letters; these were no longer addressed to 'Dear Celadon' or 'My dear Horace', but to 'dear Sir' or 'My dear Sir'. It is evident, for the rest, that he was in fact courting the Muse because, in a letter of 11 September to Wharton, he mentions that 'a few autumnal verses are my Entertainment during the Fall of the Leaf' – which has led Tovey to surmise that these were the early stanzas of the churchyard poem.

Having heard early in October that Chute and Withed had returned from Italy and were living at Withed's house at Fareham, he wrote a facetious letter to Chute; and a further letter on the 23rd, when they were in London. On the 8th he had announced to Wharton that he was returning to Cambridge with the peremptory request: 'This is only to entreat you would order mes gens to clean out my Appartments, spread the Carpets, air the Beds, put up the Tapestry, unpaper the Frames, &c: fit to receive a great Potentate, that comes down in the Flying Coach drawn by Green Dragons on Friday the 10th Instant. . . .' There was evidently ample service at Peterhouse to carry out such instructions, and Wharton had only to cross the road and issue them. The stagecoach to which Gray refers plied between the Green Dragon in Bishopsgate and the Red Lion, which has recently been demolished, in Petty Cury, on Mondays, Wednesdays and Fridays, leaving London at 7 a.m. It returned on Tuesdays, Thursdays and Saturdays. The fare was ten shillings each way.[4]

From Cambridge he wrote to Walpole on the 20th, giving his impressions of Barry, an Irish actor – 'silver-tongued Barry', brought to London by Garrick – whom Gray had seen in the title-role of *Othello*. He enclosed 'Noontide, an Ode' (later, renamed 'Ode on the Spring'), which he had written in 1742. From a letter of 11 December (1746) one learns that he had spent the first half of November junketing with Chute, Withed and Walpole in London. These were the only members of the country gentry with whom he was really *persona grata* in the 1740s. He more than once stayed with Chute at the Vyne, near Basingstoke. With Walpole he was once again on terms of easy familiarity, although Walpole admitted that he was not good company. On 22 December Gray wrote to him:

This comes du fond de ma cellule to salute Mr H. W. not so much him that visits and votes, and goes to White's & to court; as the H. W. in his rural capacity, snug in his tub on Windsor-hill, & brooding over folios of his own creation; him that can slip away, like a pregnant beauty, (but a little oftener) into the country, be brought to bed perhaps of twins, and whisk to town again the week after . . .

He inquires about the progress of the 'Memoires'; refers to Lord Lovat, who was to be beheaded later in the year; and encloses 'a scene from a tragedy'.

The odd references in the letter need to be explained. In the previous summer Walpole had rented a house at Windsor which he called 'my little tub'. The 'Memoires' were to be a record of parliamentary proceedings, but it does not appear that Walpole began to write them before 1751. The 'scene in a tragedy' was the beginning of 'Agrippina', of which only 202 verses had been composed. The excessively long speeches suggested that the play would consist more of talk than action.

December 1746 was marked by a minor scandal in Pembroke Hall, which Gray described to Wharton in a letter of the 27th. John Blake Delaval, son of a Northumberland magnate and then an undergraduate, had introduced into his rooms a certain Nell Burnet, dressed as an officer and masquerading as 'Captain Hargreaves'. The Master, getting wind of the affair, searched Delaval's bedroom, detected signs of the presence of the 'gentle-woman', but failed to discover her since she was 'locked up in a cupboard'. Even so, Delaval was requested to leave the college. Dr Long regretted his rigour – the Delavals were an important family – and tried to persuade other colleges to admit the delin-quent, but without success. This affair did not injure Delaval's career. He was created a baronet in 1761, was elected an MP, and later became a peer of the United Kingdom, as well as inheriting the Delaval estates.

Gray concludes his letter by asking Wharton: 'Have you seen the Works of two young Authors, a Mr Warton & a Mr Collins, both Writers of Odes? It is odd enough, but each is the half of a considerable Man, & one the Counter-Part of the other . . . they both deserve to last some years, but will not . . .' He adds in postscript: 'I was 30 year old yesterday, what is it o'clock by you?'

Collins's odes had appeared earlier in the month, and were destined to last. Thomas Warton, of Oriel College, is mainly remembered for his *History of English Poetry*, for which Gray later handed over to him the plan and notes he had made for his own projected work on the subject. He and his brother Joseph, Head-master of Winchester School, were friends of Johnson and Garrick.

Five letters of Gray, written between 1 January and 1 March 1747, which have been preserved, are to Walpole. In January he is praising Racine's *Britannicus* and quoting Madame de Sévigné. On 8 February, in response to Walpole's thoughtful suggestion, he discusses the plan of publishing Richard West's literary remains, and adds a list of the poems which he has in hand: poems in English, poems in Latin, imitations of Latin poets and translations from Latin. 'This is all I can find . . . You, I imagine, may have a good deal more.' He suggests that Walpole might obtain other papers from West's mother; and he encloses the twenty-nine Latin verses which conclude all he ever wrote of the 'De Principiis Cogitandi'. 'I should not care', he adds, 'how unwise the Ordinary Sort of Readers might think my Affection for him, provided those few, that ever loved any Body . . . might from such little Remains be moved to consider what he might have been; & to wish, that Heaven had granted him a long Life, & a Mind more at Ease.'

In the end, the volume of West's writings was never to appear. Walpole, who had been particularly attentive to West from the outset, was a busy man and may have felt that Gray should have undertaken the task, which would not have been arduous. But since the previous September Gray had been immersed in the literature of ancient Greece.[5] Towards 22 February he condoled with Walpole on the untimely death of his cat ('Selima, was it? or Fatima?'); and on 1 March he sent him an 'Ode on the Death of a Favourite Cat Drowned in a Tub of Gold Fishes' – surely, in the circumstances, an unfeeling and inappropriate elegy. Several sepulchral epigrams in the *Greek Anthology*, composed with sympathy and understanding, could have provided models. But Walpole appears to have appreciated it, which was what mattered. Gray even sent another copy to Wharton, who had gone to live with his people in Durham, and who was thinking of marrying. Gray inquired in this letter about the lady's name. She was Margaret Wilkinson, the daughter of another well-to-do Dunelmian, who lived in Crossgate, the steep street that leads up past the ancient church of St Margaret of Antioch and is the direct road to Brancepeth. Gray refers, in passing, to 'that old Rascal, the Master' (Roger Long), and to Christopher Smart, who is likely to be 'abîmé' because 'his Debts daily increase'.

It is true that Dr Long had been annoying the fellows, and that Smart, an inveterate tippler, had for some time been a serious problem. But the fact remains that Smart and Long, together with the butler, Dunthorne, an extremely able mathematician who assisted Long, were by far the most distinguished men in Pembroke.

In 1746 the fellows had voted unanimously to elect Henry Tuthill, of Peterhouse, to a fellowship; but Long had vetoed the proposal. In 1747 Gray, who was now acting as if he were a member of the Society, proposed his new friend, William Mason, of St John's. This again was approved by the fellows, and again vetoed by Long. The quarrel had now reached an impasse. The Master may well have been within his rights; until quite recently heads of Houses exercised far greater powers than they do today. Richard Bentley, of Trinity, made all appointments to college

offices, and filled fellowships with his own tools. Roger Long
(1680–1770) lectured on 'experimental philosophy', which
probably meant astronomy in this instance. In 1729 he had been
elected to the Royal Society, in 1750 he was to become Lowndean
Professor of Astronomy, and he was writing a book on the subject,
of which the first part had appeared in 1742. Long, furthermore,
was a practical inventor. He had erected in one of the courts 'a
hollow revolving sphere, 18 feet in diameter, representing on its
inner surface the apparent movements of the heavenly bodies'.[6]
For his amusement he had built himself a vessel in which he
paddled round the pond in the garden. And he was something of a
musician, with his pianoforte. Here then was a man of parts,
presiding over a society of undistinguished dons – respectable, if
somewhat mediocre, with the exception of Christopher Smart.

For Smart, if not respectable, was learned and brilliant, an outstanding Latinist and regarded by many people as one of the great
ornaments of Cambridge. In his letter to Wharton,[7] quoted above,
Gray mentions that Smart was composing a comedy, in which his
acquaintances were to act, but in which he also 'acts five parts
himself'. Gray regarded him as ridiculous and 'mad'. In the event,
A Trip to Cambridge, or the Grateful Fair was produced in the
college hall, with Stonhewer, a recent Peterhouse friend of Gray,
acting as prompter. It was probably quite good, otherwise able
men like Gordon, later Precentor of Lincoln, and Dr John
Randall, later Professor of Music, would not have consented to
act in it. This comedy 'must', writes Professor B. W. Downs, 'be
one of the last, if not the very last example of the College drama
so popular in the sixteenth and early seventeenth centuries'.[8]
Smart's great and original poems, 'A Song to David' and the
'Jubilate Agno', did not appear until later. Gray may have been
jealous of his abilities; however, he and others did try to help him
in his financial difficulties.

Thomas Wharton, who was now married, had taken his wife
to London for the honeymoon, and returned to live in Durham.
On 30 November Gray wrote with pleasure to hear of their safe
arrival:

> . . . yet I can not chuse but lament your Condition, so coop'd
> up in the Elvet-House with Spirits & Hobgoblins about you, &
> Pleasure at one entrance quite shut out . . . open up your Delisle

[an atlas], & take a Prospect of that World wch the cruel
Architect has hid from your corporeal Eyes, & confin'd 'em to
the narrow Contemplation of your own *Backside*, & Kitchen
Garden.

One gathers from this that the house was not, as one would
expect, one of the many Georgian buildings on the north side of
Old Elvet, but a house on the east side of New Elvet, probably (in
the writer's view) the building now painted a greyish-blue, which
stands just beyond the Three Tuns Hotel, and which has been
listed as an ancient building, to be preserved from demolition. The
ground rises behind it, and if, as is likely, there were tall houses on
the opposite side of the street, these would obstruct the view of the
cathedral.

Gray's ennuis were not confined to Pembroke; he was soon
having trouble in his own college. One day in January 1748,
Professor Whalley, who 'has hated me', remarked 'to a large
Table full of People, that I was a kind of Atheist'. It seems likely
that, under Middleton's influence, he may have expressed doubts
as to the miracles ascribed in *Acts* to some of the Apostles; and
there is reason to think that he was not conspicuously pious. One
may recall in this connexion that he had a friend named Nicholas
Bonfoy, who lived with his mother at Bishop's Ripton in Huntingdonshire; and that Gray and Brown sometimes paid them a
visit. Gray wrote of Mrs Bonfoy that 'she taught me to pray' – as
though he had not previously been in the habit of praying. Whatever the reason for Whalley's remark, Gray actually wrote a letter
to deny the charge and was imprudent enough to show it to some
of his acquaintances. Unfortunately, it fell into the hands of the
Rev. Henry Etough, Rector of Therfield in Hertfordshire. This
Etough was a notorious busybody who frequently came to Cambridge to stir up mischief. He had acquainted himself with enough
of the private lives of prominent ecclesiastics to spread gossip
about them and to make himself greatly dreaded. Gray complained
of him and of Whalley in a letter to Walpole,[9] as though he were
another thorn in his flesh; and when Mason drew a caricature of
Etough, with his large head and stunted body, Gray appended to
it an eight-line satire, entitled 'Tophet'. This was sufficiently
violent to make one think that Etough had really injured him; but
it seems more likely that he regarded any unpopular Cambridge

figure as a personal enemy, and that this 'brawling Fiend' was
merely one of them. What is certain is that Gray was far more at
home in virulent and even indecent satire than in the lyric poetry
which he found so laborious to write. Such poems as 'Tophet' and
'The Candidate' may have been dashed off at a sitting.

But it was possible to forget Long, Smart, Whalley and Etough
by reading every ancient Greek author he could find and filling
his Commonplace Book with extracts. As early as September 1746
he tells Wharton that he has been studying Aristotle's *Poetics*,
Politics and *Morals*, and finding Aristotle difficult: 'he has a dry
Conciseness, that makes one imagine one is perusing a Table of
Contents'. To this letter he appends a list of seventy-three editions
of Greek and Roman classics, and some thirty-four works by
commentators. In December he sent Wharton a 'Chronological
Table' of events in Greece down to the time of Philip of Macedon's
death. Each page contained nine columns to display the concord-
ance of events military, political and literary. He was already familiar with much of Euripides, and was now re-reading Aeschylus.
In 1747 he seems to have been studying Sophocles and Aristophanes, and also Athenaeus's *Dynosophistai*[10] (*Philosophers at
Dinner*). Athenaeus is one of the most informative, as well as
entertaining, of writers: to him more perhaps than to any author
since Homer, scholarship owes a knowledge of daily life in classical
and Hellenistic Greece, especially of the diet of the sober and the
feasting of the self-indulgent; with a host of curious and amusing
anecdotes. From Athenaeus, Gray returned to Isocrates, a
philosopher who interested him. The year 1748 was probably
filled with the same occupations. On 17 March 1749, he writes:
'I have read Pausanias and Athenaeus all thro', & Aeschylus again.
I am now in Pindar & Lysias; for I take Verse & Prose together,
like Bread & Cheese.'[11]

Pausanias's *Description of Greece* was needed to supplement
Athenaeus; while Strabo and other geographers went far to complete the picture. Gray was led by them to immerse himself in
travel books, especially those relating to the East. Yet it apparently
never occurred to him to marshal any part of this vast and varied
knowledge into book form or even essays; and, as a result, the
store of erudition which he had amassed has been, for practical
purposes, wasted.

CHAPTER 8

Fire in Cornhill:
The Elegy and 'A Long Story': 1748–1751[1]

In January 1748 Dodsley published a miscellany in three volumes under the title of a *Collection of Poems*. Volume I contained several pieces which had already appeared in magazines or as pamphlets, by Lady Mary Wortley Montagu, Samuel Johnson, Collins and others. Three pieces by Gray were published anonymously in Volume II; and in Volume III, three of Walpole's poems, also anonymously, together with West's 'Monody on the Death of Queen Caroline', and William Mason's 'Musaeus', a tribute to Pope. Walpole had caused Dodsley to add that the 'Monody' was 'by Richard West, Esq: Son to the Chancellor of Ireland, and Grandson to Bishop Burnet'. It is to be regretted that the *Collection* did not include West's other poems, which were well worth publication. Gray, in writing to Walpole, observed that '*Musaeus* seems to carry with it the promise of something good to come'.

Whether or not the appearance of his first odes gave Gray any pleasure, he suffered a real disaster from a fire in Cornhill. Breaking out in a nearby alley on 25 March, it destroyed a great number of buildings, including the house in which he had been born.[2] It no longer belonged to his mother, but to himself; and he or Dorothy had neglected to insure it for its full value. He now found that to rebuild it and meet the other expenses would cost at least £650. The London Assurance Company paid £484 in April. A further irritation was loss of the rent which had been paid by the tenant, Mrs Sarrazin, a milliner.

When one remembers that £175 (his net loss after the house was rebuilt) was equivalent in purchasing power to very many times that figure today, when one reflects that Gray had been obliged to exchange the pleasant routine of Cambridge for difficult negotiations in London, a certain degree of ill temper is understandable. It comes out in a letter of 5 June 1748 to Wharton:

Do not imagine, I am at all less sensible to your kindness, w^ch
. . . is of a Sort, that however obvious & natural it may seem, has
never once occur'd to any of my good Friends in Town, where
I have been these seven Weeks. their Methods of Consolation
were indeed very extraordinary: they were all so sorry for my
Loss that I could not chuse but laugh. one offer'd me Opera-
Tickets, insisted upon carrying me to the Grand-Masquerade,
desired me to sit for my Picture. others asked me to their Con-
certs, or Dinners & Suppers at their Houses; or hoped, I would
drink Chocolate with them, while I stayed in Town. all my
Gratitude (or, if you please, my Revenge) was to accept of every
Thing they offer'd me: if it had been but a Shilling, I would
have taken it . . . I profited all I was able of their Civilities, & am
returned into the Country loaded with Bontés & Politesses, but
richer still in my own Reflexions . . .

To offer money is always a delicate matter. It may well have
occurred to Walpole to advance a loan or even make a gift, but
after his experience on the grand tour, when Gray seems to have
resented his dependence on the other's largesse, he was wise to
refrain.[3] To give him tickets for the opera, and take him to the
masquerade in the Haymarket, were ways of diverting his mind.
The picture is supposed to have been the portrait by Eckhardt,
now in the National Gallery.

To illustrate his feelings, Gray quotes some verses of Gresset's,
and, further on, speaks enthusiastically of *Le Méchant*, which had
been first performed in 1747 and had just been published in a
two-volume Amsterdam edition of Gresset's works, together with
Ver-Vert, the *Epître à ma sœur* and other pieces. Gray held
Gresset in high esteem. *Ver-Vert*, a mock-heroic poem, relates the
adventures of a learned parrot which had ostensibly belonged to
the Visitandines of Nevers. As to the *Epître à ma sœur*, Gray later
told Mason that this had given him 'the first idea' of the ode 'On
the Pleasures arising from Vicissitude'. After his remarks about
Gresset, Gray speaks with great liking of William Mason, who 'is
really in Simplicity a Child, & loves every Body he meets with';
and he expresses anxiety on account of Henry Tuthill, who had
not yet been elected a Fellow of Pembroke, or obtained even a
curacy, as Gray puts it.

This letter was written from Mrs Rogers's house at Stoke, where

Gray's mother and Mary Antrobus were now living with their sister. Gray himself spent the summer there, apart from one or two visits to Walpole's house at Twickenham, to which he had given its old name of Strawberry Hill. Here Gray saw George Montagu, a great friend of Walpole, whom Gray and Walpole had met at Rheims in 1739; here, too, he met Richard Bentley, the son of the famous Master of Trinity, who was helping Walpole to add to, and decorate, his house. Montagu appears to have written a little later to Walpole that he did not care for Gray, because Walpole replied:

> I agree with you most absolutely in your opinion about Gray; he is the worst company in the world – from a melancholy turn, from living reclusely, and from a little too much dignity, he never converses easily – all his words are measured, and chosen, and formed into sentences; his writings are admirable; he himself is not agreeable.[4]

Gray must have conversed easily enough with middle-class men like Wharton, Brown and Mason; in the company of nobles, with their easy and natural manner, he seems to have been on the defensive. Living in a secluded and – at that time – a provincial society, he had become so much of a bookman, a *rat de bibliothèque*, that he had lost (if he had ever possessed) any gift for the quick exchanges of normal conversation. Hence he talked like a writer, if not a lecturer. Apart from this, he gave the impression of being older than his years.[5] People may well have wondered if he had ever been young. The portrait which had been made of him at about the age of thirteen – an unintentionally cruel picture which is now in the Fitzwilliam Museum – is that of a prim and elderly child. Events in 1742 had inspired an outburst of poetry, but since then he had written little, apart from the trifle about Walpole's cat and probably several stanzas of the Elegy; and most of the first Commonplace Book.

However impatient his manner made Walpole, the latter continued to treat him with every consideration, and constantly to encourage him to write verses, and to agree to publish them.

It appears that on 19 August, some three weeks before Walpole's letter to Montagu, Gray sent Wharton fifty-seven lines of a poem in rhymed couplets on 'The Alliance of Education & Government;

I mean that they must necessarily concur to produce great & useful Men'. He points out that different climates and soils nurture different kinds of people, some warlike, some industrious, others artistic, or indolent, some with no gifts at all. The subject, therefore, is the influence of climate and geography on character and the idea almost certainly comes from the Abbé Dubos and, beyond him, from Saint-Évremond. It is a philosophic poem, rather like Johnson's *Vanity of Human Wishes*, or Goldsmith's 'Traveller', which Matthew Arnold thought it might have influenced.[6] The style is, to our taste, artificial; but eighteenth-century writers or orators admired it. C. J. Fox is reported to have cited with enthusiasm the verses about the Nile:

> What wonder, in the sultry Climes, that spread,
> Where Nile redundant o'er his summer-bed
> From his broad bosom life and verdure flings,
> And broods o'er Egypt with his watry wings . . .

while Gibbon, in Volume III of *The Decline and Fall*, regretted that Gray did not 'finish the philosophic poem of which he has left us such an exquisite specimen'. He had, by that time, added a further fifty lines, and had consigned it to his Commonplace Book, without troubling to finish it. This, he explained, was because, on reading the *Esprit des Lois* (Geneva, 1748), he found that Montesquieu had anticipated 'many of his best thoughts'. He had hoped to dedicate the poem to Montesquieu, but by the time he had written 107 lines Montesquieu was dead (he was to die in 1755). In later years Gray gave his young friend Norton Nicholls a more convincing explanation, to the effect that 'he could not go on with it. He had grown used to composing short poems where he could "polish every part"; he said that "he could not write otherwise, and that the labour of this method in a long poem would be intolerable".'[7] One must agree that he had no gift for writing a long poem, which requires a sustained effort and puts a strain on the nervous temperament.

At some date in 1748 or 1749,[8] Gray wrote to Chute that he had just heard that 'Turner (the Professor of Modern History here) was dead in London. if it be true, I conclude, it is now too late to begin asking for it'. As Gray and Chute had apparently discussed Gray's ambition, and as Chute may have had a chance of men-

tioning it to Walpole, Gray would have been glad to hear what
Walpole thought of it; and whether, in short, he could, with propriety, use his influence on Gray's behalf. But Turner was so
inconsiderate as not to die until November 1762. In 1756 the
Master of Pembroke fell ill, and one has the impression that his
demise would not have been unwelcome. Gray was anxious for
Brown, the President – an excellent man – to succeed him. Long,
however, not only recovered but lived until he was ninety, dying
only in 1770. It must have been rather vexatious.

On 9 March 1749 Gray wrote to Wharton that 'peace had been
signed between Prince Roger, surnamed the Long, Lord of the
Great Zodiack, the glass Uranium, & the Chariot that goes without
Horses, on the one Part; and the most noble James Brown' and
others, on the other. In brief, the Master had agreed to the election
of Tuthill and Mason as fellows. He had particularly objected to
Tuthill. Turning to books, Gray speaks with praise of the *Esprit
des Lois*. It represented, he says, 'the Labour of 20 Years . . . the
Style very lively & concise . . . it is the Gravity of Tacitus . . .
temper'd with the Gayety & Fire of a Frenchman'.[9]

After composing part of 'The Alliance of Education and
Government' in 1745, Gray had ceased to bestir himself, except to
study Plato, to transcribe in his Commonplace Book passages from
books of travel, and perhaps to add a few stanzas to the Elegy.
Conscious of his indolence, he again reproaches Cambridge with
it, as though distaste for any great effort were something new for
him. Thus he writes to Wharton on 29 April:

> . . . the Spirit of Lazyness (the Spirit of the Place) begins to
> possess even me[10] that have so long declaimed against it; yet has
> it not so prevail'd, but that I feel that Discontent with myself,
> that *Ennuy*, that ever accompanies it in its Beginnings. Time
> will settle my Conscience, Time will reconcile me with this
> languid Companion: we shall smoke, we shall tipple, we shall
> doze together, we shall have our little jokes . . . & our long
> Stories; Brandy will finish what Port begun; & a month after
> the Time you will see in some Corner of a London Even[ng]
> Post, Yesterday, died the Rev[nd] Mr John Grey [sic], Senior
> Fellow of Clare-Hall, a facetious Companion, & well-respected
> by all that knew him. his death is suppos'd to have been

occasion'd by a Fit of an Apoplexy, being found fallen out of Bed with his Head in the Chamber-Pot.[11]

It was easier to write in this vein to Wharton than to Walpole. In the same letter he speaks of recent books he has heard of, including the elder Crébillon's *Catalina*, first performed in 1748. The characters, he considers, are 'painted with great spirit'. He ends by accepting a loan of twenty guineas which Wharton had offered. On 8 August he wrote again to Wharton to describe the installation of the Duke of Newcastle as Chancellor of the University; the success of Dr Chapman's speech of welcome, and of William Mason's Installation ode. Preparations had begun in June, and every notable in the country had been invited;[12] but the actual ceremony took place on 1 July. Gray mentions that Tuthill was to come into residence at Michaelmas, and he has hopes 'that these two (Mason and Tuthill) with Brown's assistance may bring Pembroke into some Esteem'. But it was not to work out in that way.

1749 was an eventful year for Gray. On 5 November Mary Antrobus died at West End House, the home at Stoke, and Gray wrote a letter of condolence to his mother. He had hardly dispatched this before he read in some paper that a certain Horatio Walpole had been nearly killed by a ruffian, near London. He wrote at once, on 12 November, to Horace Walpole:

> I hope in God it is your Uncle, or his Son (for News-Papers are apt to confound ye) but from the Circumstances I fear it must be you, that have had so very narrow an Escape from Death. excuse me, if I am sollicitous to know how you are after such a Surprise; & whether you have really met with no considerable Hurt . . .[13]

Gray was right in his surmise. It was the famous Horace, and not his uncle or cousin, both of whom had the same name. Two highwaymen had attacked Walpole's carriage as he was returning from Kensington to St James's. One of them, James Maclean, son of a Scottish minister, had fired, and the bullet had grazed Walpole under the eye. This Maclean had committed several robberies and was hanged in 1750.

Between 12 November 1749 and 12 June 1750, when he wrote again to Walpole, there is no record of Gray's doings. He probably remained at Cambridge until the beginning of June and then, as in previous years, spent the summer and autumn with his mother. It seems at least certain that, stimulated, or rather activated, by the death of his aunt, of whom he had been very fond, he brought himself to complete the churchyard poem. 'I have been here at Stoke a few days (where I shall continue good part of the summer),' he wrote to Walpole; 'and having put an end to a thing, whose beginning you have seen long ago, I immediately send it you. You will, I hope, look upon it in the light of a *thing with an end to it*; a merit that most of my writings have wanted, and are like to want . . .'[14]

Years later, in 1773, Walpole wrote to Mason that he thought the 'Churchyard was . . . posterior to West's death at least three or four years . . . At least I am sure that I had the twelve or more first lines from himself above three years after that period.' This still leaves one uncertain as to both when Gray had begun the poem, and when he had written the four stanzas of a *first* conclusion, stanzas which he afterwards discarded, before adding the vivid description of the young poet, of his last days and his burial.[15] These points will be discussed in Part Two of the present work. Gray's original intention had been to call the poem 'Stanzas . . .', and it was Mason who had induced him to entitle it an 'Elegy'.

The idea of a 'Meditation' among the tombs, which was a fashionable topic at the time, had probably occurred to him during his first few years at Peterhouse, when he was living next door to the graveyard of Little St Mary's, one of the most melancholy spots in Cambridge; but it is generally agreed that the scene of the poem, so far as it has one, is Stoke Poges, because 'th'unhonoured dead' whom it commemorates are a rural community of husbandmen, such as Gray could observe during his summer wanderings round West End House. The scenery of Stoke, with its meadows, elms and beeches, which had been evoked in the 'Ode on the Spring', has been beautifully described by Mr Ketton-Cremer, who notes that the place has now lost much of its rural seclusion.[16] The description of the churchyard –

> Beneath those rugged Elms, that Yew-tree's Shade,
> Where heaves the Turf in many a mould'ring Heap,
> Each in his narrow Cell for ever laid,
> The rude Forefathers of the Hamlet sleep

– fits the churchyard at Stoke, where two yew trees are still standing. Hard by the church stood the Manor-House, which had been built by an Earl of Huntingdon in the sixteenth century and purchased towards 1600 by Sir Edward Coke.

It was at Walpole's instance[17] that Gray had at last sent him the Elegy, but without intending it to be published. Walpole, however, was so deeply impressed that he lent a copy or copies to friends, and they circulated copies. One fell into the hands of Lady Cobham, who had just brought her young protégée, Miss Henrietta Speed, to occupy the Manor-House at Stoke. This house she had inherited from her mother. Her husband, a retired general, had died the year before, and she had been obliged to vacate the Hall at Stowe. Miss Speed, a girl of twenty-two, had been an orphan from childhood and Lady Cobham had brought her up. She was witty and attractive, as well as being the prospective heiress of Lady Cobham. Another, a very beautiful and brilliant person, happened to be staying at the Manor at this time: Lady Schaub, a French Protestant from Nîmes who, having lost her first husband, had been much sought after, and had married Sir Luke Schaub. Sir Luke was a Swiss from Basle, who had become a British subject and was a member of the diplomatic service. Here was cosmopolitanism in person.

Lady Cobham, having heard from the Rev. Robert Purt that the now celebrated author of the churchyard stanzas was actually staying with his mother and aunt about a mile away, asked Lady Schaub and Miss Speed to call on Mrs Gray and make the poet's acquaintance. This was probably in September. Mason in his *Memoirs of Gray* gives a discreet account of the visit, stating that the poet 'happened to be from home when the ladies arrived'. The fact was that, being afraid of ladies of fashion, he had taken refuge in 'a small closet in the garden'. On returning from this retreat, he found a note:

Lady Schaubs compliments to Mr Gray
    She is sorry to have not found[18] him to tell him that Lady Brown[19] is very well.

Gray was now obliged to return the call and, far from finding it a *corvée*, he met with a most cordial reception and was invited to dinner. After this he was frequently entertained at the great house, as he called the Manor. He became an intimate of these ladies and, in order to divert them, evoked his adventure in a humorous piece entitled 'A Long Story', which is one of his most successful efforts. As it is not in fact long, he justified the title by inserting before the final quatrain: '(Here 500 stanzas are lost)'. This was evidently completed some days after 3 October because it contains an allusion to the trial and sentence of James Maclean. In response to a copy which Gray sent to Lady Cobham, Miss Speed wrote:

> Sir,
>
> I am as much at a loss to bestow the Commendation due to your performance as any of our modern poets would be to imitate them; Every body that has seen it, is charm'd and Lady Cobham was the first, tho' not the last that regretted the loss of the 400 [*sic*] stanzas; all I can say is, that your obliging inclination in sending it has fully answered, as it not only gave us amusement the rest of the Evening, but always will, on reading it over. Lady Cobham and the rest of the Company hope to have yours' tomorrow at dinner.
>
> I am your oblig'd & obedient
> Henrietta Jane Speed.[20]
> Sunday.

Copies of 'A Long Story' circulated in London almost as rapidly as manuscripts of the Elegy; and there may have been gossip about some more particular friendship between Miss Speed and Mr Gray. A copy of the verses had reached Durham by December, because on the 18th Gray wrote to Wharton to explain himself:

> . . . but for my Heart it is no less yours that it has long been; & the last Thing in the World, that will throw it into Tumults, is a fine Lady. the Verses you so kindly try to keep in countenance were wrote to divert that particular Family, & succeeded accordingly, but, being shew'd about in Town, are not liked there at all . . .

He adds that a lady of fashion had told Walpole that she did not know what to make of 'a Thing by a Friend of his . . . for it aim'd at every Thing, & meant nothing. to wch he replied, that he had always taken her for a Woman of Sense, & was very sorry to be undeceived'.

'A Long Story' contains in fact details and allusions which could be properly understood only by Lady Cobham's circle; yet the general drift of the story and the gaiety of the style – in a metre imitated from Matthew Prior – are such as to amuse most readers.

In the letter to Wharton, cited above, Gray encloses the 'Stanzas',[21] that is, the churchyard poem, which

> have had the Misfortune by Mr W.ˢ Fault to be made still more Publick, for wᶜʰ they certainly were never meant, but it is too late to complain. they have been so applauded, it is quite a Shame to repeat it. . . . I should have been glad, that you & two or three more People had liked them, wᶜʰ would have satisfied my ambition . . . I have been this month in town . . . diverting myself among my gay Acquaintance; & return to my Cell with so much more Pleasure. I dare not speak of my future Excursion to Durham[22] for fear – but at present it is my full Intention.[23]

One is left to surmise that Gray's 'gay Acquaintance' included Lady Cobham and her friends, as well as Walpole and his; and that, if Miss Speed had not thrown his heart 'into Tumults', she had not left it untouched. The 'Misfortune' of having his stanzas 'made still more Publick' was one of his eccentricities, and this was not the only time that Walpole was to be censured and reproved.

On 11 February 1751, in fact, he wrote to Walpole: 'As you have brought me into a little Sort of Distress, you must assist me, I believe, to get out of it . . .'. A copy of the Elegy had fallen into the hands of the *Magazine of Magazines*, a not very reputable monthly, which had written to Gray to say that they were printing it; that they had learned 'that the *excellent* Author of it is I . . ., & that they beg not only his *Indulgence*, but the *Honor of his Correspondence*, &c . . . I have but one way left to escape the Honour they would inflict upon me . . .' and, in short, Walpole is asked to make Dodsley print it in less than a week from his copy, but without the author's name, 'in his best Paper & Character. he must correct the Press himself . . . if he would add a line or two to say it came into his Hands by Accident, I should like it better. . . .'[24]

Walpole at once executed Gray's commission and the Elegy

appeared on the 15th in a quarto-sized pamphlet at sixpence, the day before the *Magazine of Magazines* published a copy full of spelling mistakes; while, to make things worse, it was stated that the verses were 'by the very ingenious Mr *Gray* of *Peter-house, Cambridge*'. The official copy was headed as follows:

The following Poem came into my Hands by Accident, if the general Approbation with which this little Piece has been spread, may be call'd by so slight a Term as Accident. It is this Approbation which makes it unnecessary for me to make any Apology but to the Author: As he cannot but feel some Satisfaction in having pleas'd so many Readers already, I flatter myself he will forgive my communicating that Pleasure to many more.

The Editor.

Tact and complacency could hardly have gone further, and Gray was pacified:

My dear Sir,

You have indeed conducted with great decency my little *misfortune*: you have taken a paternal care of it, and expressed much more kindness than could have been expressed from so near a relation. But we are all frail; and I hope to do as much for you another time . . . I thank you for your advertisement, which saves my honour, and in a manner *bien flatteuse pour moi* . . .[25]

He adds that he is going to send a copy of Mason's drama, *Elfrida*, for Walpole's opinion.

Meanwhile, Dodsley's edition of the Elegy was quickly sold out, and was to be reprinted several times in the next few years, and again and again since then. It was to be translated scores of times into other languages, especially into Latin, and also into French, Italian, Greek, German, and Welsh; even into Sanskrit and Bengali; but not, as far as I can ascertain, into Spanish or Russian.

In the second reprint of 1751 Gray inserted, before the Epitaph, the stanza about the robin and the violets – a very lovely stanza. One regrets that he afterwards discarded it.

CHAPTER 9

The Six Poems and the death of Dorothy Gray: 1752–1753[1]

Anxious to secure recognition for Gray, Walpole now began to plan an edition of the English poems which Gray had written, to be illustrated by Richard Bentley. As a member of the 'Committee of Taste', with Chute and Walpole himself, he was designing the decorations for the house at Strawberry Hill, and Walpole felt sure that he would do justice to Gray. Kent's designs for an edition of *The Faerie Queene*, he told Montagu,[2] were in his view very bad, whereas 'our charming Mr Bentley is doing Gray as much more honour as he deserves than Spenser'. This *seems* to imply that he thought Gray a greater poet than Spenser. However that may be, it is clear that by the spring of 1751 Bentley had begun to make drawings for the five of Gray's poems which Walpole had collected, as well as for Walpole's own verses. But Walpole was more interested in publishing his protégé's work than his own. In response to an inquiry if he had any other piece in hand, Gray sent him the 'Hymn to Adversity', which he had written in August 1742, adding:

> I send you this (as you desire) merely to make up half a dozen; tho' it will hardly answer your End in furnishing out either a Head or Tail-piece. but your own Fable[3] may much better supply the Place. you have alter'd it to its Advantage . . .[4]

It follows from this that Gray had agreed to the projected edition, although he appears at first to have 'thrown cold water' on Bentley's drawings. Bentley, however, went ahead, and in the end Gray was delighted.[5] On 8 July 1752 he wrote to Walpole:

> I am at present at Stoke, to wch I came at half an Hour's Warning upon the News I received of my Mother's Illness . . .

but as I found her much better . . . I shall be very glad to make you a visit at Strawberry, whenever you give me a Notice of a convenient time. I am surpriz'd at the Print, wch far surpasses my Idea of London Graving. the Drawing itself was so finished . . . Mr Bentley (I believe) will catch a better Idea of Stoke-House from any old Barn he sees than from my Sketch: but I shall try my Skill. . . .[6]

The print in question was a proof of Bentley's drawing of the young poet's funeral in the Elegy, a drawing engraved by Charles Grignion, who was considered more skilful than Johann Sebastian Müller. The latter had engraved the illustrations for the other poems. Gray duly sent a sketch of the Manor-House at Stoke, and Bentley used it for the head-piece to 'A Long Story'; but Gray was still feeling qualms about including this poem. It may be that Dodsley, who was to publish the *Six Poems*, had objected to it:

He has reason [Gray wrote to Walpole] to gulp when he finds one of them only a long story. I don't know but I may send him very soon (by your hands) an ode to his own tooth, a high Pindarick upon stilts, which one must be a better scholar than he is to understand a line of, and the very best scholars will understand but a little matter here and there. It wants but seventeen lines of having an end, I don't say of being finished. As it is so unfortunate to come too late for Mr Bentley, it may appear in the fourth volume of the *Miscellanies*, provided you don't think it execrable, and suppress it.[7]

He had now reconciled himself to the inclusion of 'A Long Story', which he had not wished to see in print. But Walpole, who later told Lady Ossory that humour was Gray's 'natural and original turn', obviously liked it, and Bentley's designs clinched the matter. The 'high Pindarick' to which Gray refers was 'The Progress of Poesy', which he did not finish until later. It is not, as he conceded, a model of clarity.[8] On 17 December he advised Walpole that he had received the first proofs of the *Six Poems*; 'I thought it was to be a Q^to, but it is a little Folio. the Stanzas are number'd, wch I do not like.'[9] In February 1753 he found further ground for alarm, and wrote direct to Dodsley:

> I am not at all satisfied with the Title, to have it conceived that I
> publish a Collection of *Poems* (half a dozen little matters . . .)
> thus pompously adorned would make me appear very justly
> ridiculous . . . the Verses are only subordinate, & explanatory to
> the Drawings, & suffer'd by me to come out thus only for that
> reason. . . .

The title was to be altered and to read:

Designs by Mr R. Bentley
for six Poems by
Mr T. Gray[10]

Dodsley, in the meantime, had planned to reproduce Eckhardt's
portrait of Gray as a frontispiece to the forthcoming volume, and
news of this threw the poet into a paroxysm of anxiety:

> Sure you are not out of your Wits [he wrote to Walpole]. this I
> know, if you suffer my Head to be printed, you infallibly will
> put me out of mine. I conjure you immediately to put a stop to
> any such design . . . the thing, as it was, I know will make me
> ridiculous enough; but to appear in proper person at the head
> of my works, consisting of half a dozen Ballads in 30 pages,
> would be worse than the Pillory. . . . I am extremely in earnest,
> & can't bear even the Idea . . .

He begs to be set at ease.[11]

Walpole good-humouredly complied with Gray's wishes and
sent a note to allay his anxiety. This, however, seems to have produced an effect opposite to that intended, because it provoked a
further letter, now lost, in which he must have repeated his
objection and offered to compensate Dodsley for any loss he may
have incurred in having the plate engraved to no purpose.

Walpole replied that he was 'very sorry . . . that [he] had expressed [himself] in a manner to have quite the contrary effect
from what [he] intended'. He reassured Gray about any possible
loss for Dodsley. The portrait would not appear. He thought the
title a mistake, since the drawings had evidently been made to
illustrate the poems. He did not agree that it was affected to leave
out 'the Mr before your Names'; if he ever published anything, it

would appear as by 'plain Horace Walpole'. He concluded: 'I will say no more now, but that you must not wonder if I am partial to you and yours, when you can write as you do and yet feel so little Vanity . . .'[12]

Walpole was indulgent. There was probably an unconscious, if perverse, element of vanity in Gray's make-up. His character, formed by a cruel heredity and home-life, is so complex that any conclusions must be tentative, except that pride was an outstanding characteristic. But his extraordinary anxiety about the *Six Poems*, and his dread of ridicule, suggest that Walpole may have been mistaken. An excess of modesty may be due to fear of not being a great success.

The *Six Poems* duly appeared on 29 March, entitled and printed as Gray had required: a folio of thirty-six pages, printed on one side of each leaf and in large type. The price was half a guinea. Each poem had a frontispiece, head-piece and tail-piece, five of these engraved by Müller and the one for the Elegy by Grignion. Bentley had thoroughly enjoyed himself. In place of the portrait which Gray had dreaded, Bentley had adorned the title-page with a picture in which a monkey (Bentley) is seated at an easel, making a portrait of Apollo with his lyre (Gray),[13] while one sees in the distance the twin peaks of Parnassus. Was he poking fun at Gray as well as at himself? All the designs fulfilled their purpose except those for the 'Hymn to Adversity', which fell short of the horrors Gray had imagined. For the ode on the cat he went far beyond the text of Gray's verses, turning what ought to have been an elegy, which it was not, into a piece of fun. The tail-piece depicted Selima on the prow of Charon's boat on the Styx, arching her back and spitting at Cerberus, whose three heads are barking at her. As Gray's ode had been so inappropriate, this was perhaps the best way of treating it. The frontispiece to the churchyard poem was suitably ghoulish; in the tail-piece was depicted the funeral procession bearing the coffin of the dead poet to the church-door, where a cleric is calmly awaiting it. The frontispiece to 'A Long Story' contains a story in itself. In the top left corner a winged cleric (Mr Purt) is blowing a double trumpet, while behind him two winged ladies are flying in pursuit of the poet. The latter, at the bottom, is escaping under the 'hoops' of two muses. Outside the frame, top left, Sir Christopher Hatton is dancing wildly with one leg in the air; and at the very top Queen Elizabeth, backed by a cannon, is glaring across at the Pope, backed by a 'Bull'. Not many such appropriate illustrations to a book of poems can have been made in England.

Gray was so pleased with Bentley's drawings[14] that he had already composed some 'Stanzas to Mr Bentley', seven quatrains in all, comparing the artist's 'airy fancy' and 'genuine flame' with his own 'tardy rhymes'.

> Ah! could they catch his strength, his easy grace,
>   His quick creation, his unerring line,
> The energy of Pope they might efface,
>   And Dryden's harmony submit to mine.
> But not to one in this benighted age
>   Is that diviner inspiration given,
> That burns in Shakespeare's or in Milton's page,
>   The pomp and prodigality of heav'n . . .

These stanzas, which are unique in their kind in Gray's work, strike one as the most pleasing and spontaneous that he ever wrote. They confirm to some extent Arnold's view that 'an east-wind' blowing in that age was discouraging to Gray's genius, who might have written much more and better poetry, if he had been born later.

Unhappily the publication of *Six Poems* could give him little pleasure, as his mother had died earlier in the month, on 11 March. The loss of her to whom he owed his life and his education, who had always advised him for the best, affected him perhaps more than the loss of West. On the headstone of her tomb in the churchyard at Stoke, her son described her as 'the careful tender mother of many children, one of whom alone had the misfortune to survive her'.[15] After attending the funeral, Gray wrote to Wharton, who was in London, to ask if he could find rooms near him; if not, he would go to his former lodgings in Jermyn Street, where he appears to have had rooms above the shop of a hosier named Roberts, at the sign of the Three Squirrels. He felt that Wharton was the friend most likely to be able to console him.

On the other hand, the year 1753 had set the seal on his reputation. Discerning critics now recognised him as the major poet of the day, and this he owed entirely to Walpole. It was Walpole who had been responsible for the publication of the Elegy; it was he who had planned the *Six Poems*. There is no evidence that, but for Walpole, Gray would ever have published any verses under his own name. It is true that late in 1754 he sent a copy of his first 'Ode in the Greek Manner' to Wharton, who then wished him to publish it; but Gray thought that it might simply appear in a new miscellany of Dodsley's.[16] Gray also later arranged for Dodsley in London and the Foulis Brothers in Glasgow to print a collected edition of his poems without advising Walpole of the plan. But this was only after Walpole had persuaded him to come out in print, and after he himself had printed the two Pindaric odes. Had it not been for this active friend, it is likely that Gray would have left all his verses, as he did leave most of them,[17] to Mason, who published them after Gray's death. And in that event he would have been known in his lifetime – apart from the Elegy – only to a limited circle; he would not have been offered the post of Poet Laureate; nor is it likely that Stonhewer could have induced Lord Grafton to have Gray appointed to the Cambridge professorship.

It was not that Walpole ever posed as the generous patron. His name did not appear in connexion with the Elegy or with the *Six Poems*. One might perhaps have expected Gray to dedicate an English poem or a collection to him, as the Roman Horace had dedicated several of his odes and other pieces to Maecenas.[18] But Gray did greatly assist Walpole in his historical works, and perhaps it did not occur to him to dedicate any of his English poems to his friends.

Thus it would be unfair to reproach him with ingratitude, or exaggerate the fuss he had made over the *Six Poems*. He was by nature nervous and apprehensive; he had a real distaste for publicity. He had probably feared that if a slender volume, priced at ten and sixpence (equivalent in purchasing power to some twenty times that figure today), fell into the hands of anyone in Cambridge, as it was certain to do, Eckhardt's portrait, of a young man with a gentle, dovelike face, would draw down further ridicule on him. He was aware that the fellow-commoners of Peterhouse regarded his jars of pot-pourri and window-boxes of flowers as more typical of a maiden lady than a manly don. Hence the frantic letter to Walpole, to prevent the inclusion of the Eckhardt portrait, which had made him look younger than he was.

The year 1753, with the death of his mother, marks an era in the life of Gray. He was now thirty-seven and, in habits and manner, middle-aged. His health, hitherto, even his nerves, had been tolerably good. In 1754 they began to give way, and with them the characteristics of eccentricity grew more pronounced.

CHAPTER 10

The visit to Durham:
the Pindaric Odes: 1753–1755[1]

Gray returned to Cambridge late in March 1753, and by the middle of June he appears to have recovered sufficiently from his bereavement to be interesting himself in politics and planning the visit to Durham. At the levee which the Duke of Newcastle, as Chancellor of the University, held in Clare Hall on the 16th, Gray received 'a very affectionate squeeze by the hand, & a fine compliment in a corner'. Although the Duke's appearance and manners were frequently ridiculed, he was a very capable politician and, by his visits to Cambridge, kept a firm hold on appointments to bishoprics and other senior positions. Walpole disliked him because he was one of those who had been instrumental in Sir Robert's fall from office; Gray hated 'old Phobus' (as he called him), though one does not know why. Newcastle was a man of excellent private character.[2]

In a letter to Wharton on 28 June, Gray mentions a report that Henry Vane the elder, the third Baron Barnard, intended to get his son-in-law elected 'at Durham' – which probably meant to one of the two county seats.[3] He adds that in rather over a fortnight he is setting out with Stonhewer, 'who is going down to his father's in a post-chaise'. They started on 16 July, travelling by the turnpike and hoping that their carriage would not be overturned by the mob from Leeds. In the event they suffered no injury. By way of Ripon, near which they saw Fountains Abbey and Richmond, they reached Wharton's 'Elvet-house' on 22 July.

Durham delighted Gray: '. . . suffice it to tell you', he wrote to James Brown, 'that I have one of the most beautiful Vales here in England to walk in, with prospects that change every ten steps . . . all rude & romantic, in short the sweetest spot to break your neck or drown yourself in that ever was beheld'.

This suggests that he had walked along the Banks, that is, the steep slopes that enclose the Wear where it makes a loop round the high peninsula on which stand the cathedral and the castle. Gray adds that he has seen Chapman, the Master of Magdalene, who was a prebendary of Durham, that he has dined with the Bishop, and has been twice at the races. But all was not well. He felt 'very shabby', as his dress coat, which had been packed in Stonhewer's box, had been sent by sea from King's Lynn to Sunderland, and had not yet arrived. '. . . you are desired therefore to send Lee the Bedmaker at Pet: house to the master of the Lynn boats to enquire what Vessel it was sent by, & why it does not come . . . P.S. I have left my Watch hanging (I believe) in my bed-room. will you be so good to ask after it?'

The coat probably arrived before long, and Gray stayed in Durham for over two months. Durham City was then a pleasant country town, limited in its boundaries and diminutive compared with what it is today. It housed, in addition to the clergy in the College (as the Close is called), an agreeable society of gentlefolk, many of them well-to-do, for whom the Assembly Rooms in the Bailey, and the race-course – which lay on the meadow between the houses on the north side of Old Elvet and the river – provided certain amenities. But in the absence of sanitation the place was unhealthy: 'here is a malignant Fever in the town', Gray wrote to Mason. The surrounding countryside was then entirely rural; the uplands were as bare as they are now, the great oak-forests having been felled as far back as the sixteenth century for shipbuilding on Tyneside. The collieries then lay mainly along the Tyne valley. In the absence of industrial coal-smoke and very little domestic pollution, the climate was better than it is today, colder but freer from fogs in winter, warmer in summer. The countryside was studded with castles, mainly built by Norman nobles to defend the frontier, and manor-houses – mainly belonging to the landed gentry – many of which have now disappeared or are in ruins. Great families like the Vanes and the Bowes were politically dominant. Apart from Sunderland, Stockton, Darlington and the port of Hartlepool, from where a company of Crusaders, sponsored by Bishop Pudsey, had once sailed, there were no large towns; Spennymoor and Crook, now very populous, being then only tiny hamlets.[4]

This explains why Gray enjoyed his visit to Durham, and why in later years he appreciated Wharton's manor of Old Park, one of the former residences of the bishops. If County Durham was more agreeable then than it is now, Cambridge on the contrary has improved: it is regarded by good judges as the most beautiful small city in the kingdom. In regard to Durham, it is surprising that Gray makes few references to the cathedral and the massive Norman keep beside it – one of the finest architectural units in the country.

Leaving Durham on 28 September, Gray called on Mason in York and was impressed by the stoicism with which he was bearing his misfortune. His father, a Hull clergyman, had bequeathed his estate to Mason's stepmother and entailed it to her daughter. But for Mason's fellowship, he would have been left penniless. From York Gray took the stage-coach, in which he had the company of Lady Swinburne, the widow of the Northumberland baronet of Capheaton.[5] She had been a good deal on the Continent, and was 'very chatty & communicative, so that I passed my time very well'. On reaching Cambridge he learned that his aunt, Mrs Rogers, had suffered a stroke. He went at once to her bedside; but she fortunately recovered, and he remained at Stoke until late in November.

It is interesting to record that on 3 October, that is, five days after Gray had left Durham, Richard Wharton, a younger brother of Thomas, had been involved in a quarrel with Sir Robert Eden and had challenged him to a duel. This was a statutory offence, and Richard had to find £4,000 in recognizances; of which £2,000 came out of his pocket, while his brothers Thomas and Jonathan each provided £1,000. The immediate cause of the quarrel may have been some trifling altercation. The Edens had a town house in the South Bailey, and the Whartons also owned a house there.[6] But the principal source of irritation was probably political. Sir John Eden, a country squire, was one of the two members for the city, and the corporation was probably anxious to have its own men elected.[7] However that may be, there is no mention in any surviving letter of Gray's of a misfortune which must have seriously troubled Dr Wharton – and which may explain why he soon afterwards set up in practice in London.

A letter which Gray had written to Wharton on 18 October is interesting for its observations on the journey from Durham to Cambridge, and for the evidence it supplies that the countryside was then very different from what it is now, and the climate also.

. . . at Topcliff (near Northallerton) I saw a large Vine full of black grapes, that seemed ripe . . . south of Tadcaster, I thought the Country extremely beautiful, broke into fine hills cover'd with noble woods . . . & every thing as verdant almost, as at Midsummer . . .

Gray had returned from Durham in good spirits, but the sojourn at Stoke had, not unnaturally, brought on a fit of melancholy. For Mason, in the meantime, the wheel of fortune had turned full circle. He was now secretary to Lord Holdernesse and was living in Arlington Street. On 5 November Gray wrote, requesting him 'to ask at Robert's, or some place in Jermyn-street, whether I could be there about a fortnight hence. I won't give more than ½ a guinea a week, nor put up with a second floor, unless it has a tolerable room to the street . . .'.

It seems that Mr Roberts accommodated him and that he had Mason's company for a few weeks, before returning to Cambridge. Early in 1754 he began to study a few of the Renaissance poets with a view to composing his first Pindaric ode. He also, in reply to a request from Walpole, sent him a great deal of information about the fifteenth and early sixteenth centuries, with copious extracts from English and French historians. The death of Henry Pelham in March led to a general election, in which Walpole, who had hitherto represented Torrington, became member for Castle Rising, thus continuing that long membership of the House which was to furnish later historians with so valuable a record of eighteenth-century politics. Gray, however, was now very much run down in health. He suffered from fever and fits of dizziness, as well as recurrent attacks of 'gout' and rheumatism, which he recorded in his pocket-books. It has been thought that most of these ailments were symptoms of a malady of the kidneys, and that this was ultimately the cause of his death. Travel did him good, for a time. He visited John Chute at the Vyne, near Basingstoke, Walpole at Strawberry Hill, and, later in the summer, George Montagu in Northamptonshire. This tour afforded him an opportunity of seeing Woburn and other notable mansions, especially Warwick Castle, which he described when writing to Wharton in September.[8] Of more interest is a letter of 26 December, in which he sent Wharton the full text of his 'Ode in the Greek Manner', later to be renamed 'The Progress of Poesy'. This was indeed a 'high Pindarick upon stilts'. Readers might be excused if they did not at once see that in Strophe 3 'Nature's Darling' was Shakespeare; still more if they wondered whether he was speaking of himself, as the successor of Shakespeare and Milton, when in Epode 3, he wrote:

> Oh Lyre divine, what daring Spirit
> Wakes thee now? tho' he inherit
> Nor the pride, nor ample pinion
> That the Theban Eagle bear . . .

Gray, a little hesitant about having sent the ode to Wharton, added: 'I desire you would by no means suffer this to be copied; nor even shew it, unless to very few, & especially not to mere Scholars, that can scan all the measures in Pindar, & say the Scholia by heart . . .' Wharton had at this time moved to London, where he was now practising medicine. At some date during the winter of 1754-5 the Earl of Bristol, who was expecting to be sent as Minister to Lisbon, invited Gray to accompany him as a private secretary. The change of climate and scenery would have improved his health and spirits; but he declined the offer.[9] The Earl was eventually appointed to Turin, a part of Italy which might also have been beneficial to Gray.

As it was, he continued to suffer from ill health and depression. On 1 March Mason sent him an 'Ode to Melancholy', hardly calculated to cheer the invalid. But he was not unwell enough to have to take to his bed. On the contrary, he was planning further poems, as he told Wharton on 9 March: 'I have two or three Ideas more in my head. . . . Must they too come out in the shape of little sixpenny flams . . . till Mr Dodsley thinks fit to collect them with Mr this's Song, and Mr t'other's epigram, into a pretty Volume?' One of these turned out to be 'The Bard', which he may already have begun; the other was an ode in stanzas more like those of his earlier poems. It was to treat of the 'Contrast between the winter past and coming spring – Joy owing to that vicissitude – Many who never feel that delight – Sloth – Envy – Ambition – How much happier the rustic who feels it, tho' he knows not how'.[10] Of the ode itself Gray seems to have composed some 68 verses – eight and a half stanzas – in 1754, and then laid them aside. Mason found them after the poet's death, completed the ninth stanza, added three to round off Gray's plan, and entitled the poem: 'Ode on the Pleasure arising from Vicissitude'. Mason's additions are adequate; but the eight stanzas which Gray had written may well appear to modern readers as the best he ever composed in English: they come nearest to anticipating Wordsworth and Shelley.

He had turned in 1754 from minute research into the medieval history of England and France to the study of the history and language of the Welsh; and especially of Welsh poetry. His principal sources were the information which Lewis Morris had given Thomas Carte for his *History of England*, a book which had just appeared (1747–54); but also, and of equal importance, David ap Rhys's *Cambrobrytannicae Cymraecaeve linguae institutiones* (1592), a work on the language and prosody; David Powel's edition of the *Descriptio Cambriae* (1585), and of course Giraldus Cambrensis. From these works he acquired a great deal of information which he summarised where it interested him in a second volume of the Commonplace Book. This was a folio, in which the article headed 'Cambri' occupies seven pages. Gray's principal interest was the study of Welsh prosody and the origin of rhyme in modern poetry. These speculations belong rather to his critical interest in English prosody;[11] but his researches into Welsh poetry were of immediate use to him in composing 'The Bard'. He had read in Carte's *History* that in 1284, when Edward I finally conquered North Wales, he was 'said to have hanged up all their Bards, because they encouraged the Nation to rebellion, but their works (we see) still remain; the Language . . . still lives, and the art of their versification is known, and practised to this day among them'. Identifying himself with a survivor of this alleged massacre, Gray imagines the bard as apostrophising from a crag in Snowdonia the victorious king as he leads his army up the defile; foretelling the evils that will befall his descendants, and the final triumph of the Welsh – and the perpetuation of poetry – by the accession of the Tudors to the throne. The structure of the poem is that of a Pindaric ode, but the versification is imitated from Welsh poetry, entailing an abundant use both of internal rhymes and of alliteration.

Gray appears to have composed the first strophe, and perhaps also the antistrophe and the epode, by the spring of 1755; and on 21 August he sent to Stonhewer 'a piece of the Prophecy; which [he remarks] must be true at least, as it was wrote so many hundred years after the events'.[12] This was Antistrophe 2 and Epode 2, with four verses of Strophe 3. On the same day he wrote to Wharton, who seems to have liked the first part of 'The Bard'. But Gray was very unwell and felt unable to compose any more at the time. In another letter, dated 18 October from Stoke, he speaks of listlessness, and begs Wharton 'to prescribe me somewhat strengthening & agglutinant'. It was not until his health had improved, and then only when John Parry, 'the blind harper' of Ruaben, had given a recital in Cambridge, that inspiration returned and he completed 'The Bard'.[13]

Meanwhile, in the summer of 1755 he had received a long and silly letter from Mason, who was in Hanover and finding it hard to give 'any satisfactory account of the state of Germanic Learning'. On a visit to Hamburg he had met a 'Madam Belch', who had asked him the name of 'the famous Poet that writ the Nitt toats [the "Night Thoughts"]. I replyd Doct^r Yonge. She begd leave to drink his Health in a Glass of sweet wine. . . . I asked Madame Belch if she had ever read La Petite Elegie dans La Cemeterie[14] Rustique, C'est Beaucoup Jolie, je vous Assure! . . . Oui Monsr (replyd Madame Belch) Je lu, & elle est bien Jolie & Melancholique mais elle ne touche point La Coeur comme mes tres cheres Nitt toats.'

He adds that in Hamburg he had bought 'a piano Forte,[15] and so cheap, it is a Harpsichord too of 2 Unison, & the Jacks serve as mutes . . . Pray Mr Gray write soon . . . and tell me about Rousseau or any thing . . .'. He mentions the names of a number of other Englishmen who were in Hanover, including William Whitehead, the future Laureate.

Gray was well enough in July to stay with Chute at the Vyne, and pay a visit to Portsmouth and Netley Abbey. He was charmed with the scenery, especially the tall oak-woods and 'the sea winding, & breaking in bays into the land', as he described it in a letter of 6 August to Wharton. But two days later he was suffering from 'a feverish Disposition, & little wandering pains, that may fix into the Gout . . .'; and on 10 August he cried off a visit to Strawberry Hill because 'they have order'd me to bleed', and he could not bring all his medicines with him. On the 14th he writes to tell Chute that Walpole is 'very ill of a Fever & Rash'; and that he himself has 'been bloodied, & taken draughts of salt of Wormwood, Lemons, Tincture of Guiacum, Magnesia & the Devil'. His foot aches, his head aches, he feels 'light & giddy'. A week later he was being attended by Dr Hayes, of Windsor, but still did not know whether his malady was gout or rheumatism. The doctor had drawn off ten or eleven ounces of blood, and prescribed a draught to be taken night and morning. Gray sent Wharton the formula, which he did not understand. He was still feverish and suffering from loss of sleep. On 14 October, however, he tells Walpole that he has 'been tolerably well' since he saw Montagu; but he is still fearing a relapse. The Whartons had invited him to stay with them at the house they had acquired in Coleman Street, and he hoped to come. He warned them that he might fall ill again: they 'are not to imagine my illness is in *Esse*; no, it is only in *Posse*'. He did, however, stay with them from 30 October to 26 November, and then returned to his rooms in Peterhouse.

CHAPTER 11

The move to Pembroke Hall:
the Pindaric Odes (II): 1756–1757[1]

'Notabile et insigne et quam pretiosum collegium quod inter omnia loca universitatis . . . mirabiliter splendet et semper resplenduit' (Henry VI on Pembroke Hall).

The treatment recommended by Wharton had relieved Gray's pain and other symptoms; but he was now beset with a new source of trouble. Two fellow-commoners who lived on the same staircase 'make a great progress in drunkenness', he wrote to Wharton. He feared that they might, one night, overturn a candle and set the place on fire. He therefore begged Wharton to send him a rope-ladder, at least thirty-six feet long, and with 'strong hooks' to attach to 'an iron bar to be fix'd withinside of my window'.[2]

Gray then had a bar fixed *outside* his window in such a way that he could hook the ladder on to it; the ladder arrived; these precautions of his, however, were an invitation to mischief. In the small hours of one morning early in March, his tormentors persuaded their servant to raise a cry of fire, in the hope that Gray would descend the ladder into the cold churchyard. It is very doubtful whether, as afterwards related, they had actually prepared a tub of water to receive him. In fact, when he opened the window he realised that it was a false alarm and went back to bed. In the course of time, however, this episode gave rise to some picturesque legends,[3] all of which were accepted by Edmund Gosse and woven into a piece of fiction that deserves quoting:

> . . . Gray was by no means a favourite among the high-coloured young gentlemen who went bull-baiting to Heddington or came home drunk and roaring from a cock-shying at Market Hill. Accordingly the noisy fellow-commoners determined to have a lark at the timid little poet's expense, and one night in February

1756, when Gray was asleep in bed, they suddenly alarmed him with a cry of fire on his staircase, having previously placed a tub of water under his window. The ruse succeeded only too well: Gray, without staying to put on his clothes, hooked his rope-ladder to the iron bar, and descended nimbly into the tub of water, from which he was rescued with shouts of laughter by the unmannerly youths. But the jest might easily have proved fatal; as it was, he shivered in the February air so excessively that he had to be wrapped in the coat of a passing watchman, and to be carried into the college by the friendly Stonhewer, who now appeared on the scene . . .[4]

Gosse comments indignantly about this 'almost inconceivable' outrage. The story is beautifully narrated, but practically all of it is romance. Neither Gray nor Mason refers to any such mishap. An authentic account of the affair was given by the Rev. John Sharp in a letter to the Rev. John Denne, on 12 March, that is, a few days after the event. He speaks of Gray's fear of fire, a fear due to the disaster in Cornhill, and to the rope-ladder and 'iron machine' and then adds: 'the other morning Lord Perceval and some Petrenchians,[5] going a-hunting, were determined to have a little sport . . ., and thought it would be no bad diversion to make Gray bolt, as they called it, so ordered their man Joe Draper to roar out fire. A delicate white night-cap is said to have appeared at the window; but finding the mistake, retired again to the couch . . .'.[6]

As Sharp was a Fellow of Corpus, some two hundred yards away, he was in a position to know the truth. Gosse should have had his doubts about the story of the tub of water. If Gray had really been drenched, it is most unlikely that a providential night-watchman would have appeared at the critical moment, and that Gray would have escaped an attack of pneumonia; in the latter case the culprits would certainly have been punished. As it was, Gray, who had been disturbed for weeks past by the noise made by his neighbours, now complained to the Master and Fellows; but they shrugged off the affair as a 'boyish frolic'.[7] As nothing was done to stop the nuisance, and as Gray had no real friends in Peterhouse except Stonhewer, he moved his penates, including a harpsichord and a large library, over the street to Pembroke Hall. Here he had close friends, and, although not liked by Gray, the

Master, Dr Long, raised no objection. Gray was given pleasant rooms[8] in the Hitcham Building, on the south side of the second court, which is still called Ivy Court, at a rental of £8 a year. On 25 March he reported his move to Wharton:

> This may be look'd upon as a sort of Æra in a life so barren of events as mine, yet I shall treat it in Voltaire's manner, and only tell you, that I left my lodgings, because the rooms were noisy, and the People of the house dirty. . . . All, I shall say more, is that I am for the present extremely well lodged here, & as quiet as in the Grande Chartreuse; & that every body (even the Dr Longs & Dr Mays) are as civil as they could be to Mary de Valence [foundress of Pembroke Hall] in person.[9]

The first two courts of Pembroke remain much as they were in Gray's time, except that the wing opposite the Hitcham Building has been repaired, and the Hall, to the right of the porter's lodge, enlarged. The chapel, with its handsome tower, had been designed by Sir Christopher Wren and built at the expense of his uncle, Matthew Wren, Bishop of Ely.

Founded in 1347 by Marie de Châtillon, daughter of the Comte de Saint-Pol and widow of Aymer de Valence, Earl of Pembroke, Pembroke Hall is the oldest of the *regular* Cambridge foundations,[10] with the exception of Peterhouse (1284). It has had many distinguished members: Nicholas Ridley, who had been Master for some years before the Marian reaction, when he was burned at the stake in Oxford; Edmund Spenser, who lived there for many years and perpetuated the fame of the then Master, John Young, and his friend Edward Kirke, in *The Shepherd's Calendar*; Gabriel Harvey, not to speak of a number of influential prelates.[11] 'No college but Trinity', wrote M. A. R. Tuker, 'outshines Pembroke for the fame of its scholars and none for the antiquity of its fame. Henry VI . . . speaks of it as "this eminent and most precious college, which is and ever hath been resplendent among all places in the university".'[12]

Roger Long, who was Master in Gray's time, was not deserving of Gray's disparagement. Dunthorne, the college butler, was a talented scientist who figures in the *DNB*. For the rest, by entering Pembroke Hall, Gray could feel that he had at least one illustrious predecessor who had been a servant of the muses; although he could not know that Smart, whom he considered a nuisance, would be recognised in our days as perhaps second only to himself and Goldsmith among mid-eighteenth-century poets.

Smart, however, had gone to live in London, having married the stepdaughter of Newbury, the publisher. Other fellows of the college had left, and new ones had been elected. Brown, May and Tuthill were still there, and, until July, Dr Long seemed to be a permanency. But he then, at the age of seventy-six, fell ill, and it looked as though this would be the end. On 30 July Gray, who was at Stoke, wrote anxiously to Walpole, informing him that 'Dr Long . . . (I am told) is either dying or dead', and begging Walpole to use his influence with Henry Fox or the Duke of Bedford on behalf of James Brown, the President (who would have made an excellent Master) – '. . . the Antagonist I apprehend is a Mr Addison, a *Creature* of your Uncle'.[13] Walpole began to draft a letter to Henry Fox; but Gray's appeal had been based on a false alarm, for Dr Long disappointed expectations and lived on to the age of ninety, displaying his 'Zodiack' and paddling about the pond in his velocipede.

Among the fellows whom Gray mentions in a letter to Mason, Edward Hussey Delaval, third son of a Northumberland magnate, was by far the most distinguished. While a good classical scholar, he had made his reputation in chemistry and physics, and was to be elected to the Royal Society in 1759. Gray appears to have done nothing in the spring and summer. The usual sojourn at Stoke made him, as usual, melancholy. In August, however, he went to London to see Chute, who had had a severe attack of gout, and, later, at the Vyne, did what he could to help the invalid. Mason, in the meantime, devoted his leisure hours to writing verses in imitation of Gray. It must have been pleasant to read his ode 'To a Friend':

> Through this still valley let me stray,
> Rapt in some strain of pensive GRAY,
> Whose lofty genius bears along
> The conscious dignity of Song;
>
> He too perchance, (for well I know,
> His heart can melt with friendly woe)
> He too perchance, when these poor limbs are laid,
> Will heave one tuneful sigh, and sooth my hovering shade.

He continues:

> While through the west, where sinks the crimson day,
> Meek twilight slowly sails, and waves her banners gray[14]

– a couplet which Gray called 'superlative'. This may have been ironical; or Gray may, perhaps, have thought the ode no more than his due. In any case, he encouraged Mason's poetisings. What Mason had read of 'The Bard' had suggested to him a blank-verse tragedy, *Caractacus* (which Gosse thought inferior to 'To a Friend'). For this project, he applied to Gray for information about the Druids, and on 19 December Gray sent him the titles of five recent works on the subject. 'Odickle', he added, 'is not a bit grown, tho' it is fine mild open weather. Bell Selby has dream'd that you are a Dean or a Prebendary.'[15] Miss Selby was one of the waitresses in the coffee-house. Her dream had already come true, since the Archbishop had made Mason a Prebendary of York Minster.

Gray had sent extracts of 'The Progress of Poesy' and 'The Bard' to his new friend Bedingfield, in August and December, but 'Odikle', as already mentioned, was still unfinished. During the early months of 1757 he seems to have got through the days with the aid of his usual 'narcotic' (as Gosse called it), this time probably in the study of Icelandic, that is, Old Norse poetry. 'The Bard' would probably have never been completed, but for the visit of John Parry, who gave a recital in May.

> . . . Mr Parry has been here, & scratch'd out such ravishing blind Harmony, such tunes of a thousand year old, with names enough to choak you, as have set all this learned body a'dancing, & inspired them with due reverence for Odikle, whenever it shall appear. Mr Parry . . . has put Odikle in motion again, & with much exercise it has got a *tender Tail* grown, like Scroddles, & here it is . . .

The 'tender tail' which he sent in this letter to 'Scroddles' (as he called Mason) consisted of Antistrophe 3 and Epode 3, concluding with the melodramatic suicide of the bard.

After making a few alterations in the text, Gray wrote to Mason: 'I send you enclosed the breast & merry-thought & guts & garbage of the chicken, wch I have been chewing for so long, that I would give the world for neck-beef or cow-heel . . .'. Bonfoy[16] and Neville – a classical scholar of Emmanuel College – preferred the first ode and objected to the conclusion of 'The Bard'; but Gray had already altered the last line and considered 'To triumph & to die are mine' better than 'Lo! to be free, to die, are mine'. Mason wanted the odes to be printed, and Gray, with an air of unwilling-ness, negotiated with Dodsley, who paid him forty guineas (a large sum in the currency of those days) for the copyright. Walpole, in the meantime, urged Gray to allow him to print the odes on the press he was establishing at Strawberry Hill, and Gray consented, not very graciously. Walpole then suggested that 'The Bard' needed explanatory notes.[17] Gray, who had left Cambridge for Stoke, replied on 11 July:

> I will not give you the trouble of sending your chaise for me. I intend to be with you on Wednesday in the evening. If the press stands still all this time for me, to be sure it is dead in child-bed.
>
> I do not love notes, though you see I had resolved to put two or three. They are signs of weakness and obscurity. If a thing cannot be understood without them, it had better be not under-stood at all . . .[18]

Printing began on 16 July and on 8 August two thousand copies were published by Dodsley with the title:

Odes by Mr Gray: ΦΩΝΑΝΤΑ ΣΥΝΕΤΟΙΣΙ –
Pindar, Olymp. II. Printed at Strawberry Hill for
R. and J. Dodsley in Pall Mall.

The quotation from Pindar meant 'Vocal to the intelligent', as Gray translated it. But what was needed to understand the odes was not intelligence but specialised knowledge. In spite of his modest disclaimers to Brown and Mason, Gray took special pains to obtain publicity for the little quarto volume, which Dodsley had priced at one shilling. Brown was warned that 'a poetical Cargo' would reach him in August, and he was asked to distribute copies to the Master and Fellows of Pembroke and to various other people in, or connected with, Cambridge. Dodsley was instructed to send copies to Lady Swinburne, to Bedingfield and his mother, and to 'Miss Hepburn at Monkridge near Haddington, if there be any such Person, wch I little doubt.[19] . . . you are desired to give me your *honest* opinion about the latter part of the Bard, . . . for I know it is weakly in several parts . . .'. He also asks for a report on how the book will be received in the north of England. He regrets the 'sulkyness' he has recently displayed, and any words which may have hurt Dodsley's feelings, 'for in reality I have been ill ever since I left Cambridge'.

Gray remained at Stoke until November, living in company with Mrs Rogers at West End House. 'The Cobhams are here, and as civil as usual,' he told Wharton. Mr and Mrs Garrick paid Lady Cobham a visit. Gray whiled away the time reading the first two volumes of the *Encyclopédie*, and awaited news of the way the odes were being received. Hurd[20] wrote that in Cambridge 'every body would be thought to admire. 'Tis true, I believe the greater part don't understand them.' Reports from London were no better, and Gray concluded that he was 'not at all popular. the great objection is obscurity . . . one Man (a Peer) . . . thinks the last stanza of the 2^d Ode relates to Charles I & Oliver Cromwell. in short the Συνετοι appear to be still fewer, than even I expected', he wrote to Wharton. The particularly obscure verses were the first eight in Epode 3, and it can be seen that they refer to Shakespeare and Milton, when one is told; but the first two lines –

> The verse adorn again
> Fierce War, and faithful Love . . .

– could mislead any reader. On 25 August Gray wrote to Hurd, relating that a 'very good man' had read the odes 'seven or eight times' and that 'when he next sees them, he shall not have above thirty questions to ask.' Gray's friends had written to console him – 'in short', he adds, 'I have heard of nobody but a player and a doctor of divinity that profess their esteem for them'; and also 'a lady of quality' who, however, did not understand the references to Shakespeare and Milton. The 'player' was Garrick, the DD, John Brown, and the lady of quality, Lady Holdernesse. Gray concluded his letter by asking Hurd not to be 'too happy' in the college living he had received, 'nor forget entirely the quiet ugliness of Cambridge'! Hurd replied at once that everybody in

Cambridge 'that knows anything of such things, applauds the Odes. And the readers of Pindar dote upon them'.

Gray was far from pleased when, on 7 September, he wrote to Mason, who had obtained notable preferments: 'You are welcome to the land of the Living, to the sunshine of a Court, to the dirt of a Chaplain's table', and so on, with further derogatory remarks, before returning to his personal obsession: 'I would not have put another note to save the souls of all the *Owls* in London. it is extremely well, as it is. nobody understands me, & I am perfectly satisfied.' He then adds a list of the unfavourable comments which had been made. It is interesting to notice that on the same day he wrote in a very different tone to Wharton, dwelling on some favourable verdicts. Miss Speed had seemed to understand the odes, and had repeated φωναντα συνετοισι to those who did not. Dr John Brown had called his poems 'the best Odes in our language. Mr Garrick, the best in ours, *or any other*'. (Better than Pindar's? Garrick was not perhaps the best judge.) Shenstone and Lord Lyttleton admired the poems, while wishing that the meaning had been clearer; while Walpole, in a letter to Lyttleton, said that 'perhaps no composition ever had more sublime beauties than are in each' of the odes. Mrs Garrick, he added, had been struck by the expression 'many-twinkling feet', and had declared that 'Mr Gray is the only poet who ever understood dancing'.[21] This was praise indeed, though Gray may not have heard it until later. At the time, he was pleased by the notice in *The Monthly Review* for September, 'particularly that observation, that the *Bard* is taken from *Pastor, cum traheret*, & the advice to be more original, & in order to be so, the way is (he says) to cultivate the native flowers of the soil . . .'.[22] This unsigned notice had been by Goldsmith, and he was certainly right. The subjects of Pindar's odes had been familiar, and interesting, to everyone in ancient Greece; the subject of 'The Bard' was of interest to cultured Welshmen, but only to a limited number of Englishmen. In 'Pastor, cum traheret' (Horace, *Odes*, Book I, No. 16) Nereus forecasts the ills that will befall Troy in consequence of Paris's betrayal of Menelaus's hospitality. It seems unlikely that Gray had been thinking of this ode; but the similarity of the theme also struck Johnson and Algarotti, who thought 'The Bard' 'far superior' to Horace's ode.[23]

Meanwhile, in the long and thoughtful notice which Goldsmith had written for *The Monthly Review*, he had ventured to advise Gray to 'study the people' as Pindar had done.

> He chose the most popular subjects, and all his allusions are to customs well known, in his days, to the meanest person. [Gray lacked these advantages. Yet] it is by no means our design to detract from the merit of our author's present attempt: we would only intimate that an English poet, – one whom the Muse has *mark'd for her own*, – could produce a more luxuriant bloom of flowers by cultivating such as are natives of the soil . . . such a genius as Mr Gray might give greater pleasure, if . . . he did justice to his talents, and ventured to be more an original . . .

Goldsmith, in fact, had put his finger on Gray's essential defect, his lack of originality, and his great mistake, namely, that since Pindar's odes had celebrated contests which no longer existed in modern Europe, odes which were to be sung and accompanied by dance, it was impracticable to adapt this form of verse to the needs of a world so different. Goldsmith preferred 'The Bard' to 'The Progress of Poesy'. It 'will give as much pleasure to those who relish this species of composition, as anything that has hitherto appeared in our language, the Odes of Dryden himself not excepted'.[24]

Walpole, in the meantime, proceeded to print in pamphlet form six stanzas in which Garrick urged Gray to ignore those who had failed to understand him, and not to 'quit his heav'n born art'.[25] This should have pleased the most exacting of poets, but Gray was too unwell to appreciate it. He wrote to Walpole to say that he had been in a 'much worse state of health' than usual. As to the printing: '. . . tho' I admire rapidity in writing and perseverance in finishing, being two talents that I want; yet I do not admire rapidity in *printing*, because this is a thing, that I or any body can do'.[26]

Neither Goldsmith's eulogium nor Garrick's encouragement seems to have greatly pleased Gray. He resented the fact that most people had been unable to understand the allusions in his odes. To these compositions he had devoted more time and trouble than to any of his other work, and he thought they had been a failure. On the contrary, over 1300 copies had been sold by the autumn, and he was now recognised as England's most eminent poet. On the death of Colley Cibber, the Laureate, the Duke of Devonshire directed his brother, Lord John Cavendish, whom Gray had met at Peterhouse in the 1750s, to ask Mason to sound Gray on the matter. Would he accept the position? Gray declined; and then wrote to Mason disparaging the office and the men who had recently held it, anticipating Shelley's disdain of the holders of this office. For several months, Gray had been sick in mind and body: much of his ill humour must be put down to ill health. He had no heart for writing that history of English poetry which he had planned and for which he was well qualified.

CHAPTER 12

Gray and Miss Speed: London and the British Museum: 1758–1759[1]

During the first half of 1758 Gray devoted most of his time to the second volume of the Commonplace Book. In this he entered notes on Norse and Welsh poetry, under the headings of 'Gothi' and 'Cambri'. The heading 'Metrum' contained notes for a study of English prosody, to which he believed that both of the former had contributed. On receiving news that Dr Wharton's little boy, Robin, had died in April, he wrote a sympathetic letter of condolence and composed an epitaph, which is obviously imitated from an epigram in the Greek Anthology, and is not an improvement on it. In June he made a tour of the principal cathedrals and abbeys in and near the Fen country; but when he returned to Cambridge he learned that his aunt, Mrs Oliffe, had suffered a stroke, and that Mrs Rogers had been very ill. This meant, he feared, that he would perhaps have to spend 'some years . . . in a house with two poor bed-ridden Women', as he wrote to Wharton, asking if he could find him quarters in London for a week. But before leaving Cambridge he wrote to Mason, who was now Rector of Aston, near Sheffield, to describe the new University Library. 'I keep an Owl in the garden' (of Pembroke), he added, 'as like me as it can stare; only I don't eat raw meat, nor bite people by the fingers.'

From the temporary quarters which had been given him in 1756 he had moved to another and more roomy set in the same building. The principal room, which served as his library, had windows overlooking Ivy Court, and is still preserved as 'the Gray Room', partly as a museum, partly for receptions. It has a fireplace at each end. Over one, hangs a copy of Benjamin Wilson's portrait of Gray in middle age; over the other, the portrait of Henrietta Speed. The bedroom, on the south side, overlooked the Master's garden. Gray enjoyed here the same liberty as in Peterhouse for cultivating

flowers in window-boxes, such as hyacinth and jonquil bulbs
which he grew indoors, as well as anemones and mignonette. Over
one fireplace stood two large Japanese vases, blue and white.
During the daytime, when not reading, he would stroll in the
fields, probably in Coe Fen and on Sheeps' Green, and, further
away, note the date of sowing wheat, and record the arrival and
departure of migrant birds.[2] He was now taking an even closer
interest in nature than he had done as a young man. It is recorded
that in the early evenings he would play on his harpsichord pieces
by Pergolesi and the younger Scarlatti.

But such pleasures had to be forgone towards the end of June,
when he went to visit his aunts, now aged respectively seventy-
seven and eighty-two. As, however, they had servants, he was able
to accompany Lady Cobham and Miss Speed to Hampton, to visit
Hampton Court, and also to see Walpole at Strawberry Hill. His
duties at Stoke were not arduous. He was often entertained at the
Manor, where Miss Speed cheered him with her witticisms. Lady
Cobham was trying to promote a match between them, and
Henrietta appears to have been not unfavourable to the scheme,
although she would not have wished to leave Lady Cobham while
the latter was still alive. At all events, Gray was becoming more
intimate with them. Some sixty years later, Admiral Sir John
Duckworth recalled that, as a small boy, he had been struck by the
sight of Gray 'being driven by Miss Speed about the country-lanes
in a butcher's cart'.[3] Not that visits to Stoke Manor were always
so agreeable. On 31 August he wrote to Wharton:

. . . I have been obliged to go every day almost to Stoke-house,
where the Garricks have been all the last week. they are now
gone, & I am not sorry for it, for I grow so old, that, I own,
People in high spirits & gayety overpower me, & entirely take
away mine. I can yet be diverted with their sallies, but if they
appear to take notice of my dullness, it sinks me to nothing . . .

The company of women – and of strangers – fatigued him: he
could not help it. Two years later, at a picnic near Henley, he only
once uttered a few words. When newcomers arrived in Cambridge,
he was apt to take refuge in the 'facunda silentia linguae', as he
called it. 'He never spoke out' – James Brown's words, repeated by
Matthew Arnold, have been regarded by some critics as relating

only to Gray's last illness; but there is no proof of it. Brown's form of expression sounds like a general statement: if referring to the one occasion, he would surely have stated: 'He did not say how ill he was feeling.'

Gray remained at Stoke until the early winter. At the end of September Mrs Rogers died, having left him £500 and made him joint executor of her estate with Mrs Oliffe, whom he did not like. It is quite probable that this old lady, feeling somewhat helpless in spite of her servants, was often querulous; but one wonders whether she deserved the hard things that Gray said of her in a letter to Brown, or again when he wrote to Wharton: 'I am agreeably employ'd here in dividing nothing with an old *Harridan*, who is the spawn of Cerberus & the Dragon of Wantley.' It took him a little time to fulfil his duties as executor, writing to his young cousin, Mary Antrobus, to assure her that she had not been forgotten. Then, as Mrs Oliffe had decided to move to her old home in Suffolk, he disposed of West End House and dispatched a cargo of furniture, glass, china, kitchen utensils and books, to be looked after by the kindly Wharton in London. He himself appears to have decided to migrate there – at least for a time.

Early in January 1759 he took lodgings in Gloucester Street, near Southampton Row, and probably furnished them with the effects he had sent from Stoke. Had he, in fact, as Mr Ketton-Cremer thinks, 'made up his mind to leave Cambridge and settle for an indefinite period in London'? It seems possible and, if so, it was an unusual move. Had he failed to appreciate all the advantages, personal and financial, which he had enjoyed in Cambridge, or was he attracted to London by having heard that the British Museum was soon to be opened? He would be able to study there the collections of medieval manuscripts. It seems that he had not burned his boats, and that he had left his books, harpsichord, music and window-boxes in his Pembroke rooms. He must have had an understanding with the college that he could return whenever he wished. There is no evidence of this; but it is recorded that he was back in the college from 15 February to 4 March.

Meanwhile, on 18 January, he had reported to Mason that Christopher Smart was not dead, as had been feared, and that an adaptation of Voltaire's *Mérope*, together with a farce adapted from Fagan, had been performed for his benefit. Aaron Hill had been responsible for the English version of *Mérope*. G.-B. Fagan's *La*

Pupille (the ward) had also been adapted; this play – reckoned by Voltaire as the best one-act farce of the century – had appeared under the title of *The Guardian*. Dr Arne seems to have been referring to this when he entitled his parody of Gray's Elegy: 'The Guardian outwitted'.[4]

Smart had suffered attacks of insanity since 1756, and was being looked after by friends. He was, when sane, amusing and very good company.

Gray had been a victim of gout early in February, and in April another attack brought him 'nearer being a Cripple'. This, however, had not prevented his hearing Cocchi's *Ciro riconosciuto*, a new opera, or visiting the British Museum, which had opened in Montagu House on 15 January. It housed Sir Hans Sloane's books and MSS, the Cottonian MSS and the Harleian. Parliament appears to have voted £1,400 a year to the Trustees for the acquisition of new books and the expenses of maintenance. In June Gray returned to Cambridge for a few days, and in July moved to rooms above a baker's shop in Southampton Row. Wharton, who seems to have had no great enthusiasm for the practice of medicine, had gone back to Durham; in July Gray sent him news of the hot weather, and described the various fruits available in London, and the flowers with which he had been adorning and scenting his rooms. As he had no means of recording the first blooming of wild flowers, he sent Wharton a long list which he had made at Stoke in 1754, when there had been 'a cold rainy Summer'.

He was much interested at this time in the war on the Continent with its varying fortunes, the defeat of the French at Minden, followed by the victory scored by the Russians and Austrians over Frederick of Prussia at Kunersdorf on 12 August. This news he sent to Miss Speed, who replied in one of the few interesting and revealing letters which he received at this time:

25th August 59

My dear Sir,

I wonder whether you think me capable of all the gratitude I really feel for the late marks you have given me of your friendship, I will venture to say if you knew my heart you wou'd be content with it, but knowing my exterior so well as you do You can easily conceive me Vain of the Partiallity you show me; in return for putting me in good humour with myself I will [assure] you Lady Cobham is surprizingly well & most extremely oblig'd to you for the Anxiety you express'd on her account – We now take the Air ev'ry Day. . . .

We are both scandaliz'd at your being in Town at this time of year . . . because we think it very unwholsome from the heat of the Season – now I know you are insensible to heat or cold . . . but you have not attention enough to your self to seek a remedy, we beg now to point out one against the Excessive heat of London, by desiring you wou'd come down to Stoke where you will find Ev'ry thing cool but the reception we shall give you – there is always a Bed Air'd for you & one for your Serv[t]; indeed I can make use of the Strongest argument to tempt you which is that at this time it will be a deed of Charity as we are absolutely alone. . . . if you are at present an invalide let that prompt you to come, for from the *affected creature* you know me, I am nothing now but a comfortable nurse . . .

I am au desespoire [*sic*] about my friend L. G. S. . . . I hope to talk all these matters over with you soon therefore shall add no more at present but that I am with great truth Dear Mr Greys
faithful Serv[t]
Henrietta Jane Speed
never make Excuses about franks for I never shall grudge the Expence you put me to by your Letters.[5]

This letter sounds like a declaration, or at least an encouragement. Gray must have written to excuse himself for not at once accepting the invitation, because he remained in London until late September, studying documents which related to Richard III. In a long letter to Wharton he gave the exact temperatures on thirty-two days from 20 July to 20 August, and identified a 'fish', which his friend had mentioned, as 'the Ink-fish', that is a squid or cuttle fish. For this he gave the Greek, Latin, French and Italian names, and explained that the Italians eat the smaller ones as a delicacy. He added that he was going 'to Stoke for a time, where Lady Cobh[m] has been dying' (contrary to the report in Miss Speed's letter).

After spending three weeks at Stoke, he accompanied the ladies to Lady Cobham's town house in Hanover Square, where Dr Duncan gave her treatment; and here he remained until about 18 November, when he returned to Southampton Row. Being now a good deal better off, he had engaged a manservant named Stephen Hempstead, a thoroughly reliable man who remained with him to the end. Keenly interested, like everyone, in news of the war, he had now heard of the fall of Quebec. He could not, of course, know that before leaving England, General Wolfe had been given a copy of the churchyard Elegy; that he had actually made notes in it; and that when, on the eve of the battle, that is on 12 September, someone in a boat near the General's, as they were moving along the river, quoted the poem, Wolfe was said to have observed: 'I would rather have been the author of that piece than beat the French tomorrow.'[6] The truth is, that Wolfe was himself a sick and melancholy man; he may indeed have had a premonition of his end.[7]

CHAPTER 13

Macpherson and Ossian:
studies in Welsh and Norse Poetry:
1760–1761[1]

In January 1760 Gray was reading Jehan Froissart's *Chroniques de France et d'Angleterre* – 'a favourite book of mine', he told Wharton in one of his voluminous letters. This mention was to catch the eye of Sainte-Beuve, who speaks of 'le charmant poète Gray qui, dans sa solitude mélancolique de Cambridge, étudiait tant de choses avec originalité et avec goût' – but, as the French critic did not realise, merely as a pastime. In March Gray was saddened by the death of Lady Cobham, which, however, must by now have been expected. He subsequently learned that she had left her estate to Miss Speed, and to himself £20 for a ring, perhaps as a hint that he should propose marriage to the heiress. His subsequent movements may be explained by this legacy; at the time, however, he was delving more deeply than before into the study of ancient Welsh poetry, and his interest in this was further enhanced by some extracts from Ossian which Walpole sent him in April. He replied with enthusiasm:

> I am so charmed with the two specimens of Erse poetry, that I cannot help giving you the trouble to enquire a little further about them, and should wish to see a few lines of the original, that I may form some slight idea of the language, the measures, and the rhythm . . .

Later in the year he told Wharton that he had been 'so struck with the infinite beauty' of Macpherson's 'translations from the Erse-tongue' that he had written to the author, who sent him a further fragment without, however, revealing whether they were genuine translations or mainly inventions of his own. Other inquiries elicited a letter from David Hume, which appeared to confirm their authenticity. These poems, wrote Hume, were 'in every body's mouth in the High-lands', and he named various reputable people who already knew them. He and others were raising a subscription to enable Macpherson to visit the Highlands with a view to recovering other fragments. Gray then was very near believing that these *Fragments of Ancient Poetry, collected in the Highlands of Scotland and translated from the Gaelic or Erse Language* – Ossian, in short – which appeared in the summer of 1760, were genuine. While entertaining some doubts, he continued to be fascinated by *Fingal*, an alleged epic which came out in December 1761, and by *Temora* in 1763.[2] Basing his so-called epics on a few genuine fragments which he had come across, Macpherson had invented whole poems with a skill akin to genius, and a keen sense of what would exactly hit the taste of the age – in France and in Italy even more than in England. In the history of the European literatures, the Ossianic poems contributed far more to the influence of 'English' literature than the works of such poets as Coleridge, Wordsworth and Shelley.[3]

Gray's thoughts had not always been on this lofty and mystical level. A letter of 22 April to Wharton, who had by now gone to live in the Manor of Old Park, contained news of a duel between two notables, and of the trials of Lord George Sackville and Lord Ferrers. The letter continued:

I thank you heartily for the Sow. if you have no occasion for her, I have; & if his L[dp] will be so kind as to drive her up to Town, will gladly give him 40 shillings and the Chitterlings into the bargain. I could repay you with the Story of my Lady F:r, but (I doubt) you know my Sow already.

Edmund Gosse was mystified by this passage, possibly because he had read it in Mason's bowdlerised version. 'It is rather difficult to know what, even in so pastoral a Bloomsbury,[4] Gray did with a sow, for which he thanks Wharton heartily in April 1760.'[5] Gosse did not realise that since his undergraduate days Gray had used 'Sow' to refer to any woman,[6] and also as a story, especially an improper one, about a woman – as in the above passage. Small wonder if he was not quite at ease in feminine society. Of this he had a great deal in June and July. He wrote to Wharton late in June:

. . . for these three weeks, I have been going into Oxfordshire with Madame Speed; but her affairs, as she says, or her vagaries, as I say, have obliged her to alter her mind ten times within that space: no wonder, for she has got at least 30,000£ with a house in Town, plate, jewels, china, & old-japan infinite, so that it would be ridiculous for her to know her own mind. I, who know mine, do intend to go to Cambridge, but that Owl Fobus is going thither to the Commencement.

Hatred of Lord Newcastle, the Chancellor, was one of Gray's obsessions, although this year his interest in Ossian, about which he wrote to most of his correspondents, had put Newcastle into the background. In July he spent some time at Shiplake, as the guest of Mrs Jennings, who was there with her daughter and Miss Speed. These ladies talked and laughed too merrily for Gray's peace of mind: he became very much fatigued by the chatter. One day they all dined 'on a cold loaf', which means that they had a picnic. Walpole reported to a friend that, according to Lady Ailesbury, Gray only once opened his mouth and that was to say: 'Yes, my Lady, I believe so.' In the end he escaped to London and Cambridge; and after this, though he occasionally saw Miss Speed, the relationship cooled off. Many years later, Lord Harcourt, who had known Gray at Cambridge, described Miss Speed as witty and good-humoured, but cold-hearted. '. . . she really loved nobody', he thought.[7] And it has been suggested that Gray had detected this alleged coldness.[8] But the kind letter she had written to him in August 1759 gives an opposite impression. One is inclined to conclude that it was Gray who was cold, that he was not attracted to women, and was completely set in bachelor ways. The sequel was not long in coming. In January 1762 he wrote to Wharton:

My old Friend Miss Speed has done what the World calls a very foolish thing. she has married the Baron de la Peyrière, Son to the Sardinian Minister, the Comte de Viry. he is about 28 years old (ten years younger than herself)[9] but looks nearer 40. this is not the effect of debauchery, for he is a very sober Man; good-natured & honest, & no Conjurer.[10] the estate of the family is about 4000£ a year. the Castle of Viry is in Savoy a few miles from Geneva, commanding a fine view of the Lake . . . I do not think she will make quite a *Julie* in the country.

He is referring to the *Nouvelle Héloïse*, of which the heroine, Julie, is perfectly contented with the rural life at Clarens. So far from having committed an error, Miss Speed had made a wise choice. She had acquired a home in one of the most beautiful parts of Europe, and was destined to a brilliant career as the wife of an ambassador, as the baron became after his father's death.

Apart from the Ossianic volume, 1760 was an *annus mirabilis* in the history of English literature. The first two volumes of *Tristram Shandy*, which had appeared in January, met with Gray's approval; while *The Sermons of Mr Yorick, Published by the Rev. Mr Sterne, Prebendary of York*, issued by Dodsley in May, proved even more to his taste. In June Gray asked Wharton: '. . . have you read his Sermons (with his own comic figure at the head of them)? they are in the style I think most proper for the Pulpit, & shew a very strong imagination & a sensible heart: but you see him often tottering on the verge of laughter, & ready to throw his perriwig in the face of his audience'.[11] *D'Alembert's Lettre à M. Rousseau*, contained in his *Mélanges de Littérature* (from 1753) . . . did not appeal to him: it was cold and dry, like its author. Later in the year, or possibly in January 1761, Walpole, who had been reading the first volumes of the *Nouvelle Héloïse*, which had begun to appear,[12] sent them to Gray for his opinion, and received the following reply:

> I have been very ill this week with a great cold and a fever. . . . Rousseau's people do not interest me; there is but one character and one style in them all . . . I . . . am not touched with their passions; and as to their story, I do not believe a word of it . . . because it is absurd . . . now she (Julie) has gone and (so hand over head) married that monsieur de Wolmar, I take her for a vraie Suissesse, and do not doubt but she had taken a cup too much, like her lover.

After reading the whole of the novel he wrote to Mason:

> . . . the Dramatis Personae . . . are all of them good Characters. I am sorry to hear it, for had they been all hang'd at the end of the 3ᵈ volume, no body (I believe) would have cared. in short I went on & on in hope of finding some wonderful denouement that would bring . . . something like Nature & Interest out of absurdity & insipidity. no such thing: it grows worse & worse . . .

Authors are often not good critics of their contemporaries, but this judgement stands out as one of Gray's most unfortunate. Whatever the faults of the novel – which is very long for the modern taste, though not for that of the eighteenth century or the Romantics – it is the exact opposite of insipid, and its interest increases towards the end. Here is indeed 'le style qui brûle le papier'. The last letter in Part IV, in which Saint-Preux describes the excursion to Meillerie and the return across the lake by moonlight, is one of the great passages in French literature. At the end of March 1761, in a letter to Mason, Richard Hurd, the future Bishop of Lichfield, noted the real reason for Gray's dislike of the novel: 'I am not surprized that Mr Gray and other fine readers should dislike *Nouvelle Héloïse*. I see a hundred reasons for this. The admirers of Crébillon are out of their element here. To tell you my opinion in one word, this is the most exquisite work of the kind that ever was written . . . The reason is the author is a man of virtue, as well as genius.'[13]

Gray's correspondence with Wharton in this period was concerned less with literature than with natural history, a subject on which he could write with some competence. In a letter of 31 January 1761 he sent details of the first blooming of flowers and the first appearance of birds, in the year 1755, at Uppsala in Sweden, at Stratton in Norfolk, and at Cambridge, in parallel columns: fifty-one items, from 23 January in Norfolk, corresponding with 12 April at Uppsala, to 9 October in Norfolk, corresponding with 6 October at Uppsala. Many of the observations are of interest to bird-lovers, such as the arrival of the swallow (6 April in Norfolk, 9 May at Uppsala); of the cuckoo a few days later; and the silence of the cuckoo and departure of the swallow. The dates for Norfolk had been supplied by Stillingfleet; Gray himself had noted many of the dates for Cambridge, which were of course about the same as for Norfolk. For Uppsala the information was provided by a correspondent. Later in the same letter he lists the dates for the first singing and arrival of birds in Norfolk. Such observations were to occupy him more and more in later years.

As early as April 1760 Gray's interest was kindled in Welsh poetry when he received a copy of the *De Bardis Dissertatio*, perhaps in manuscript as it had not yet been published. This was by the Rev. Evan Evans, a Denbighshire clergyman. Evans was a genuine scholar who had included in his treatise a number of ancient poems, for some of which he had provided translations into Latin. Gray recorded in his Commonplace Book some stanzas by Taliessin, which he dated *c.* AD 570; 'Gwalchmai's Delights', *c.* 1260; and 'Gruffudd's Lamentation for Prince Llewellyn', *c.* 1284.[14] He made no use of these, but he adapted the translation of Gwalchmai's 'Ode to Owen Gwynedd' (a prince of North Wales in the twelfth century) in 'The Triumphs of Owen', an impressive little poem in forty seven-syllable lines. 'The Death of Hoël', which had taken place near Catterick, was based on 'the *Gododin* of Aneurin, Monarch of the Bards'. This contained twenty-five verses; while 'Caradoc' and 'Conan', which are fragments, were also taken from Aneurin, a poet of the late sixth century. Thus Gwalchmai had lived some six hundred years after Aneurin and Taliessin, and Evans's work had enabled Gray to range over a vast period of Welsh poetry. Despite its originality and beauty, Gray seems to have been less impressed by it than by Macpherson's inventions.

In addition to his study of Evans's work, Gray had been investigating the poetry in Old Norse or Icelandic. As early as 1755 a poem he had found in Torfaeus's *History of Norway and the Orkneys*[15] had given him the first idea of 'The Fatal Sisters'; while he had inserted in 'The Bard' the refrain of the 'Web of Fate' which belongs to Norse and not to Welsh poetry. His first notes on, and extracts from, Snorro Sturlaeus and Thormodus Torfaeus were entered in the second volume of the Commonplace Book. In 1761 he returned to the subject, but now to poetry rather than history. Several pages of the third volume of the Commonplace Book are devoted to notes for 'The Fatal Sisters' and 'The Descent of Odin', and he was now using Thomas Bartholin's *Antiquitatum Danicarum de causis contemptae mortis*.[16] In one column he copied the original Old Norse and, facing it, Bartholin's Latin version; and he added notes full of minute erudition. Though he never mastered Icelandic, it was not difficult to understand and imitate the main features of the prosody, the rhythm and especially the use of alliteration and repetition.[17]

'The Fatal Sisters' consists of the song of the three Valkyries and is derived from a poem in the *Njàls Saga* of the eleventh century. It contains sixty-four seven-syllable verses and is the most 'grisly' of Gray's adaptations. 'The Descent of Odin' is adapted from the 'Baldrs Draumar' (the Dreams of Balder), elsewhere called the 'Vegtamskvida', of which Bartholin had provided a Latin version. Gray's poem contains ninety-four verses and is more informative about Norse mythology. It is also of more interest, since it may possibly have suggested to Arnold the theme of 'Balder Dead'.[18] Here again Gray inserted explanatory notes in the Commonplace Book and also in the 1768 edition of his poems, in which these pieces first appeared. 'The Descent of Odin' might have had, as its sub-title, 'The Twilight of the Gods', as Gray commented:

> *Ragnarockr*, the *Twilight of the Gods*, is the End of the World, when not only all the human Race are to perish, the Sun & the Stars to disappear, the Earth to sink in the Sea, & Fire to consume the Skies, but Odin himself & the Gods (a few excepted) must come to an end. after wch a new heaven & a new earth will appear, the Ruler of all things (a nameless God) will come to Judgement, & *Gimle*, the Abode of the Good, & *Nastrond*, that of the wicked, will subsist for evermore.[19]

These few pieces were all that Gray produced in 1761 from so great a mass of learning. They were, however, well written, and, while 'The Fatal Sisters' was obscure, 'The Descent of Odin' was easier to understand than the Pindaric odes, and evocative of a 'romantic' past which was quite new to most readers. The picture of Odin on 'his coal-black steed', pursuing his way, despite the yells of 'the dog of darkness', to 'Hela's drear abode . . .

> Till full before his fearless eyes
> The portals nine of hell arise

. . . could not fail to kindle the imagination, and win the approval of Walpole.

A few readers of the Welsh pieces in the 1768 edition may have been led to study Evans's work for themselves, and take an interest in matters vaguely described as 'Celtic';[20] though Ossian influenced a wider public. Scott may have read the Norse poems before his voyage to the Shetlands; but what he saw and learned on the spot would have served to account for the local colour in *The Pirate*. He could have read about the Nornes in the *Edda*. Our romanticists as a whole were inspired by Italy, although some Scandinavian influence reappeared in Arnold.

Gray's letters to Brown and Wharton in the first half of 1761 are mainly concerned with small talk and anecdotes about the aristocracy, a topic of perennial interest. He had grown tired of London and was planning a return to his rooms in Pembroke College. On 13 June he wrote to Brown with a request that 'Bleek' (the bedmaker) should 'make an universal rummage of cobwebs, and massacre all spiders, old and young, that live behind windowshutters and books'. One of the fellows had aired the rooms. Gray was determined to come, even if 'Fobus' should preside at Commencement; and he did in fact reach the college on the 15th. But as Newcastle arrived early in July, Gray made a tour of various Suffolk villages and manors, returning to Cambridge after the Chancellor's departure and going to London at the end of July. He urged Mason to join him 'in your way to the Coronation [of George III], & then we may go together to Town . . . do, & then I will help you to write a bawdy Sermon on this happy occasion'.[21]

Thomas Percy, who had received a living in Northamptonshire, came to Cambridge in August and spent a fortnight in the Pepysian Library, copying many of the ancient ballads of which the Library possessed a great store. A former Fellow of Magdalene assisted him. On 1 September Gray, who had come back from London, invited him to tea at Pembroke. They discussed ancient poetry, including perhaps the Norse pieces which Gray had transcribed; and it has been suggested that these included the 'Five Runic Pieces' which Percy was to publish in 1765 in his *Reliques of Ancient English Poetry*; but not the 'Voluspa' and the 'Havamaal' which Mr Powell Jones regarded as of more value.[22] Percy had already exchanged letters with Evan Evans. On 7 September Gray returned to London; and for the coronation, which was to take place on the 22nd, Lord George Cavendish obtained for him a seat in the Duke of Devonshire's box in Westminster Hall. The officials who organised the show made many amusing mistakes, such as providing the right food for the wrong people. The spectacle, however, was magnificent, and Gray described it to Wharton in a long and enthusiastic letter, not omitting the substantial meal he enjoyed: 'great cold Sirloins of Beef, legs of mutton, fillets of veal . . . and liqueurs'.[23]

On 22 October he sent Brown a list of the twenty-eight articles which the carrier would be delivering at Pembroke in a few days, and which Brown was requested to have put in Gray's rooms.

These included two chests of drawers, four tables, a wash-stand, two feather-beds, a fire-grate, two chests of books, etc. 'Those marked with a cross are easier to break, & therefore pray observe if they appear to have received any damage.' As all but three were so marked, Brown would have no very easy task. Gray continued:

> . . . You will take notice of No 6, & 7 for another reason, because in them are Papers & other things of value to me. they may all stand pack'd up as they are, till I come, wch will be in about three weeks, I guess: in the mean time I beg no fire may be made, nor any body go flaunting in with a candle, for so many mats & so much packing will make it very dangerous.

By early December he was back in his old rooms and thoroughly enjoying himself. The appearance of Macpherson's *Fingal* enchanted him. 'For my part', he wrote to a friend, 'I will stick to my credulity . . . The Epic Poem is foolishly so called, yet there is a sort of plan and unity in it very strange for a barbarous age; yet what I more admire are some of the detached pieces – the rest I leave to the discussion of antiquarians and historians . . .'

CHAPTER 14

A visit to Old Park:
Nicholls, Algarotti and others:
Lord Sandwich: 1762–1764[1]

Early in January 1762 Mason appears to have announced the fulfilment of his ambition. 'The Rev. Mr Herring, chancellor of the diocese' of York, had died, and Mason, thanks to Frederick Montagu's influence, had succeeded him as canon residentiary. Gray congratulated him in a somewhat cynical letter: 'It is a mercy, that Old Men are mortal . . . I heartily rejoice . . . to see your insatiable mouth stopt, & your anxious perriwig at rest & slumbering in a stall. the BP of London (you see) is dead: there is a fine opening. is there nothing farther to tempt you? . . .' He may not have been yet aware that Lord Holdernesse had obtained for Mason the office of Precentor. The news, when he received it, gave Gray an opportunity for further raillery, in February: 'I wish all your choir may mutiny, & sing you to death.' To Wharton, whom he hoped to visit in the summer, he was always polite. He informed him of Miss Speed's marriage, representing her as four years older than she was, and added that the *Nouvelle Héloïse* had 'cruelly disappointed' him; 'but it has its partisans, among wch are Mason & Mr Hurd. for me I admire nothing but Fingal . . .'.

On 28 February he thanked Walpole for a copy of his *Anecdotes of Painting in England*, and urged him to proceed with his next work, on a history of the manners, customs, etc., of England. The first is an excellent book. For both books Gray had supplied a certain amount of material from his researches in the British Museum. Meanwhile he appears to have become acquainted with a circle of notables even wider than before. These included Thomas Lyon, a younger brother of Lord Strathmore, who had a small property in Durham. Thomas Lyon, now a Fellow of Pembroke, was a studious young man. It is doubtful if Gray became really intimate with this set, except in the case of a few of the clergy, like Clarke and Palgrave.[2] But he had succeeded in imposing himself on public opinion as a great man, and – stranger still – he was so regarded by the Fellows of Pembroke Hall. It was probably in June that Norton Nicholls, then an undergraduate at Trinity Hall, who had been longing for an introduction, was presented to him. Nicholls described the meeting in a letter to a young friend in London:

My dear Temple.

Now I give you leave . . . that you Envy me! Last Friday I had the Happiness of drinking Tea with the great Mr Gray at Lobb's Room . . . I did not find him as you found Johnson, surly, morose, Dogmatical, or imperious. But affable, entertaining and polite. He had no other opportunity of showing his superior abilities but such as naturally presented itself from the subject of Conversation, which however he never propos'd.[3]

Conceive if you can how happy I find myself when he told me he hop'd to have the Pleasure of my Company some Afternoon at Pembroke. He has not yet fix'd on any. I am under a thousand Anxieties whether or no he will . . . That I should be acquainted with one of the greatest Men who ever existed in the World! That he should (as it is probable he may!) visit me at my own Room!

We had some discourse about Dante and he seem'd very much astonished that I should have read any of it . . .[4]

In his *Reminiscences of Gray*, composed towards 1805, Nicholls recalled that 'the conversation turned on the use of bold metaphors in poetry; & that of Milton was quoted – "The sun was pale, & silent as the moon &c", when I ventured to ask if it might not possibly be imitated from Dante: *mi ripingeva la dove il sol tace.* Mr Gray turned quickly round to me & said "Sir, do you read Dante?" & entered into conversation with me'.

It was not surprising after this that Nicholls became an ardent disciple of Gray, regarded him as a model of virtue and even obeyed his injunction not to call on Voltaire! He learned much about the more agreeable side of Gray's character, and his opinions of contemporary and earlier writers. His detailed record of these is of great interest for the study of Gray as a literary critic.[5]

In 1762, and probably in subsequent years, he often visited Gray 'at his own room, you may be sure, for I believe he fears some deadly infection in mine. I drink tea there when I please and stay till nine . . .'. So he wrote to Temple, adding that Gray played on his harpsichord and that they sang duets, 'and then we go in great form to the coffee-house, where we doze over the news and pamphlets till the last stroke of eleven . . .'.[6] In a later letter, dated 17 September 1763, Nicholls expressed pleasure that Temple himself had been admitted to the friendship 'of a man whom I . . . reverence with the most awful respect for his Sublime Genius, and profound knowledge; and whom I am persuaded that I should esteem, love and confide in, for his disposition, and goodness'.[7] Temple, who later became rector of a Devonshire parish, formed a curious link between Gray and Boswell, with whom this young clergyman was on terms of great intimacy. While in Holland, Boswell received from Temple a letter which filled him with the highest notion of Gray's character; although it does not appear that they ever met.[8]

In July 1762 Gray spent a fortnight at York with Mason who, he said, '*tranche du Prélat*', and reached Old Park about the 18th. The manor house stood by the road which slants downhill from Spennymoor to Crook.[9] When Surtees published his *History of Durham* in 1832, he says that two tall elms stood in front of it and there was a marshy slope behind. It was then deserted. In 1762 it was swarming 'with labourers and builders', wrote Gray. 'The books are not yet unpacked, and there is but one pen and ink in the house. Jetty and Fadge (two favourite sows) are always coming into the entry, and there is a concert of poultry under every window . . .' Despite such surroundings Gray remained at Old Park until early November. He then travelled slowly southward, visiting Fountains Abbey again, then Kirkstall Abbey, Leeds and Sheffield 'in a valley by a pretty river's side, surrounded with charming hills'; and, after that, the Peak, 'a country beyond comparison uglier than any other I have seen in England, black, tedious, barren, & not mountainous enough to please one with its horrors'. Chatsworth House, however, pleased him, and he described the improvements to the grounds recently effected by Capability Brown. He found Hardwick Hall so full of memorials of Queen Mary Stuart that she seemed 'but just walk'd down into the Park'. On reaching London and hearing that Shallet Turner had died in November, he caused his name to be proposed to Lord Bute for nomination as the next Professor of Modern History. Bute, however, had other views, and before Christmas Laurence Brockett was appointed – an unsuitable choice.

The year 1763 brought Gray into touch with 'Count' Francesco Algarotti, well known as author of *Il Newtonianismo per le Dame* (1737). He was not a real count, but had received the title from the King of Prussia. W. T. How, sometime Fellow of Pembroke, had met him in Italy and shown him copies of Gray's Pindaric odes and Mason's dramas (which Gray had spent many hours in correcting). Algarotti could hardly contain himself for admiration. On 25 April, How wrote to Gray from Pisa, enclosing a letter from Algarotti to the 'Illustrissimo' author of the Pindaric odes. He had long doubted whether a dilettante like himself ought to send any of his little things ('coserelle') to an arbiter of every kind of poetical elegance; but he trusted that they would be accepted. Italy was going to be informed 'that England, rich already in having a Homer, an Archimedes and a Demosthenes, is now not lacking in a Pindar'. The 'little things' which Algarotti had promised were essays on painting, the opera and the French Academy in Rome. They reached Gray in the autumn, and on 10 September he thanked their author in a long and polite letter mostly concerned with Italian operas and operatic singers. He himself was gratified to have won Algarotti's 'approbation, having no relish for any other fame than what is confer'd by the few real Judges, that are so thinly scatter'd over the face of the Earth'.

In the previous June, Mason had been collecting subscriptions to enable Christopher Smart to publish a *Translation of the Psalms of David*. 'I have seen his *Song to David* & from thence conclude him as mad as ever', he wrote to Gray. The 'Song to David', which had been published in April, is not only an entirely original poem, but might be regarded as equal to the best of Gray's, and in a class altogether higher than Mason's. The latter Gray was regularly correcting; but he also had a low opinion of Mason himself. The Precentor was unwise enough to reveal that he was planning marriage, though it is not clear with whom, and the news was enough to provoke Gray to perhaps the unkindest letter he ever wrote:

I rejoice. but has she common sense, is she a Gentlewoman? has she money? has she a nose? I know, she sings a little, & twiddles

on the harpsichord, hammers at sentiment & puts herself in an
attitude, admires a cast in the eye, & can say Elfrida by heart;
but . . . let her have some wifelike qualities, & a double portion
of prudence. . . . however we are very happy, & have no other
wish than to see you settled in the world. we beg you would not
stand fiddleing about it, but be married forthwith . . .[10]

and he adds a grossly indecent suggestion as to how the couple
should proceed on their honeymoon journey. Mason appears to
have had a slight squint – hence the personal allusion. But he
cannot have been so innocent as not to see the implication behind
'has she a nose?'[11] Mason apparently bore no resentment.

Gray spent the summer, autumn and winter of 1763 in Pembroke Hall, and remained there until September 1764. He then
made a leisurely tour of Hampshire and Wiltshire, spending some
time in Southampton, once again admiring Netley Abbey and its
oak-woods, inspecting Winchester Cathedral and, later, visiting
Salisbury and Stonehenge. The death of Lord Hardwicke had left
a vacancy in the office of Lord High Steward of the University, and
the Earl of Sandwich, who wished to succeed him, was supported
by a number of clergy, as well as by the Lady Margaret Professor
of Divinity, by Laurence Brockett and Dr Roger Long. He was
dissolute and heartless and, as an office-holder in various adminis-
trations, thoroughly incompetent. Young Lord Hardwicke, who
opposed Sandwich, appears to have been well suited for an office
which enjoyed a certain amount of patronage and influence in the
disposal of university properties. One evening, apparently in
February 1764, when *The Beggar's Opera* was being performed,
Macheath's exclamation: 'that Jemmy Twitcher should 'peach, I
own surpriz'd me' was seized on by the public, and the name was
applied to Sandwich. Hence the use of it in a satire entitled 'The
Candidate', which has been ascribed to Gray and has been accepted
as his by Mr Ketton-Cremer and by the editors of *The Complete
Poems* (Oxford, 1966). Walpole had a copy in Gray's handwriting,
and both he and Mason believed it to be by Gray, though not
necessarily under that title. It is clear from Gray's correspondence
that he was one of the 'Anti-Twitcherites',[12] but there is absolutely
no proof that he wrote 'The Candidate'. For vulgarity and indecency
it is in a different class from 'Tophet' and 'On Lord Holland's Seat
near Margate', which are certainly by Gray, and not indecent.

When Walpole sent a copy of the verses to Mason in 1774, the latter replied on 2 October: 'I remember when he repeated them to me (for I never before saw them in writing) . . .'. Messrs Starr and Hendrickson cite this letter in a footnote to the text of 'The Candidate' (*Complete Poems*, p. 78); but in the 'Explanatory Notes' at the end of the volume they state: 'In Sept. 1774 Walpole, who had heard Gray recite the poem much earlier, found a copy in Gray's hand and at some later date may have printed it' (*Poems*, p. 238). So, according to the editors of *The Poems*, Gray had recited the verses to Mason, which seems to be a fact; but also to Walpole, at some date not specified. The curious way in which information is divided here between footnotes to the text and Explanatory Notes, is puzzling. There is no proof that Walpole ever printed 'The Candidate'. It first appeared in the *London Evening Post* in February 1777, preceded by a letter which begins: 'The following verses are said to be the production of the late celebrated Mr Gray . . .'. A similar version appeared in the *Gentleman's Magazine* in January 1782, under the title of 'Jemmy Twitcher, or The Cambridge Courtship'.[13]

What further complicates the question is the fact that Charles Churchill, a friend of Wilkes and therefore, in 1764, a bitter enemy of Lord Sandwich, also attacked Sandwich in a satire entitled 'The Candidate',[14] which appeared in May of that year – a fact to which neither the editors of Gray's *Correspondence*, nor the editors of his *Poems*, make any allusion.[15] Churchill was not a friend of Gray's; the latter indeed wrote rather unpleasantly about his death in a letter to Mason of January 1765, Churchill having died at Boulogne-sur-Mer on 4 November 1764.

If Gray's editors are right in ascribing to Gray the shorter satire, it can do nothing but discredit him. The first four lines are humorous enough; but the speech by 'Divinity', in remonstrating with 'Physic' and 'Law', borders on the profane, while the last two lines so alarmed Walpole that he and Mason thought they should be simply omitted. They read:

> D—n ye both for a couple of Puritan bitches!
> He's Christian enough that repents, and that——

The last word might have been 'twitches' or 'switches'; unfortunately it was 'stitches'.[16]

To revert to Churchill's satire, it is surprising that neither Gray's editors, nor Mr Douglas Grant, who has edited *The Poetical Works of Charles Churchill*, have noted that there are two different satires entitled 'The Candidate', directed against Lord Sandwich, appearing in editions both of Churchill and of Gray. Churchill's satire is a long piece of 806 verses. After dismissing the classes of people whom he had previously attacked, he turns to Sandwich, who is the object of about five hundred lines of ridicule and invective, reaching a climax in verses 621–8. But nowhere is Churchill guilty of the indecencies which disfigure the piece ascribed to Gray. The latter may have been familiar with Churchill's 'The Candidate', because he commented on Churchill's death in his 'Notes on Churchill'.[17] One can only suppose that if he himself satirised Sandwich, he intended not to let anyone but a few intimates know about it.

It was not that Sandwich was an unfit object for satire; but the satirist should not have gone beyond the limits which, for example, Juvenal had imposed on himself.

The voting in Senate for the High Stewardship seems to have ended in a draw, and in 1765 the Court of King's Bench decided in favour of Hardwicke. Meanwhile, in 1764, Gray had been suffering from an ailment which frightened him; and in July Thomas Thackeray, an eminent surgeon, operated on him. The trouble, it was found, arose from piles, though in 'an extreme degree'.

In this same month Walpole was writing his Gothic romance. The idea had come from an extraordinary dream he had had in June. On the following evening he began the novel, not quite knowing how it would develop and end. It seems to have grown, as it were, of itself. He finished it on 6 August, printed it at Strawberry Hill and published 500 copies on 24 December under the title of *The Castle of Otranto, a Story, translated by William Marshal, Gent., from the original Italian of Onuphrio Muralto*. In the Preface he stated that the work had been printed at Naples in 1529, but had probably been written during the age of the Crusades. It caused an immediate sensation. On 30 December Gray wrote from Cambridge to Walpole:

I have received the C: of O:, & return you my thanks for it. it engages our attention here, makes some of us cry a little, & all in general afraid to go to bed o' nights. we take it for a translation, & should believe it to be a true story, if it were not for St Nicholas . . .

The book was so successful that in the following April Walpole published another edition, in which he acknowledged that he was the author. It is very odd to learn that many people had ascribed the book to Gray.[18] He himself does not appear to have understood that it was a literary event of some importance. He could not, of course, have foreseen that from it would spring a whole succession of tales of terror and mystery – those of Mrs Radcliffe, of Lewis, of Mary Shelley and a host of others.

CHAPTER 15

Glamis Castle and the Highlands; Madame de la Peyrière in London; The First Visit to the Lakes: 1765–1766[1]

Gray was finding it increasingly difficult to spend most of the year in 'silly dirty Cambridge'. At the same time he felt no desire to revisit the Continent; for, even if he had wished to see Italy again, he would have had to cross France. And he disliked the French – a 'childish people', he called them. He had followed the events of the Seven Years' War with the keenest interest, and the effect had been to confirm him in his chauvinism. This attitude appears to have coloured his critical opinion of French writers, Voltaire foremost, and also J.-J. Rousseau (who was counted as French). His remarks on the *Lettres écrites de la Montagne* and on the earlier *Contrat social*, as well as on Rousseau personally, are strangely intemperate.[2] The Continent being excluded, he extended the length of his visits to other parts of the United Kingdom. Towards 29 May he stayed for some little time with Mason at York, where he found the Precentor annotating Shakespeare in a specially interleaved copy of the latter's works. Of this he disapproved: there had been too many annotators. Subsequently he composed a little poem on the subject: 'William Shakespeare to Mrs Anne, Regular Servant to the Revd Mr Precentor of York'. In this he imagines the poet as deprecating all commentaries, and declaring that he would prefer his pages to be used to 'bottom' the pies and tarts in the making of which 'Mrs Anne' was an expert:

> So York shall taste what Clouet[3] never knew;
> So from *our* works sublimer fumes shall rise:
> While Nancy earns the praise to Shakespeare due
> For glorious puddings, & immortal pies.

This, even having regard to 'A Long Story', is quite the most successful of his humorous pieces. Mason declared that he would paste it in his copy of Shakespeare and that it would enhance the book's value.

After leaving York, Gray stayed for about two months at Old Park, during which time he visited Hartlepool and took great interest in the healthy fisherfolk and the nature-life of the sea-shore, especially the habits of the hermit crab. In the meantime the Honourable Thomas Lyon, with whom Gray was already acquainted, must have presented him to Strathmore; for Gray was now invited to accompany Strathmore and his brother, and a cousin, Major Lyon, who were all returning from Strathmore's Durham property to the ancestral castle of Glamis. Leaving Hetton, today Hetton Lyon, the Strathmore seat near Durham, on 19 August, they travelled post to Edinburgh. On the following two days Gray was taken by Major Lyon to see the Castle and Holyrood House. The journey and the sightseeing had evidently fatigued him, since he afterwards described Edinburgh as 'that most picturesque (at a distance) and nastiest (when near) of all capital cities'. Dr John Gregory, a distinguished physician, invited him to supper to meet a few friends, including the well-known historian, William Robertson, then Principal of the University. Gray was tired and not equal to the occasion. When the Elegy was praised, he replied that it 'owed its popularity entirely to its subject, and that the public would have received it as well if it had been written in prose'.[4] Robertson did not share in the general reverence which was felt for Gray, and Norton Nicholls was shocked on being told that when the historian 'saw Mr Gray in Scotland, he gave him the idea of a person who meant to pass for a very fine gentleman'.[5]

On the following day the passage of the Firth of Forth in stormy weather proved frightening to Gray; but he was able to rest that night at Perth, and the party reached Glamis in good time on the morrow. Gray was much impressed by the imposing avenue of Scotch pines and lime trees which led to the castle, and by the castle itself and the great trees that surrounded it. The estate lay in the long, fertile valley known as Strathmore, well tilled under the supervision of the Earl, who was effecting various improvements. After a few pleasant days at the castle, Gray enjoyed an experience beyond anything he had foreseen: a tour of the central

Highlands under the care of Major Lyon. They went up the Tay valley, saw Schiehallion, loftiest of the mountains in that region, and Ben More, which 'rises to a most awful height, & looks down on the tomb of Fingal'; and pushed as far as the Pass of Killie-crankie. The Ossian country was to inspire Wordsworth. It impressed Gray without, however, inspiring him to poetry. 'Since I saw the Alps I have seen nothing sublime until now,' he wrote to Wharton;[6] and to Mason: '. . . none but these monstrous creatures of God know how to join so much beauty with so much horror'.[7]

Meanwhile James Beattie, who occupied the Chair of Moral Philosophy and Logic at Aberdeen, had written to invite Gray to visit the city: 'Will you permit us to hope, that we shall have an opportunity at Aberdeen, of thanking you in person, for the honour you have done to Britain, and to the poetic art, by your inestimable compositions . . .?'[8] As Gray was not disposed to undertake a further journey, Beattie was invited to spend a day or two at Glamis Castle. Gray, who was feeling better and was, besides, much flattered by Beattie's expressions of esteem and affection, received the young man with more than his usual cordiality. Beattie was delighted with the interview. He was im-pressed, he told his patron, Sir William Forbes, by Gray's sound judgement and 'extensive learning . . . His conversation abounds in original observations, delivered with no appearance of senten-tious formality, and seeming to arise spontaneously without study or premeditation . . .' As this was the opposite of his manner with Walpole and Montagu, and generally with the ladies, it seems that he was at ease and most himself in the society of younger men.

In response to an inquiry from Marischal College as to whether he would accept an honorary degree of Doctor of Laws, Gray presented his 'most grateful acknowledgement' of the honour which had been proposed, but declined it on the ground that it might 'look like a slight' on Cambridge. He would 'avoid giving any offence to a set of Men, among whom I have pass'd so many easy, & (I may say) happy hours of my life . . .'.

Gray left Glamis about 7 October and, to avoid crossing the Firth of Forth, returned by way of Stirling. He again stayed with Wharton at Old Park and, on reaching London, lodged for a few weeks with the hosier Roberts in Jermyn Street. Learning that Walpole had suffered an attack of gout and had gone to Paris, he wrote solicitously, advising him to keep his legs warm and to make no sudden changes in diet. On 19 November Walpole replied that he was much better, though still weak. Paris seemed different from the city they had known in 1739; it was ugly and without trees or verdure.[9] He had been surprised at the slightly indecent conversation he had heard at Madame du Deffand's. Many of the women were agreeable, but the men generally vain and ignorant. The 'Philosophes' were fanatical atheists. 'Voltaire himself does not satisfy them'; one of them said: 'Il est bigot; c'est un Déiste'. Nevertheless Walpole had found some pleasant society and would have been sorry not to have come. In the weeks that followed he had still more reason to enjoy the society of Madame du Deffand and her friends. His wit and his easy command of French won the hearts of the Parisian ladies, and in a letter of 25 January 1766 he wrote that he was being 'sent for about like an African prince or a learned canary-bird'.[10]

Earlier, in December 1765, having learned that the Baronne de la Peyrière was in London, where her husband was now ambassador, Gray 'sate a morning with her before I left London. She is a prodigious fine lady, & a Catholick . . . not fatter than she was . . . They were all exceeding glad to see me, & I them', he told Wharton.

Back in Cambridge, he sank into his habitual melancholy. He sought to dissipate it by taking out the notebooks in which he had recorded the observations of insects, sea-creatures and birds which he had made the previous autumn. He now possessed the three volumes of Linnaeus's *Systema Naturae*, which he had had interleaved; and to this he transferred his notes, illustrating them with beautiful and accurate drawings of birds, beetles, moths and butterflies. His picture of the Swallowtail, with its caterpillar and chrysalid, is particularly attractive. Less sensible, in Walpole's eyes, was the habit of composing Latin verses about insects, and going even further in the direction of pedantry;[11] but it made him happy.

The coming of spring gave him an opportunity to escape from Cambridge, and he spent the whole of June with William Robinson, a former Cambridge acquaintance, and now Rector of Denton in Kent. They visited Margate and Ramsgate, and Gray was enchanted with the landscape and distant views from Denton. 'In the east', he wrote to Norton Nicholls, 'the sea breaks in upon you, & mixes its white transient sails & glittering blew expanse with the deeper & brighter greens of the woods & corn. This last sentence is so fine I am quite ashamed. But no matter! you must translate it into prose . . .' In the autumn the Rev. William Palgrave entertained him at Thrandeston in Suffolk, and this enabled him to visit parts of Norfolk and see the handsome but unpretentious manor which Sir Robert Walpole had had built for himself at Houghton. From Thrandeston he moved into his London lodgings and, while in London, met Mason's wife, who impressed him as 'a pretty, modest, innocent, interesting figure'. She was suffering from tuberculosis, and the medical science of the time was incapable of saving her. The winter of 1766–7 was exceptionally severe, and she died in March. Mason was heartbroken, and Gray wrote him a sympathetic letter of condolence.

In the previous December the Comte de Viry had died and the Baron de la Peyrière, who now succeeded to the title, was appointed minister in Madrid. Gray had not attempted again to see his old friend, now Comtesse de Viry and a most brilliant and socially successful ambassador's wife. He was more preoccupied than ever with his health. On 28 January he had written to tell Mason that something was growing in his throat 'which nothing does any service to, and which will, I suppose, in due time, stop up the passage'. Tending the bulbs of narcissus and hyacinth[12] which he grew in glasses diverted his mind, and his throat seems to have got better by April, when he again took lodgings in Jermyn Street and enjoyed the pleasures of the town, going to operas and plays, meeting old friends, seeing Walpole, and consorting with Frederick Hervey, a brother of Lord Bristol, and now Bishop of Cloyne. 'He is very jolly,' Gray told James Brown; '. . . we devoured four raspberry puffs together in Cranbourn-alley standing at a pastrycook's shop . . .' In the same letter he reports that Rousseau had left England, after writing letters to the Lord Chancellor and to General Conway[13] which showed that his mind had been temporarily unhinged. Hume, who had sponsored his visit to England in January 1766, had arranged for him and Thérèse to stay as the guests of Mr Davenport at Wootton in South Derbyshire. Here he had been quite happy for over a year, but had then suffered an attack of paranoia – a partial insanity which occasionally affected him, and which seems to have been inherited. George III, at the suggestion of General Conway, had granted him a pension of £100 a year. Voltaire ridiculed him in public, but most people were sorry for him.

In the middle of June Gray set out, in the company of James Brown, on the most ambitious of his tours. From Mason's Rectory at Aston, in 'an Elysium among the coal-pits,' he wrote as follows to Wharton on 21 June:

> tomorrow we visit Dovedale & the Wonders of the Peak, the Monday following we go to York to reside, & two or three days after set out for Old Park, where I shall remain upon your hands; & Mr Brown about the time of Durham-races must go on to Gibside, & for aught I know to Glamis . . .
>
> Mr B: owns the pleasantest day he ever passed was yesterday at Roche-Abbey. it is indeed divine.

July and August were spent at Old Park, from where Wharton took him on short excursions to Richmond and Rokeby, and again to Hartlepool. In August, the Hon. William Hervey, a younger brother of the Bishop of Cloyne and in later life a General, visited Durham. 'he danced at the Assembly with a conquering mien', Gray wrote to Mason, '& all the Misses swear, he is the genteelest thing they ever set eyes on, & wants nothing but two feet more in height . . .'. Finally, on the 29th, after going to Gibside to pay his respects to the Countess of Strathmore, the former Miss Bowes, the Durham heiress whom the Earl had recently married, he and Wharton left for a tour of the Lakes. They went by way of New-castle, and by the road to Carlisle which runs parallel with Hadrian's Wall. Rain had begun to fall, and continued to fall at Penrith and Keswick. Clouds hung low over the mountains and they caught no more than a glimpse of Skiddaw. They pushed on as far as Cockermouth; but Wharton had been 'taken ill' with asthma, so they returned by the most direct route from Penrith, that is, by way of Appleby, Brough, Bowes Moor and Barnard Castle. It was probably after inspecting, in the church at Appleby, an epitaph composed by a former Countess of Dorset, who owned six castles in Cumberland, that Gray was moved to write the following burlesque:

> Now clean, now hideous, mellow now, now gruff,
> She swept, she hissed, she ripened and grew rough
> At Brougham, Pendragon, Appleby and Brough.

He stayed on for a time at Old Park, enjoying the peaches and grapes – which must have been grown in a hot-house, since the climate is scarcely warm enough even to ripen apples. In November he spent some time in Jermyn Street, and returned to Cambridge in December. Here he suffered another attack of gout, but had recovered sufficiently by the 24th to thank Beattie for the arrangement he had proposed to make with the Foulis brothers in Glasgow, with a view to a Scottish edition of the *Collected Poems*. It appears that Gray had agreed with Dodsley, some months before, on the production of an edition in London. This was to include all his poems (except 'A Long Story'), including the Norse and Welsh pieces; and Gray had decided to annotate it, indicating the sources of the various phrases and expressions which he had used. On the same day as his letter to Beattie, Gray wrote to Walpole to explain a point in connexion with Walpole's *Historic Doubts on Richard the Third*. This was an important work which Walpole had begun in the previous winter and which he was to publish in February 1768. The first edition was of 1,200 copies, and these sold so quickly that 1,000 more were printed forthwith.

On the 28th Gray wrote to Wharton, inquiring about the children, of whom he was very fond. And so the year 1767 drew to its end.

CHAPTER 16

The Professorship of Modern History: A Second Visit to the Lakes: 1768–1769[1]

In the small hours of the night of 17–18 January 1768 Pembroke Hall suffered the kind of disaster which had obsessed Gray since the destruction of his house in Cornhill. This time a fire had broken out in the north wing of the second court, that is, in a room facing Gray's, a room vacant at the time. The damage might have been serious but for an alarm given by two Methodists. Gray described the event in a letter to Nicholls: 'two Saints, who had been till very late at their nocturnal devotions, & were just in bed, gave the first alarm to the college & the town. we had very speedy & excellent assistance of engines & men'. It does not appear that the fire spread much beyond one set of rooms, and probably the flooring of the set above. It is not stated whether the 'Methodists' were members of the college. Perhaps they lived in what is now Pembroke Street.

On 1 February Gray sent instructions to Dodsley, and probably on the same day to Beattie, for the printing of his poems in the new edition. They were to be arranged in the following order: the 'Ode on the Spring', the 'Ode on the Cat', the Eton College ode, the 'Ode to Adversity', the 'Progress of Poesy', 'The Bard', 'The Fatal Sisters', 'The Descent of Odin', 'The Triumphs of Owen', the churchyard Elegy. 'A Long Story' was on no account to be included. Notes were to be printed at the foot of each page. In these he elucidated the Pindaric odes, but also indicated the sources of a great number of phrases and expressions in all the pieces: from Lucretius, Virgil, Dante, Petrarch, Shakespeare, Milton, Dryden, Matthew Green and others; some of them more than once. Without acknowledging all his sources – for his mind was so full of these expressions that he was probably unaware at times of their not being original – he went beyond what Walpole and others had desired in the way of an explanation of the Pindaric odes.

The result reveals, as nothing else, Gray's conception of poetry. A poem was not to be, as it would be for most of the Romantic and Victorian poets, an original composition, but one in which the language could often be a mosaic of phrases taken from earlier poets. This, to Gray's mind, seems to have been not only legitimate but normal. The inference is that he was simply continuing, in his English poems, the principles which he had been taught as a schoolboy at Eton. A schoolboy could hardly be expected to compose original verses in Latin: he would be advised to use phrases which occur commonly in Virgil, Horace, Ovid and other classical authors. Gray in fact did this in his Latin poems, and he carried over the practice into his English pieces. He frankly reveals this, which shows that he did not regard the practice as plagiarism, but as perfectly natural – at least for a learned poet.

On 14 February he wrote a long letter to Walpole about the latter's *Historic Doubts*, which he had re-read. He still suspected Richard 'of the murder of Henry VI'. The chronicler of Croyland charged him with this crime (and Commines repeated this charge, possibly because he was following the chronicler). Gray found it strange that Richard, who had been acclaimed by the nobility and the common people, should 'within a few months' be deserted by 'Buckingham, his best friend, and almost all the southern and western counties'. He admitted that Walpole had 'shown Henry the seventh to be a greater devil than Richard'. It was inevitable that Walpole's book should provoke incredulity. Tudor propaganda had effectively blackened the character of Richard; while Shakespeare, who had naturally accepted the only account available in his time, had fixed in the public imagination the image of an infamous king. Accepted notions are not easily discredited. Amid so much that is uncertain in regard to Richard III, one fact emerges. Richard had no sufficient motive for contriving the murder of the little princes if their sister survived; and there was also doubt of their legitimacy. He could have foreseen that, to have been guilty of so foul a crime could only have prejudiced him in the eyes of the public. The facts remain obscure, and therefore, to suspend judgement is the wiser course.

It is amusing to read, in Gray's comments, the extent to which Walpole had shocked the *idées reçues* of 1768. 'I have heard you charged with disrespect to the king of Prussia; and above all to King William, & the revolution,' he wrote. In fact Walpole did not

regard either William III or Frederick of Prussia as above criticism. To the charge mentioned he replied on 18 February: 'A
newspaper has talked of my known inveteracy to [Frederick] –
Truly, I love him as well as I do most kings.' In the *Historic
Doubts* he had pointed out that the various circumstances surrounding the coronation of Richard III

> have not at all the air of an unwelcome revolution, accomplished
> merely by violence. On the contrary, it [the accession of Richard
> III] bore great resemblance to a much later event, which, being
> the last of the kind, we term *The Revolution*. . . . Though the
> partisans of the Stuarts may exult in my comparing King
> William to Richard the third, it will be no matter of triumph,
> since it appears that Richard's cause was as good as King
> William's, and that in both instances it was a free election.[2]

On 12 March 1768 *Poems by Mr Gray* was published in a small
octavo volume, with none of the éclat of the 1753 edition. 1,500
copies were printed and sold at half a crown. The Glasgow edition,
which appeared in May, was printed in large and handsome type,
and was altogether more worthy, in the author's eyes. Meanwhile,
Walpole had seen in *The Public Advertiser* a notice of *Poems by
Mr Gray*, and on 18 February he wrote to Gray:

> . . . I called directly at Dodsley's to know if this was to be more
> than a new edition . . . his foreman told me he thought there
> were some new pieces, and notes to the whole. It was very
> unkind, not only to go out of town without mentioning them to
> me, without showing them to me, but not to say a word of them
> in this letter . . .

'This letter' refers to Gray's missive of the 14th, in which he had
mentioned certain objections to the *Historic Doubts*, and added:
'My own objections are a little more essential: they relate chiefly
to inaccuracies of style.' Gray had not seen fit to include a mention
of the forthcoming edition of his poems. Walpole might well have
thought this strange, since he had sponsored the Elegy, had
arranged for the illustrated edition of 1753, and had printed the
Pindaric odes. Gray had never before made a move to publish
anything under his own name. His rise to celebrity had been
entirely due to Walpole.

On 25 February Gray replied: 'To your friendly accusation, I am glad I can plead not guilty with a safe conscience.' He then described the arrangement he had made with Dodsley, observed that Walpole had seen the two Norse poems, and said that he had included

> . . . a bit of something from the Welch, and certain little notes, partly from justice (to acknowledge the debt, where I had borrowed anything), partly from ill temper, just to tell the gentle reader, that Edward I was not Oliver Cromwell, nor queen Elizabeth the witch of Endor. This is literally all; and with all this I shall be but a shrimp of an author . . . I will be candid . . . and avow to you, that till fourscore-and-ten, whenever the humour takes me, I will write, because I like it . . . If I do not write much, it is because I cannot.

He meant that he could not write any more poetry: inspiration had deserted him. He could no doubt have written interesting prose works, if he had been so minded. In the same letter he gives further information relating to Richard III, and the correspondence on this topic continued until 8 March. Walpole discovered 'A Paradox, or apology for Richard III by Sir William Cornwallis', and asked Gray to look it up. Gray found that it was contained in *Essayes of certaine Paradoxes*, published in 1613; declared that Cornwallis had read only the common chronicles, gave details and concluded that it was 'an idle declamation'. Several writers had disagreed with Walpole; Guthrie had criticised him angrily, and Hume politely. Hume Walpole recognised as a serious historian, and he asked him to elaborate his arguments. He dealt with the objections in a *Supplement to the Historic Doubts*, but told Gray that 'the few Criticisms I have suffered have done more than my own arguments could: They have strengthened my opinion, seeing how little can be said to overturn it'. He concluded by saying: 'I think you will like Sterne's sentimental travels,[3] which tho' often tiresome, are exceedingly goodnatured & picturesque.'[4]

If Gray answered this letter, his reply has not been preserved. He spent part of April and the whole of May in Southampton Row and in June again stayed with William Robinson at Denton in Kent. On this occasion he visited the picturesque mansion which

Lord Holland had built for himself on the North Foreland. This nobleman had incurred the greatest obloquy not only from having enriched himself, but from having quarrelled with all his colleagues. If he were not the most cynical and self-seeking of all the politicians of the time, he appears to have been the most generally hated. He had beguiled his retirement by building a house in classical style, and setting up around it, in accordance with the 'Gothicism' of the age, a sort of ruined castle, a convent and cloisters to provide quarters for his guests; and an inn, disguised as a chapel of St Peter, where visitors could obtain food and drink. It is not known whether he kept a tame hermit to occupy a grotto. However that may be, the sight of this eccentric domain galvanised Gray into writing the verses 'On Lord Holland's Seat near Margate', which is the only satire of any length (twenty-four verses in rhymed couplets) which can confidently be ascribed to him. The invective is not perhaps stronger than Churchill might have used, but the language is quite different from that of 'The Candidate' (that is, the satire ascribed to Gray), a fact which reinforces doubts as to Gray's authorship. The satire on Lord Holland is said to have been left in Gray's dressing-table drawer at Denton. It was posted on to him, and he apparently then showed it to Wharton and Mason. Walpole urged Mason not to publish it, on the ground that it would be an unkind blow to Lord Holland, who was then (1775) a very sick man.

Gray had returned to London and was staying in Jermyn Street when he heard from his cousin, Mary Antrobus,[5] that Laurence Brockett had died. Brockett had dined with Lord Sandwich at Hinchingbrooke, and while returning to Cambridge with his servant along the Huntingdon Road twice fell from his horse, and died on the following Sunday. This news must have reached Stonhewer earlier, for Stonhewer, as the Duke of Grafton's secretary, immediately proposed the name of Gray as a suitable successor. Grafton, who was then acting as virtual head of the ministry, recommended Gray to the King, and wrote to say that he had the King's command to offer the appointment to Gray. He added: 'he must take the warmest part in approving so well judged a measure as he hopes I do not doubt of the real regard & esteem with which he has the honour to be, etc.' – as Gray quoted the Duke's letter in writing to Wharton. Gray was overjoyed at the fulfilment of a long-cherished ambition and wrote:

My Lord,

Your Grace has dealt nobly with me; and the same delicacy of mind that induced you to confer this favour on me, unsolicited and unexpected, may perhaps make you averse to receive my sincerest thanks and grateful acknowledgements . . . these are indeed but words; yet I know and feel they come from my heart . . .

He then attended a levée at the Palace, kissed the King's hand, and was assured that he owed the appointment to the King's 'particular knowledge' of him. The weather, however, was so hot that he was hardly able to follow the proceedings. He did nevertheless pay his duty calls on the various members of the Cabinet, and, in spite of the heat, remained in Jermyn Street until the end of August. He wrote to his principal friends, including Nicholls, who was living very agreeably in his parsonage at Blunderston, near Lowestoft. Thomas Barrett, of Lee Priory in Kent, wished to take Nicholls as his companion on a tour of France and Italy, and Gray was commissioned to make the offer. There would be an honorarium of £100 a year, and all expenses provided. Gray advised Nicholls not to accept the offer, and Nicholls declined it – for the time being.[6]

Gray returned to Cambridge early in September. According to Mason, he at once began to prepare an inaugural lecture, and the notes that have been preserved show that it set out methods of study and research. The Statutes of 1724, which governed the professorship, required the incumbent to read 'lectures in the publick schools at such times as shall hereafter be appointed'; these times, however, had never been specified. Furthermore, the professors in Oxford and Cambridge were required 'to maintain with sufficient Salarys, two Persons, at least, well qualified to teach and instruct in writing and Speaking the Said Languages' (French and Italian); the said teachers would 'be obliged to instruct gratis in the Modern Languages twenty Scholars of each University, to be nominated by us' (i.e. by the Crown). The language teachers were able to supplement their income by giving private lessons in addition to the above. It seems that the object of these foundations was not simply to provide for instruction in medieval and modern history but, quite as much, to qualify young men for the diplomatic service.

Harris, of Peterhouse, the first professor, had delivered an inaugural lecture in Latin, had appointed Monsieur Masson and Signor Piazza to teach their respective languages, and done nothing further. Turner, who succeeded him, and Brockett, had merely drawn their stipends, and Brockett had not paid the language teachers more than a pittance. At Oxford the situation had been even worse. Joseph Spence, who had assisted Walpole in so timely a manner at Reggio, had held the Oxford chair since 1742, and had not even troubled to reside. Now, on 20 August (1768), Spence had been drowned in a pond in his garden at Byfleet; whereupon the Vice-Chancellor and Heads of Houses, conscious of the way in which Spence had abused his position, submitted a memorandum to the King, in which they proposed that all future Professors of Modern History should reside during Full Term, deliver fifty lectures every year, and pay the language teachers £50 a year each. The King agreed that 'this office should never any more be held as a sinecure'.

John Vivian, who wished to succeed Spence, would evidently be subject to any new regulations, though Gray, who had been appointed unconditionally, would not. Even so, the matter weighed on his conscience, the more so as the Government now invited him, as well as Vivian, to submit their views on their duties. Vivian proposed that he should deliver one public lecture each term, reside long enough 'to direct the study of his pupils', and pay the language teachers £20 a year each. This was not considered satisfactory. Gray went to more trouble. The professor, he proposed, should

1 'desire the Heads of Colleges to recommend one or more young men who would be instructed without expense in some of the modern languages, & attend such lectures as He [the Professor] shall give'. The number of students would amount to nineteen.
2 He should 'nominate & pay two Praeceptors, qualified' to teach French and Italian.
3 He should reside at least 'the half of every term' – about 110 days in the year – and 'read publickly once at least in every Term a lecture on modern History to his Scholars . . .'
4 that 'at short & regular intervals', he should 'give private lectures to his Scholars on the same subject, prescribe a method of study, direct them in their choice of Authors, & from time to time

enquire into the progress they have made in the Italian & French tongues'.

5 'That if he neglect these duties, he shall be subject to the same pecuniary mulcts, that other Professors are according to Statute.'[7]

This sounds very satisfactory, on paper. In practice, all he seems to have done was to confirm René La Butte and Agostino Isola[8] as teachers of their respective languages, and perhaps he supervised the work of a few undergraduates. He had planned to deliver his Inaugural in Latin, but in fact he was so far from being accustomed to perform any regular duties, that he could not bring himself to lecture in public. He did, however, reside in Cambridge for longer periods than heretofore. On 2 January 1769 he wrote to Nicholls:

Here am I once again, & have sold my estate, & got a thousand guineas, & fourscore pound a year for my old Aunt, & a £20 prize in the lottery, & Lord knows what arrears in the Treasury, & am a rich Fellow enough, go to. . . .

The Duke of Newcastle had died in 1768 and at the end of November Grafton had been elected as Chancellor of the University. As the Chancellor usually presided at Commencement, the ceremony of installation was planned for 1 July. This required, by tradition, the composition of an ode, and also of music to which the verses would be sung. Gray felt that the least he could do was to offer to compose the verses, and he set to work, probably in February. He foresaw that it would make him unpopular. Grafton was being attacked – from under cover – by 'Junius', while the letters of Junius and the agitation due to refusal of the Commons to admit Wilkes as MP for Middlesex, roused the London mob to a fury of rioting and violence. Gray, however, completed the ode about the middle of April, handed it to the Vice-Chancellor, and went to stay in Jermyn Street for a fortnight. Spring came early that year, and he paid a short visit to Windsor to enjoy its beauty.

One gathers from Norton Nicholls's *Reminiscences*[9] that he and his wife had been in Cambridge, perhaps earlier in April.

All would now have gone smoothly if Charles Burney, who was

anxious to be awarded a doctorate, had not asked Grafton to commission him to compose the music to which the ode would be sung. Grafton agreed, and Burney then engaged a distinguished Italian, Giardini, to lead the orchestra, and also a special choir. When he presented the bill to Grafton, the Duke told him to halve it. Thereupon Burney withdrew, and it was arranged for John Randall, the Professor of Music, to compose the music and engage a less expensive choir. Gray and Randall coordinated their efforts and supervised the rehearsals. Gray expected the 'Odickle', as he called the Installation Ode, to be 'torn piece-meal in the North-Briton, before it is born. the music is as good as the words: the former might be taken for mine, & the latter for Dr Randall's'. Most of the political and ecclesiastical notables in the country, including Lord Sandwich and Lord North (who, before long, was to succeed Grafton as Prime Minister), had been invited, as well as foreign ambassadors. The visitors were to be lodged mainly in colleges, but one bishop stayed at the Dog and Porridge Pot, and other guests in rooms offered by local tradesmen at rates varying from eleven to twenty guineas for three days.[10]

The 'Ode to Music', as the Installation Ode was entitled, was a meritorious effort. The second 'Air', supposedly sung by Milton, contained gleams of genuine poetry. The general tone of airs and recitatives was necessarily rhetorical.[11] Gray might be reproached with having gone further than was necessary in his eulogy of Grafton: to make 'the venerable Marg'ret', that is, the Lady Margaret Beaufort (wife of Edmund Tudor), who had founded St John's College, trace in the 'lineaments' of her 'noble son' 'A *Tudor's* fire, a *Beaufort's* grace', was, to say the least, injudicious. The Duke's enemies could point out that his royal ancestry had been through an illegitimate child of Charles II, and that the Beauforts were descended from John of Beaufort, an illegitimate son of John of Gaunt.[12] Not that Grafton – or Lady Margaret Beaufort – could be reproached with the irregularities of their forebears; but Grafton and Frederick North belonged to the 'King's Party'; Junius and Wilkes had been inciting the London mobs against them; and Gray found himself, as he had feared, involved in the same odium. The 'Ode to Music' was immediately parodied in *The St James's Chronicle*, while *The London Chronicle* at the end of July published a parody of the 'Epitaph' which concludes the Elegy, in a manner very vicious and unjust. Junius also attacked him. A letter of 8 July, which poured insults on Grafton, concluded with the words: 'The learned dulness of declamation will be silent [after Grafton's death]; and even the venal Muse, though happiest in fiction, will forget your virtues.'

Gray, however, felt too happy in the contemplation of a plan to revisit Keswick, to be worried by all this spitefulness. On 17 July he wrote to tell Wharton that he and Brown were setting out next day; that they would come to Old Park; and 'about the end of August we may cross the Apennine, & visit M: Skiddaw . . . I am so fat, that I have suffer'd more from heat this last fortnight than ever I did in Italy. the Thermom. usually at 75. . . .'. They probably reached Old Park about the 26th and stayed until the last week in September. On the 29th of that month, Brown having probably returned to Cambridge, Gray and Wharton once again set out for the Lakes, travelling this time by way of Barnard Castle and Bowes Moor. At Brough (on the Cumberland side), where they spent the night, Wharton 'was seized with a fit of the asthma . . ., & obliged in the morning to return home', Gray wrote to Brown. 'I went by Penrith to Keswick, & passed six days there lap'd in Elysium; then came slowly by Ambleside to Kendal and this day arrived here.' This letter was written from Lancaster on 10 October. He was to be back in Cambridge on the 22nd.

The tour of the Lakes, which occupied a bare ten days, constituted the happiest holiday he had taken since the visit to Italy: so happy that he composed a careful and detailed journal of his experiences, which he sent in four long instalments to Wharton, to console him for the pleasures he had missed. The weather was mild and often sunny throughout. Between Brough and Appleby a horse and cattle fair was being held, and festive crowds of farmers and gentry were out to attend it. At Penrith on 30 September he 'dined with Mrs Buchanan . . . on trout and partridge'; then walked up the Beacon Hill. On the morrow, the sky being overcast, he made his way to the lower end of Ullswater. From a low hill top above the eastern bank he obtained a good view of the lake, with the white farmhouses among the trees near the water's edge, and the hills rising 'very rude and aweful' above them. By means of what Mason calls 'a Plano-convex Mirror . . . on a black foil', he was able to select views, as can be done in the viewfinder of a camera. Retracing his steps, he crossed the Eamont where it issues from the lake at Pooley Bridge, and walked a little way along the north-western shore, gaining a view of Helvellyn in the distance. On 2 October he took a chaise to Keswick, passing under Saddleback, and reaching the Queen's Head in time for dinner at 2 p.m. After this, he took a short walk 'alone to the *Parsonage*, fell down on my back across a dirty lane, with my glass open in one hand, but broke only my knuckles: stay'd nevertheless, & saw the sun set in all its glory'.[13]

Although only fifty-two, Gray was old for his years, and not disposed to go far except with a companion. In these circumstances he engaged a man named Hodgkins to take him to Borrowdale, carrying a cold tongue for lunch. Hodgkins 'described him as difficult to be pleased, and peevish from ill-health', and said 'that he could not ride on horseback, and would not go on the water'.[14] On 3 October the day dawned promisingly and they made an early start. Walla Crag, 'cut perpendicularly down above 400 feet, as I guess, awefully overlooks the way'. At Lodore the crags 'now begin to impend terribly over your way'. There had recently been a rock-fall, which scared him. He turned aside to see the lower part of the gorge, then pushed on under Gowder Crag, which was still more frightening. It reminded him of those passes in the Alps, 'where the Guides tell you to move on with speed & say nothing, lest the agitation of the air should loosen the snows above, & bring down a mass . . .'. So they 'hasten'd on in silence' to Grange, where a young farmer and his mother entertained them with oat-cakes, butter, milk and ale (supplemented with cold tongue). The view up Borrowdale, overhung by lofty mountains, scarcely invited further exploration. The little path was 'for some weeks in the year passable to the Dale's-men', he averred, supposing that up here lay 'mysteries' and 'the reign of Chaos & old Night'.

The farmer told him how, in the previous year, he had been let down with ropes from a cliff-top, to rob the nest of a pair of eagles, which had been carrying off lambs, as well as hares and grouse.

After returning to Keswick at leisure, Gray in the evening walked down to the lakeside

& saw the solemn colouring of night draw on, the last gleam of sunshine fading away on the hill-tops, the deep serene of the waters, & the long shadows of the mountains thrown across them . . . at distance heard the murmur of many waterfalls not audible in the day-time, wish'd for the Moon, but *she was dark to me & silent, hid in her vacant interlunar cave.*

Matthew Arnold, who was to admire and quote this description, seems not to have realised that the words in italics are from *Samson Agonistes.*[15]

On the days that followed, Gray made further short excursions, including one to Bassenthwaite Water and Armathwaite Hall; and on the 8th, in gloomy weather, left by chaise for Ambleside. The sight of Grasmere village delighted him; Rydalmere was 'of inferior size & beauty' to Grasmere, he thought. He would have slept at Ambleside but, finding the best bedroom 'dark & damp as a cellar', pushed on to Kendal. Here he spent two nights '& fared & slept very comfortably'. On the 10th he went on to Lancaster, on the 11th travelled up the Lune valley to Settle, admired 'that huge creature of God *Ingleborough*' and on the 12th visited Gordale Scar and Malham, where the roaring torrent and 'perpendicular' rocks 'threaten visibly some idle Spectator with instant destruction'. Travelling south, he admired the Wharfe valley, and Kirkstall Abbey, and so, by way of Leeds, Nottingham and Huntingdon, regained Cambridge on 22 October.

This *Journal* appears to be the first literary description of the Lake country, and is the best of Gray's prose works.

CHAPTER 17

Bonstetten: 1770[1]

Gray might now have sunk back into the kind of apathy which had recently been overcoming him in Cambridge, if at the end of November he had not received unexpected news from Nicholls. That lively young parson had been taking a holiday at Bath, where he had met Charles-Victor de Bonstetten, son of the Treasurer of Berne, and a member of the small but powerful aristocracy which governed the city. He had given Bonstetten a letter of introduction to Gray, and thought it well to advise the latter. Bonstetten was a very gifted young man, but, as his anxious father observed, his mind was 'ardent and inconstant'. Every wind of circumstance affected him. He had once made careful preparations for suicide, and then changed his mind. He had, like Gibbon, fallen in love with Suzanne Curchod at Lausanne, and again changed his mind. He had called on J.-J. Rousseau and on Voltaire, both of whom were anathema to the Bernese. After this, his father had sent him to pursue his studies in Holland, where the atmosphere would be less heady than in gay Lausanne; and subsequently he had obtained permission to cross to England and learn the language. In London he heard of a family in Berkshire which would lodge him and teach him English; and he was then not long in learning of the amenities and entertainments for which Bath was famous.

Years later, in a letter of 1827 to Heinrich Zchokke,[2] he related the circumstances of his meeting with Nicholls. On reaching Bath he knew no one, though some families he met in the boarding house were friendly. One evening, when a ball was being held in the Assembly Rooms, he climbed on to a table in order better to see the dancing. 'Un jeune Anglais s'y était déjà installé. Pour ne pas tomber nous nous jetâmes dans les bras l'un de l'autre. Cet homme était Nicholls, l'ami et le confidant de Gray . . . Nicholls resta mon ami jusqu'à sa fin . . .'

In his letter to Gray of 27 November Nicholls says that he

picked him out from among the mob in the rooms here . . . I
think he is vastly better than any thing English (of the same age)
I ever saw; and then I have a partiality to him because he was
born among the mountains; and talks of them with enthusiasm
– of the forests of pines which grow darker and darker as you
ascend, till the *nemorum nox* is completed . . .; of the cries of
eagles and other birds of prey adding to the horror . . . When I
go into Switzerland I am to be so directed! . . . and to travel
with such advantages! but it is absolutely necessary to pass a
month at Zürich to learn German;[3] and the mountains must be
traversed on foot; avec des grimpons aux mains, and shoes of a
peculiar construction. I'd give my ears to try.

Bonstetten had made his way to London with letters of introduction to Mrs Hay and Thomas Pitt. He was presented at Court, and
generally created a most favourable impression. Gray, whom
Nicholls's letter had inspired with enthusiasm, went up to town
to meet him and show him some of the sights. One of the most
typical, but also unexpected, of these is said to have been Dr
Johnson, whose enormous body was seen 'rolling before them'.
Gray stopped, whispering to his companion: 'Look, look, Bonstetten! – the great bear! – There goes Ursa Major!' – according
to Sir Egerton Brydges's *Autobiography*.[4] It is a pretty story, but
somewhat suspect. It was Lord Auchinleck who was to describe
Johnson as 'Ursa major', after the latter had been gratuitously rude
to him; and since Brydges could have read this in Boswell's *Tour
of the Hebrides* it is not unlikely that he was confused and ascribed
the remark to Gray.

Captivated by Bonstetten's charm, good looks and vivacity, Gray
brought him to Cambridge a few days before Christmas and found
him a room in the coffee-house opposite Pembroke. Here, for the
first fortnight or so, he took his meals, although before long he was
being entertained at dinner in most of the colleges. At Pembroke,
William Cole, the Rector of Milton, met him on 29 December. In a
letter of 6 January 1770 to Nicholls, Bonstetten described his doings:

Tho' I wear not yet the black gown, and am only an inferior
Priest in the temple of Meditation, yet my countenance is
already consecrated. I never walk but with even steps and mus-
ing gate, and looks commercing with the skyes . . .

I am in a hurry from morning till evening. At 8 o Clock I am roused by a young square Cap, with whom I follow Satan through Chaos and night. He explained me in Greek and latin the *sweet reluctant amorous Delays* of our Grandmother Eve. We finish our travels in a copious breakfast of muffins and tea. Then apears Shakespair and old Lineus strugling together as two ghost would do for a damned Soul. Sometimes the one get the better sometimes the other. Mr Gray . . . is so good as to shew me Macbeth, and all witches, Beldams, Ghost and Spirits, whose language I never could have understood without his Interpretation . . .

In a sort of postscript to this letter Gray wrote: 'I never saw such a boy . . . he is busy from morn to night, has no other amusement than that of changing one study for another. . . .'

A letter which Bonstetten wrote to his mother on 6 February paints a more circumstantial picture of Cambridge manners than one finds elsewhere. Social life, he tells her, is stiff and ceremonious, entirely lacking in ease and gaiety. To sit with crossed legs, pay a pretty compliment to a lady, or address civilities ('honnêtetés') to a man, or pick up a handkerchief that someone has dropped, would be considered ridiculous and indecent. It is only in England that the art of silence is practised. He has seen some fifteen men and women seated in a circle and not uttering a word for a quarter of an hour. Although England has produced witty writers, wit is not appreciated. He himself has been very kindly treated and, thanks to Gray's friendship, everyone takes pains to oblige him. Gray is

. . . certainly the premier writer and the premier poet in England . . . I eat every day in his rooms; he lives in great retirement, and is so kind as to show pleasure in seeing me. I call on him at any hour, he reads with me what I wish, I work in his room; we read natural history for amusement . . . I shall leave Cambridge on Monday, and will be in Paris for perhaps a fortnight . . .[5]

In the event he lingered in Cambridge until late in March, studying Milton and Shakespeare, and taking lessons in botany from the Curator of the Botanic Garden. While reading English poetry with him, Gray could not be persuaded to speak of his own verse or to say anything about himself. 'Between the present and the past, there was an impassable gulf.'[6] If he was reticent and excessively reserved with Bonstetten, who charmed him, it seems likely that he was equally, or even more so, with others. One imagines him seated at dinner in Pembroke or Trinity,[7] or afterwards in the parlour, and scarcely uttering a word except to agree or disagree. People would suppose him to be sunk in profound meditation; hence the prestige which he enjoyed.

Bonstetten had attracted him from the outset, but, as the weeks went by, he found himself more and more obsessed with this handsome youth, and feeling for him an affection that alarmed him. He realised his infatuation without being able to overcome it. Bonstetten, however, had an inkling of the truth and decided to leave Cambridge and cross the Channel. Gray accompanied him to London. On 20 March he wrote to Nicholls:

On Wednesday next I go (for a few days) with Mons: de B: to London. His cursed F.r will have him home in the autumn, & he must pass thro France to improve his talents & morals. he goes for Dover on Friday . . . he gives me too much pleasure, & at least *an equal* share of inquietude . . . I have never met with so extraordinary a Person. God bless him! I am unable to talk to you about anything else, I think . . . as to Wales, doubtless I should wish it this summer, but I can answer for nothing, my own employment so sticks in my stomach, & troubles my conscience . . .

Life was indeed becoming too hard for Gray. Thoughts of Bonstetten tormented him, and the consciousness that he was not fulfilling his duties as professor was an added torment. He lent Bonstetten £20, returned sadly to Cambridge and, after receiving a letter which Bonstetten had dispatched from Abbeville, wrote on 4 April to Nicholls:

At length, my dear Sr, we have lost our poor de B:n. I pack'd him up with my own hands in the Dover-machine at 4 o'clock in the morning on Friday, 23 March, the next day at 7 he sail'd & reach'd *Calais* by noon, & *Boulogne* at night. the next night he reach'd *Abbeville* . . . from thence he wrote to me, & here I am again to pass my solitary evenings, wch hung much lighter on my hands, before I knew him. this is your fault! . . . for this (as Lady Constance says) *Was never such a gracious Creature born*![8] & yet – but no matter! burn my letter that I wrote you, for I am very much out of humour with myself & will not believe a word of it. you will think I have caught madness from him (for he is certainly mad) & perhaps you will be right. oh! what things are Fathers & Mothers . . . the translation of *Gruner* can not be had this month or six weeks, so I am destitute of all things. this place never appear'd so horrible to me, as it does now. could not you come for a week or fortnight? it would be sunshine to me in a dark night! . . .

He was anxious to read a French or English version of G.-S. Gruner's *Die Eisgebirge des Schweizerlandes*, which had appeared at Berne in 1760–2, possibly because he was already contemplating a visit to Switzerland to see the glaciers – and Bonstetten. The latter wrote to him from Paris on 5 April, and on the 12th Gray took up his pen to reply:

Never did I feel, my dear Bonstetten, to what a tedious length the few short movements of our life may be extended by impatience & expectation, till you had left me . . . I am grown old in the compass of less than three weeks, like the Sultan in the Turkish Tales, that did but plunge his head into a vessel of water and take it out again . . . & found he had pass'd many years in captivity. The strength & spirits that now enable me to write to you, are only owing to your last letter, a temporary gleam of sunshine . . . I did not conceive till now (I own) what it was to lose you, nor felt the solitude & insipidity of my own condition, before I possess'd the happiness of your friendship.

Then, because (as he hinted) he had seen in Bonstetten 'the principal features' of a 'Genius truly inclined to Philosophy', as drawn by Plato in Book VI of the *Republic*, and because he foresaw 'with trembling anxiety' the dangers which would beset such a genius in Paris, he summarised the virtues of this species of mind by copying an extract which he had made years before in his Commonplace Book, adding that the

. . . endowments so necessary to a soul form'd for philosophy are often the ruin of it (especially when join'd to the external advantages of wealth, nobility, strength and beauty) that is, if it light on a bad soil; and want its proper nurture, which nothing but an excellent education can bestow . . .

Bonstetten must have seen that this was intended to apply to him. He wrote from Paris on 30 April and again on 16 May, but these letters have been lost. Gray wrote, in the interval, on 19 April, and on 9 May answered Bonstetten's letter of 30 April. Meanwhile, on the 14th, he had sent Bonstetten's Paris address to Nicholls, and one may assume that Nicholls wrote to him. That Bonstetten was (Nicholls imagined) 'in the midst of every danger and seduction, and without any advantages, but from his excellent nature and understanding', disquieted him, he had told Gray; 'I own I am very anxious for him on his account . . .'. And Gray, even more anxious, repeated this when writing to Bonstetten on 19 April:

Alas! how do I every moment feel the truth of what I have some-where read: '*Ce n'est pas le voir que de s'en souvenir*', & yet that remembrance is the only satisfaction I have left. My life is now but a perpetual conversation with your shadow. – The known sound of your voice still rings in my ears. – There, on the corner of the fender you are standing, or tinkling on the Pianoforte, or stretch'd at length on the sofa. – Do you reflect . . . that it is a week or eight days before I can receive a letter from you . . .

After quoting parts of Nicholls's anxious letter, and praising Bonstetten's 'noble and generous understanding', he warns him of the perils which he supposes surround him:

Shall the Jargon of French Sophists, the allurements of painted women *comme il faut*, or the vulgar caresses of prostitute beauty, the property of all, that can afford to purchase it, induce you to give up a mind & body by Nature distinguish'd from all others, to folly, idleness, disease, & vain remorse?

There is no evidence that the young Bernese was in any such peril. He had met the Duchesse d'Enville (a La Rochefoucauld) and her daughter-in-law in Geneva four years before, and had the entry into the best circles of Parisian society. He later informed Gray that he was going to stay with the Duchesse at La Roche

Guyon on the Seine, below Paris. On the other hand, he could hardly have spent the summer in the capital without hearing about the doctrines of the Philosophes, or even reading something by D'Holbach, Helvétius or Diderot. This would have been enough to alarm Gray, to whom anything smacking of scepticism was anathema.[9] At the beginning of May Beattie had asked Dilly, the bookseller, to send Gray his *Essay on . . . Truth, in opposition to Sophistry and Scepticism*, the publication of which had been financed by Beattie's friends. He had, himself, posted to Gray the manuscript of Book I of *The Minstrel*. On 2 July Gray complimented him on the poem, adding a few suggestions that might improve it. He had read the *Essay on Truth* (which was an unmannerly attack on Hume) and added that he himself was partial to Beattie's views:

> . . . I have always thought David Hume a pernicious writer, & believe he has done as much mischief here as he has in his own country. A turbid & shallow stream often appears to our apprehensions very deep. A professed sceptic can be guided by nothing but his present passions (if he has any) & interests; & to be masters of his philosophy we need not his books or advice, for every child is capable of the same thing, without any study at all. Is not that *naïveté* and good humour, which his admirers celebrate in him, owing to this, that he has continued all his days an infant, but one that unhappily has been taught to read & write? That childish nation, the French, have given him vogue & fashion, & we, as usual, have learned from them to admire him at second hand.

By this time (early July) other interests also had begun to divert Gray's mind from thoughts of Bonstetten. Thomas Warton of Oxford, who was planning a *History of English Poetry*, had been told by Hurd that Gray had studied the subject and drawn up an outline. He had asked Gray if he would let him have any such 'fragments or sketches of a design', and on 15 April Gray wrote to apologise for his delay in responding and sent a fairly detailed plan which comprised an introduction and four parts. The introduction is of more particular interest, since it proposes a study of the origin of rhyme in poetry; but the whole scheme represents the fruit of serious research, and is perhaps the most scholarly of

Gray's productions. Warton thanked him on the 20th. He had already written a good deal on Chaucer, and had considered the influence of other peoples on the formation of English poetry properly so called. He agreed with Gray that his work should exclude the history of dramatic poetry, which would require a volume to itself.

Later in the month Gray stayed for a few days with Nicholls at Blundeston and, on his return, found a letter from Bonstetten which he acknowledged on 9 May:

> . . . Your letter has made me happy . . . It is impossible with me to dissemble with you. Such as I am, I expose my heart to your view . . . – All that you say to me, especially on the subject of Switzerland, is infinitely acceptable. It feels too pleasing ever to be fulfill'd . . .

The letter had not, however, entirely pleased him, because he told Nicholls that its style was 'un peu trop alembiqué'; and he was disappointed that Bonstetten had let over a fortnight go by without writing again. Gray had gone to stay in Jermyn Street, and from here on 22 May he wrote to Nicholls about the long letter which he thought too finicky or affected,

> . . . & yesterday I had another shorter, & making bad excuses for not writing oftener: he seems at present to give in to all the French nonsense & to be employ'd much like an English boy broke loose from his Governor. I want much to know, whether he has wrote to you yet: if not, I am seriously angry, tho' to little purpose . . .

The young Marquis de Villevieille had called on Gray and made a good impression. He was learning English and, 'by way of exercise', translating Gray's verses into French. Apart from this tribute to his fame, life was by no means without diversions. He had had breakfast with Lord Strathmore and Thomas Lyon, and seen Strathmore's infant daughter; he had dined at Hampton Court with Stonhewer, and again with him and others in London.

Just before Nicholls received the above-mentioned letter (of 22 May), he wrote to Gray to mention that he was expecting to hear from him, and to say that Bonstetten had not written. Temple, who, as will be remembered, had a living in Devonshire, had decided on a separation from his wife and had written to Nicholls about it. Temple was in great distress and apparently wished Gray to suggest to him some historical studies which might divert his mind, and also – an embarrassing request – to advise him about his marital difficulties. In some perplexity as to what he should do, Nicholls enclosed Temple's letter. Gray, who had returned to Cambridge, replied with a touch of understandable asperity:

> . . . I would wish . . . to oblige & serve T: in any way I am able, but it cannot be *in his way* at present, he & you seem to think, that I have nothing else to do but to transcribe a page from some common-place-book on this head: if it were so I should not hesitate a minute about it.

As he had arranged to leave for Aston three days later, he had no time to look up and write out all the material which Temple required. He suggested that Temple should begin by reading Bacon's *History of the Reign of King Henry VII* and Lord Herbert's *Life and Reign of King Henry VIII* (hardly the most suitable subject for Temple) and said that he would perhaps give him more help on his return to Cambridge. Nicholls was advised to say nothing about 'the article of separation'.

At Aston, where he spent about a fortnight, he seems to have told Mason that he wished to resign his professorship. Since he was unable to perform the fairly light duties which he had prescribed in his memorandum, it would have been a reasonable step and would have eased his mind. Mason dissuaded him, although with difficulty.[10] He returned to Cambridge about 23 June, and was joined by Nicholls early in July for the projected visit to North Wales. They travelled across country to Shropshire, but here changed their plans and made their way south in a leisurely manner. They saw the principal castles, like Ludlow; the cathedrals of Worcester, Hereford and Gloucester; spent a week at Malvern; visited Shenstone's garden at Leasowes; and concluded the tour by sailing down the Wye from Ross to Chepstow. Among the 'ever new delights' of this trip, which he described to Wharton and Mason, were the new weir on the river and Tintern Abbey. 'Monmouth . . . lies on the same river in a vale, that is the delight of my eyes, & the very seat of pleasure', he told Wharton. On the

way back to Cambridge he passed two days in Oxford 'with great
satisfaction'.

The chief account of this tour in Nicholls's *Reminiscences* con-
firms the impression which others received of Gray's character.
He had agreed to stay in Malvern for a week 'most obligingly on
my account, as I found some acquaintances whom I was glad to
meet. He had neither inclination to mix much in conversation on
such occasions, nor I think much facility, even if he had been willing. This arose perhaps partly from natural reserve, & what is
called *shyness*, & partly from having lived retired in the University
during so great a part of his life . . .' But a little further on, Nicholls
quotes from Gray's letter to West (Florence, April 1741), in which
he admits 'a want of love for general society, indeed! an inability
to it'.[11] This aversion for sociability was therefore a part of his
character, and not the result of having lived in Cambridge.

Gray felt much better in health and spirits as a consequence of
this travel, and he might have looked forward to a very tolerable
Michaelmas Term. It seems that for some years past, he had been
distantly acquainted with Richard Farmer, a Fellow of Emmanuel.
Thomas Percy had corresponded with Farmer in respect of the
Reliques, and had sought Gray's opinion of them; but Gray was
negligent in replying, and this gave offence. Thus, when Percy
asked Farmer for information about the Earl of Surrey's poems,
and Farmer had suggested that Mason might supply it, Percy had
replied (in March, 1768): 'I would rather go a hundred miles in
search myself, than ask a single question either of him or his
Brother Gray . . .' Farmer, on the other hand, appears always to
have been well disposed to Gray and, according to William Cole's
recollections, they became intimate after dining together with a
Mr Oldham at Peterhouse in 1770. Farmer, Cole wrote, was considered 'one of the most ingenious' of Cambridge men,

. . . yet Mr Gray's singular Niceness in the Choice of his
Acquaintance made him appear fastidious to a great Degree to all
who were not acquainted with his Manner. Indeed there did not
seem to be any Probability of any great Intimacy, from the Style
& Manner of each . . .: the one a chearful, companionable,
hearty, open, downright Man . . . the other, of a most fastidious
& recluse Distance of Carriage, rather averse to all Sociability
. . .: nice & elegant in his Person, Dress & Behaviour, even to a

Degree of Finicalness & Effeminacy . . . [yet] They were ever after great Friends, & Dr Farmer & all of his Acquaintance had soon after too much Reason to lament his Loss . . .[12]

CHAPTER 18

The end: 1770–1771[1]

During the first three weeks of October, 1770, Gray was kept in his rooms by a sharp attack of gout. 'I am only now beginning to walk alone again', he wrote to Mason on the 24th, adding several items of college news. Lord Richard Cavendish, a son of the Duke of Devonshire, 'having digested all the learning & all the beef this place could afford him in a two months' residence is about to leave us . . .' He had come up in 1768, when Gray had called on him and described him as 'a sensible boy, awkward & bashful beyond all imagination'. He was to receive his MA in November. Meanwhile, his younger brother, Lord George Augustus, had entered Trinity, while Alleyne Fitzherbert, a son of the squire of Tissington in Dovedale, had entered St John's as a Pensioner; and Gray called on him, apparently before his (Gray's) illness. Fitzherbert, who afterwards became a distinguished member of the diplomatic service, related the episode to Rogers, who passed on the story to Mitford. According to Rogers, Gray had been

> . . . accompanied by Dr Gisborne, Mr Stonhewer and Mr Pal-grave, and they walked one after one, in Indian file. When they withdrew, every College man took off his cap as he passed, a considerable number having assembled in the quadrangle to see Mr Gray, who was seldom seen. I asked Mr Gray, to the great dismay of his companions, what he thought of Mr Garrick's Jubilee Ode, just published? He answered, He was easily pleased.

It has been objected that Gray's alleged companions are unlikely to have been all in Cambridge at the same time, or to have behaved so quaintly, and that the marks of respect shown by an assembly of undergraduates are only slightly less improbable.[2] Rogers may have exaggerated, or added to, what he had been told. Fitzherbert had certainly not used the word 'quadrangle', which alone makes the story suspect.

That autumn torrential rains caused flooding in the Fen country, and this kind of weather must have contributed to Gray's ill health. Having ventured out one day in November to seek fresh air on the Gog Magogs, he caught cold and was tormented by a racking cough. On 25 November, he told Nicholls that Bonstetten had written from Aubonne on Lac Léman, near Lausanne, but that the portrait he had promised had not arrived.

On 16 December Dr Long died and five days later was buried in circumstances which shocked William Cole, who had come from Milton to attend the funeral. A leakage from the pond in the garden had flooded the vault of the chapel, and, after a service lacking in decency, the coffin was lowered into a foot of water. On his return to Milton, Cole found a letter from Walpole, who wished him to inquire at what date Gray proposed to come to London. Cole returned to Pembroke but, Gray 'being in the Combination I would not call him from his Company . . . I wrote the next day a Note to him, of the unceremonious & indecent Manner of the Funeral, & concluded by saying, that after what passed in the Chapel to compleat all, they had taken the poor Mr [Master] from a warm Hall & a noble Fire & flung him into a Well or Ditch half full of water'.

This note was delivered by Cole's servant to Gray, who replied on the 22nd:

How did we know, pray? No Body here remember'd another Burying of the Kind: shall be proud of your Advice the next opportunity, which (we hope) will be some Forty years hence. I am sorry you would not send for me last night . . .

After a visit to Walpole, Gray was feeling in better spirits. James Brown had been elected Master and, the stipend being only £150 a year, Grafton had persuaded the King to present him with the living of Streatham, near Ely, which was worth about £300. The fellows raised enough money between them to decorate the Lodge. It 'has got rid of all its harpsicords [*sic*] & begins to brighten up: its inhabitant is lost like a mouse in an old cheese', Gray wrote to Wharton. He was, however, exchanging more frequent letters with Nicholls, discussing Froissart, who delighted Nicholls, and advising him to read Villehardouin, Joinville, Monstrelet and Commines. Nicholls replied with enthusiasm. Froissart was indeed the 'Herodotus of a barbarous age'; Nicholls understood his fourteenth-century French better than early sixteenth-century English. On 16 March Nicholls, who had just received a letter from Bonstetten, wrote: 'he entreats us à deux genoux to come, and I you in the same posture and with equal earnestness . . . He promises us, if we come, that he will visit us in England the summer following. Let us go then, my dear Mr Gray, and leave low thoughted care at the foot of the mountains . . .' He was going 'to bespeak a curate from the first of June to the last of October', so that no obstacle could prevent the visit. As Gray did not reply, he wrote again on 29 April to say that they ought to answer Bonstetten's letter. He himself had arranged for a curate and had adequate funds; he proposed that they start not later than the second week in June. On 3 May Gray replied that he was glad that Nicholls had decided definitely to visit Switzerland; though he himself was uncertain whether he could go. He had received a strange letter from Bonstetten, who declared that he had been 'le plus malheureux des hommes', that he was 'décidé à quitter son pays', and could not bear 'la morgue de l'aristocratie'. 'I am quite at a loss about it,' said Gray. He added: 'I have had neither health nor spirits all the winter.'

In a letter of 14 May Nicholls informed Gray that he had told Bonstetten he would visit Berne in the summer. Soon after receiving this letter, Gray went to stay in Jermyn Street again, lodging this time with an 'oilman' named Frisby. From here he wrote that 'all things consider'd, it is best not to keep you in suspense about my journey. the sense of my own duty, which I do not perform, my own low spirits . . . & a bodily indisposition make it necessary for me to deny myself that pleasure, which perhaps I have kept too long in view . . .'

Only about eleven letters from Gray, in 1771, have been preserved, and he may not have written many more. On 8 March he thanked Beattie for a copy of Book I of *The Minstrel*, commended certain stanzas and criticised many expressions, and especially his use of obsolete words; but he repeated his praise of the *Essay on Truth*.[3] On the 17th he wrote angrily to Walpole about Voltaire's latest publication – probably the *Dictionnaire philosophique*, in which Goldsmith was to find useful material for his *Essay on the*

Theatre (January, 1772): 'Atheism is a vile dish, tho' all the cooks of France combine to make new sauces to it. As to the Soul, perhaps they may have none on the Continent . . .' Voltaire was not an atheist; but his name now always made Gray see red. When Nicholls called on him in June, Gray made him promise not to call at Ferney. Nicholls agreed, though he could not see that a visit, such as was made as a matter of courtesy by most visitors to Geneva or the Pays de Vaud, would matter.

But Gray was now very sick. An attack of gout was followed by fever, and another complaint which he feared might involve an operation. His London doctor advised him to take a room in Kensington for a week or two, and he did so. On his return to Jermyn Street, he saw Walpole, who was about to leave for Paris. He himself went back to Cambridge on 22 July, but at dinner on the 24th he was overcome with a feeling of nausea and had to be taken to bed. Stephen Hempstead looked after him, and Mary Antrobus came to help. He knew that the end was near: convulsions and periods of delirium left no doubt in the matter. 'Molly, I shall die,' he told Mary, and repeated much the same 'now and then'.[4] Dr Glynn diagnosed the trouble as 'gout in the stomach' – a vague expression. Sir Humphrey Rolleston has regarded the symptoms as indicating an affection of the kidneys, which had resulted in uraemia.[5] Whatever the trouble, the doctors could do nothing for him. Early on the evening of the 30th Brown wrote to Wharton: 'I think him dying and that he has been sensible of his approaching Death.' After a few hours of unconsciousness, he died about 11 p.m. the same evening. Brown, on reading his will, found that he wished to be buried by his mother's grave at Stoke Poges, and this wish was carried out. Brown accompanied the coffin to Stoke, and after his return wrote again to Wharton, whom he had kept posted with the news, on 17 August: 'Every thing is now dark and melancholy in Mr Gray's Room, not a trace of him remains there . . .'

In Paris, Walpole, who saw the notice of Gray's death in a newspaper, was astounded, and wrote at once to Cole for information. Cole obtained details of the will from Brown, and on 24 August sent Walpole a very full account. Gray had managed his income most sensibly and was a comparatively well-to-do man. He appears to have been worth nearly £7,000. He left £500 each to Stonhewer, Brown and Mason; and, Cole thought, about £1,000 to each of his Antrobus cousins. They also had the furniture; and Mary seems to have been left the house in Cornhill. To Mason Gray bequeathed his coins and his books, manuscripts 'and papers of all kinds to preserve or destroy at his own discretion'. Brown and Mason were the executors and residuary legatees. As Gray had bought himself an annuity, it was difficult to know exactly what would remain over, after the various bequests had been made. These seem to have amounted to at least £4,000. The house in Cornhill must have been worth nearly £1,000; and if his estate was valued at about £7,000, it is possible that this figure included the furniture and books. The residuary legatees may have received a substantial sum.

He was not apparently rich enough to make a substantial bequest to the college; doubtless he felt, and rightly, that his cousins had the first claim on him, and, after them, his friends. It seems strange, however, that he left no personal memento, such as a ring, to Walpole. Since the quarrel and reconciliation, Walpole had certainly entertained warmer feelings for Gray than he for Walpole. Many people would rather be benefactor than beneficiary.

Brown's remark in his letter of 17 August to Wharton: 'He never spoke out', has been the subject of some controversy. The context implies that he did not tell his friends that he realised his end was near. He had, however, told Mary Antrobus – as Brown himself reported. Arnold has been criticised for extending Brown's remark to Gray's life as a whole. But there is no evidence that Gray was in the habit of speaking out, except to younger men like Nicholls – and in his letters. Even with Bonstetten, he would not speak of himself or his verses. In a group of people, like Mrs Jennings and her friends, he was noticeably tongue-tied. Walpole admitted to Montagu that Gray was poor company. While this evidence is inconclusive, it is certain that he was not expansive. His letters, on the other hand, are exceptionally long and outspoken. While most men would have expressed their dislike of Dr Long, their hatred of Newcastle or their scorn of the French (if such had been their feeling) in private conversation and been cautious in writing to friends, Gray's behaviour was the exact converse of what is normal. If there is no proof of the view that Gray 'never spoke out', there is no evidence whatever that he was in the habit of doing so.

PART TWO

The Works

CHAPTER 1

The Poet[1]

INTRODUCTORY REMARKS

The critic Roger Martin states his conviction that Gray's heredity not only determined his character and behaviour, but was also a major influence on his writings. To this determinant must be added the environment in which he grew up: the atmosphere of the house in Cornhill, vitiated by his father's outrageous conduct; and finally the equivocal influence of Eton. To have taken part in at least some games would have strengthened him physically, whereas he seems to have devoted his time partly to reading English poetry and some French, but especially to studying the Latin classics. The composition of Latin verse was a routine school exercise; but for Gray it became a habit which continued to occupy him for long after he had left Eton. He even wrote eight or nine pieces in hexameters on the various orders of insects – Coleoptera, Hemiptera, Lepidoptera etc., probably as late as the 1760s. This continuance of a schoolboy habit seems odd by modern standards, but the writing of Latin verse was not unusual at the time. The Elegy, to take one instance, was several times translated into Latin.

A further consequence of Gray's reading as a schoolboy was to store his mind with phrases and verses from Virgil, Horace, Ovid and others, and from a large number of English poets, especially Shakespeare, Milton and Dryden; his own verse is full of these reminiscences. Except for the humorous pieces, all his poems are derivative, and some are simply mosaics of borrowings. It is only fair to recall that, apart from the novelists, mid-eighteenth-century writers, especially poets and dramatists, were not conspicuously original and did not value originality, as did the Romantic poets. 'Tout est dit, depuis cinq mille ans qu'il y a des hommes et qui pensent,' La Bruyère had said.

There are always exceptions. One may cite Goldsmith in *The Deserted Village*, and pre-eminently Christopher Smart. Gray's genius was at the opposite pole to Smart's, the result not merely of a difference in outlook (Gray was never an original thinker), but also of this habit of writing Latin verse. It is difficult to compose Latin poems without using phrases consecrated by their appearance in the great classics, thereby insuring their correctness. Hence Gray may have thought that the best way to compose English poems was to employ phrases consecrated by their appearance in the *English* classics, as well as the Latin. But, for whatever reason, he proceeded always in this manner, except for the composition of the humorous pieces. To readers accustomed to take the Romantic and Victorian poets as their standard, the effect is often startling. Some of Gray's most famous lines, including those which have become standard quotations, were taken literally, or closely paraphrased, from earlier writers. On the other hand, his practice is sometimes justified on the ground that a verse of his represents 'What oft was *writ*, but ne'er so well expressed'.

I   THE LATIN POEMS[1]

Gray's principal Latin verses were written between about 1730 and 1742; a few pieces date from later years. They may be divided into three classes: poems suggested or 'commanded' by his masters at Eton or by the authorities at Cambridge; poems inspired by some public event; and, lastly, personal poems. His education had been almost entirely classical. He and his friends had been familiarised with the major Latin poets, and with some of the minor, even with Claudian. From Virgil he had learned the vocabulary of rural activities, and of heroic action. Horace had furnished models of felicitous language and the art of concision. Ovid was regarded as having come nearer than others to the 'imitation of nature', especially in love-poetry. If all Gray's pieces are derivative, this was because the young Latinist was allowed, and probably taught, to fit into his verses phrases taken from the Latin poets. But it was not to be expected that, as he acquired greater mastery of the language, he would continue this practice, except where the borrowings were deliberate and intended to be appreciated as such. Two at least of the ancient Latin poets afforded a pretext for this kind of reference or allusion. Virgil occasionally borrows subtly from Homer in a way which the scholarly would appreciate. Ausonius went much further. He composed the *Cento Nuptialis* simply by fitting phrases and half-lines from Virgil into an entirely new pattern, with a new meaning, sometimes obscene. It was a kind of game, and quite different in effect from Virgil's pleasant allusiveness.

In the verses which Gray wrote before 1738, the numerous borrowings can only be regarded as plagiarisms. But the Sapphics addressed 'Ad C: Favonium Aristium' are intended to echo Horace's ode to Septimius; and West would know that this was a scholarly game. Playful too, in this sense, were the verses he sent to West from Italy. These are of course more personal than the early poems. The so-called 'Liber secundus' of the 'De principiis Cogitandi' contain the best of his Latin verses.[2] He never learned to write original Latin, and yet he expressed himself more intimately in that language than in English.

The first of the extant pieces is a paraphrase in eleven Alcaic stanzas of Psalm 84. The opening lines –

How amiable are thy tabernacles, O Lord of Hosts!
My soul longeth, yea, even fainteth for the courts of the Lord;
My heart and my flesh crieth out for the living God

– are expanded into two stanzas:

> Oh! Tecta, mentis dulcis amor meae!
> Oh! Summa Sancti Relligio[3] loci!
> Quae me laborantem perurit
> Sacra fames, et amoenus ardor?

> Praeceps volentem quo rapit impetus!
> Ad limen altum tendo avidas Manus.
> Dum lingua frustratur precantem,
> Cor tacitum mihi clamat intus.

The second stanza merely expands the paraphrase, and, indeed, the last two lines are of Gray's invention: 'while my tongue mocks my prayers and my silent heart is clamouring within'. 'Sacra fames' and 'tendo avidas Manus' are of course Virgilian phrases.

The next verses of the Psalm are rendered rapidly enough:

Yea, the sparrow hath found her an house,
And the swallow a nest for herself, where she may lay her young,
Even thine altars, O Lord of Hosts.

Illic loquacem composuit Domum,
Laresque parvos Numinis in fidem
   Praesentioris credit Ales
   Venis amans, vetus Hospes arae.

Here Gray has deliberately avoided some of the obvious renderings.
He could have used *Hirundo*, but 'the bird that loves the Spring'
also means the swallow. *Loquaces nidi* (noisy nests) is a Virgilian
phrase,[4] which would have obviated the need to transfer the sound
of twittering to the nest itself – *loquacem Domum*. It would also
have been more direct than 'little Lares'. This is imitated from
parvo lare in Horace's *Odes* (Book III, No. 29), where the sense,
which is that of 'humble', seems not to have been appreciated by
Gray.

The hexameters, headed by a passage from Persius's third Satire,
and labelled by Gosse as 'Play-verses', probably date from 1734.
Although the thoughts are in no way original and the language
contains phrases from the *Aeneid*, the *Georgics*, from Lucretius,
Persius and Pope, yet the expression is clear enough, particularly
in lines 31 to 37:

Non super aethereas errare licentius auras
Humanum est, at scire hominem; breve limite votum
Exiguo claudat, nec se quaesiverit extra.
Errat, qui cupit oppositos transcendere fines,
Extenditque manus ripae ulterioris amore;
Illic gurges hiat late, illic saeva vorago,
Et caligantes longis ombragibus umbrae.

[It is not for man to wander unrestrained above the ether, but to
know man (Pope). Let him shut in his brief aspirations with a
scanty boundary, and let him not seek outside himself (Persius).
He errs, who desires to go beyond the limits fixed for him, and
stretch out his hands in longing for the further shore (Virgil);
for there stretches a wide whirlpool, there a savage abyss; and
. . . vast shadows.]

The whole of line 35 is virtually copied from *Aeneid*, VI, and the pathetic tone of the original is out of place in a poem which sets limits to scientific inquiry; as also is the language descriptive of the nether world in lines 36 and 37. Gray seems to have recalled that the Styx marked the boundary for the progress of the dead on their way to the nether world, but this also was inappropriate for his argument. Furthermore, the various borrowings are out of harmony with each other.

The 'Hymeneal', a 'Gratulatio' in sixty-one hexameters in honour of the Prince of Wales's marriage with Princess Augusta of Saxe-Gotha, was printed at Cambridge in 1736. It is a conventional, if not perfunctory piece, servile in tone, and servile in its dependence on Virgil. The old schoolboy exercise in arranging expressions furnished by the Roman poets is here carried to excess. In the first seven lines, half the phrases are borrowed:

> *Ignarae* nostrum *mentes, et inertia corda,*
> Dum curas regum, et *Sortem miseramur iniquam,*
> Quae Solio affixit, vetuitque *calescere flamma*
> Dulci, quae *dono Divum, gratissima serpit*
> Viscera per, mollesque animis lene implicat aestus;
> Nec teneros sensus, *Veneris nec praemia norunt,*
> *Eloquiumve oculi,* aut *facunda silentia linguae.*

Here, and in the following lines, the *Aeneid* is the main source of supply, while Horace is not spared. The reference to Pygmalion in line 52 comes from Ovid.

The poem entitled 'In Diem: 29^{am} Maii' was probably written in the Spring of 1737 in honour of the birthday of Charles II, and to celebrate his escape from the battlefield of Worcester in 1651:

> Quam tremui, cum laeva tuas Vigornia turmas
> Fudit praecipites, hostemque remisit ovantem!

The picture is vivid and concise. Unfortunately Gray is borrowing from *Aeneid*, VI, 694, 'Quam tremui ne quid Libyae tibi regna nocerent', where the dead Anchises is warning Aeneas that Dido's charms may prove dangerously tempting. Such a reference was hardly applicable to Charles II in this juncture. The poet next apostrophises the oak tree among whose leafy branches Charles hid himself until the hue and cry had subsided:

> Tuque, Arbor, nostrae felix tutela coronae,
> Gloria camporum, et luci regina vocare: (15, 16)

After embroidering on this theme, he declares (line 19) that the oak, sacred to Jupiter in ancient Latium, must now be held sacred in Britain:

> Sacra Jovi Latio quondam, nunc sacra Britanno.

This is the most spontaneous of Gray's early poems: its tone is not merely that of a scholastic exercise. On the other hand, the longer piece in elegiacs: 'In 5^{tam} Novembris', again lapses into the conventional and the obvious.

> Cui tribuenda modo sceleratae premia palmae? (1. 3)

Was Guy Fawkes as evil as Phalaris and Nero? It would seem so, Gray suggests, because, had he not been discovered, his unaided hand would have destroyed the Members of Parliament and so ruined the country:

> Jure salus se jactaret, procerumque ruina
> tantam una gentem perdomuisse manu. (11. 33, 34).

'Luna habitabilis' – the tripos verses composed in 1737 – is an extraordinary poem. Who, Gray asks the Muse, will give him wings to explore the ocean of air? No need of wings, she replies; learn rather to draw the moon nearer to yourself:

> Disce Puer potius caelo deducere Lunam . . .

Apply yourself to the little tube (the telescope) –

> Quin tete admoveas (tumuli super aggere spectas,
> Compositum) tubulo . . .

– and you will see the lunar realms. Can you doubt whether so great a world lacks dwellers? They till fields and build cities; nay, they must even now be inspecting our greater planet. They will discover Gaul and Germany and the snowy Apennine; but lo! far to the north, tiny England displays her shores. Thronging princes (of the moon) gaze on this lovely radiance, and continue gazing late into the night. Soon, communications will be established and treaties of commerce signed:

> Fœdera mox icta, et gemini commercia mundi . . .

And he foretells that England, which has harnessed the winds and ruled the waves, will rise victorious over the conquered realms of air:

> Anglia, quae pelagi jamdudum torquet habenas,
> Exercetque frequens ventos, atque imperat undae,
> Aëris attollet fasces, veteresque triumphos
> Huc etiam feret, et victis dominabitur auris.

This contradicts the warning in the 'Play verses at Eton' (1734), with which it actually shares some phrases, such as 'vastique aulae theatri' (line 17 in the 'Play' exercise, line 13 in 'Luna habitabilis') – a phrase apparently original. For the most part, however, Gray was indebted to Virgil; he drew liberally from the first four books of the *Aeneid*, from Book XII, from the *Georgics*, and once from Ovid's *Metamorphoses*.

The Sapphics 'Ad C: Favonium Aristium'[5] were sent by Gray to West in June 1738. While assenting to their parents' desire that they should enter their names for study at the Inner Temple, the two friends much preferred to live at ease and write verses. The opening stanza deliberately recalls Horace's 'Ode to Septimius' (II, 6):

> Septimi, Gadis aditure mecum et
> Cantabrum indoctum iuga ferre nostra et
> Barbaras Syrtis, ubi Maura semper
>   Aestuat unda . . .

So Gray begins:

> Barbaras aedes aditure mecum,
> Quas Eris semper fovet inquieta,
> Lis ubi late sonat, et togatum
>   Aestuat agmen!

[(O thou) about to go with me to the barbarous inner places (the Temple) which restless Eris is ever stirring up, where Strife resounds far and wide, and the togaed multitude rages.]

> Dulcius quanto, patulis sub ulmi
> Hospitae ramis temere jacentem
> Sic libris horas, tenuique inertes
>   Fallere Musa?

[How much sweeter (would it be), lying at ease under the spreading boughs of a friendly elm, to beguile the idle hours with books and with the Muse?]

Temere jacentem is only one of the Latin phrases which Gray carried over into his English verse: in the 'Ode on the Spring' it reappeared as 'at ease reclin'd'. The remaining stanzas of the Latin poem, which contains thirteen in all, refer to classical sites, Parnassus and Calpe (Gibraltar?) and mythological beings. Mason regarded 'Ad C: Favonium Aristium' as 'original' in the sense that it was not written at the bidding of schoolmasters or dons; it was not intended to be original in other ways, but to be the kind of game which young scholars would sometimes play with each other. West would at once see that Gray had parodied the 'Ode to Septimius', and the closer the imitations, the greater the pleasure; because both young men were seeing their present situation, as it were, through the eyes of Horace. The same motive animates some of the Latin verses which Gray sent from Italy in 1740 and 1741.[6] Meanwhile, Gray posted to his friend a fragment in Alcaics which has been eulogised as 'at once perfectly Horatian and wholly unlike Horace':[7]

> O lachrymarum Fons, tenero sacros
> Ducentium ortus ex animo; quater
>   Felix! in imo qui scatentem
>   Pectore te, pia Nympha, sensit!

It is difficult to understand the motive, or the point, of these verses; particularly the use of the word *quater*. They may be roughly paraphrased as 'O Fount of tears which have their sacred springs in the tender soul: four times is blest, he who has felt thee, holy Nymph, springing up from deep in his breast'.

With this exception, all Gray's Latin poems written before 1740
were more or less dependent on phrases borrowed from Virgil,
Horace and others; sometimes almost wholly dependent.

In 1740, however, the sight of Genoa, Florence, the Roman
Campagna and the environs of Naples kindled Gray's imagination
and inspired a number of pieces which are more spontaneous and
rather less closely imitative. All of them were sent by post to
'Favonius', and one of the best is an invocation in Alcaics, entitled
'Ad C: Favonium Zephyrinum'. Writing as from the falls of the
Anio at Tivoli – falls which have heard him cry to the winds the
name of his friend – Gray calls upon the 'Mater rosarum' to tell
him how at this moment his friend is occupied:

> Dic, non inertem fallere qua diem
> Amat sub umbra, seu sinit aureum
>   Dormire plectrum, seu retentat
>   Pierio Zephyrinus antro
> Furore dulci plenus . . .

[Say, under what shade does Zephyrinus love to while away the
not idle day, whether he lets the golden lyre lie in slumber or,
full of sweet frenzy, reawakens it in the Pierian cave.]

Gray is here recalling Horace's

> Et te sonantem plenius aureo
> Alcaee, plectro . . . (Odes, II, 13)

but less closely than he had been used to plundering Virgil. Moreover, the allusion, or parody, is intended to be appreciated. West,
too, must dwell imaginatively in the ancient world ('in the Pierian
grotto'); while Gray, who was now in the very haunts of Horace,
could more easily imagine the presence of fauns and naiads:

> Dilecta Fauno, et capripedum choris
> Pineta, testor vos, Anio minax
>   Quaecunque per clivos volutus
>   Praecipiti tremefecit amne,
> Illius altum Tibur, et Aesulae
> Audisse sylvas nomen amabiles,
>   Illius et gratas Latinis
>   Naiasin ingeminasse rupes.

[O Pine-groves beloved by Faunus and the goat-footed choir, I call you to witness, whichever of you, menacing Anio, as he pours over the cliff, causes to tremble with his headlong torrent, that lofty Tibur and the pleasant woods of Aesula have heard the name (of Favonius) and that the rocks dear to the Naiads of Latium have echoed it.]

The Naiads, he says, have seen him on the same moist bank where the sweetly-singing bird of Venusia so often bathed – which obviously refers to Horace, whose birthplace was Venusia, and who had celebrated the falls of the Anio and the grove of Tivoli in *Odes*, I, 7: '. . . et praeceps Anio, ac Tiburni lucus'.[8] The poem also contains a reference to Lucretius, who had spoken of the 'genitabilis aura Favoni'; while lines 33 and 34 –

> Haerent sub omni nam folio nigri
> Phoebia luci (credite) somnia

– ('For, believe me, dreams inspired by Phoebus cling under every leaf of the dark forest') are adapted from *Aeneid*, VI, 283–4:

> . . . quam sedem Somnia vulgo
> Vana tenere ferunt, foliisque sub omnibus haerent.[9]

This poem was written in May. A month or so later Gray composed a piece in hexameters on the Gaurus, now known as the Monte Barbaro, north-west of Naples. Most of the verses describe the fearful eruption which threw up, near to the Monte Barbaro, a new volcano, the Monte Nuovo: the clouds of volcanic dust which darkened the sky, the rain of red-hot lava, the terror of wild beasts in flight, and of farmers who, after the eruption had subsided, found no trace of their wives or parents. The mountain still bears marks of the catastrophe. It may be that the streams of black bitumen have dried up:

> . . . seu forte bituminis atri
> Defluxere olim rivi . . .

But perhaps, oh horror! (the mountain) is gathering fires in its secret bowels for the destruction of future peoples, and is again gathering together its scattered flames:

Sive in visceribus meditans incendia jam nunc,
Horrendum! arcanis glomerat genti esse futurae
Exitio *sparsos* tacitusque *recolligit ignes*.

'Sparsos' and 'recolligit' come from Lucan I, 157. In the piece as
a whole, the *Eclogues*, the *Georgics* and the *Aeneid* are laid under
contribution, as well as Horace, *Satires*, II, 8.

Gray would have preferred to remain in Rome throughout the
summer of 1740, but August is always an unhealthy month there,
and Walpole was well advised to settle in Florence. His friend had
no taste for the round of dances and merrymaking which delighted
Walpole. Gray consoled himself by copying out music; yet, when
the time came, in the spring of 1741, to move to Venice for
Ascensiontide, he felt real regret at having to leave the Tuscan
Athens. Hence the 'Farewell to Fiesole', a short piece in 8½ hexameters, which he posted to West on 21 April 1741:

> . . . oh Fæsulae amœna
> Frigoribus juga, nec nimium spirantibus auris!
> Alma quibus Tusci Pallas decus Apennini
> Esse dedit, glaucaque sua canescere sylva.

[O hills of Fiesole, pleasant with cool breezes which do not blow
too hard! To them kindly Pallas gave the gift of the charm in the
Tuscan Apennine and of being hoary with her grey-leaved tree.
(He continues:) I shall see you no more from Arno's vale, girt
about with porticoes and a crown of white villas, as you rise
aloft on your shining ridge; nor shall I gaze and marvel at the
antique temple, behind the line of ancient cypresses and roofs
rising above roofs.]

In the line: 'Non ego vos posthac Arni de valle videbo' Gray is
repeating Virgil's *Eclogue*, I, 75–6:

> Non ego vos posthac . . .
> Videbo . . .

which likewise expresses sorrow at quitting a beloved haunt.

After quarrelling with Walpole and spending some time, perforce, in Venice, Gray returned home by the Mont Cenis and
again visited the Grande Chartreuse. The place seemed more

solitary; the weather (it was in August) was calmer; and in the
dark pinewoods, whose silence was broken only by the roar of the
torrent, he felt the presence of the Deity whom he invoked in an
Alcaic ode:

> O Tu, severi relligio loci
> Quocunque gaudes nomine (non leve
>   Nativa nam certe fluenta
>   Numen habet, veteresque sylvas:
>
> Praesentiorem et conspicimus Deum
> Per invias rupes, fera per juga,
>   Clivosque praeruptos, sonantes
>   Inter aquas, nemorumque noctem
>
> Salve vocanti rite, fesso et
>   Da placidam juveni quietem . . .

[O thou, holy Spirit of this solemn place, by whatever name
thou art pleased to be called (for surely no minor Deity com-
mands (these) wild torrents and ancient forests; and we feel God
more present to us amid untrodden crags, wild ridges, precipi-
tous cliffs, roaring cataracts and the gloom of sacred groves . . .)
    Hail! and grant to a weary youth, if he calls on thee aright,
peaceful rest.]

Gray ends by praying that he may pass his old age (*horas
senectae*) in some sequestered spot, free from the tumult of the
crowd and the anxious cares of men:

> Tutumque vulgari tumultu
> Surripias, hominumque curis

This ode contains reminiscences of Horace. The expression:
'Salve rite vocanti' is in Book I, 13; while the last two lines recall
the second tercet of Petrarch's 'Solo e pensoso i più deserti
campi'. They may also, it has been noted, have suggested 'Far
from the madding crowd'.
    Equally personal, even moving, is the short piece in Sapphics
which he wrote after his return to London. He had felt here a
stranger in his own country, people had looked askance at his

foreign clothes, and he longed to be back at Fiesole, or Formia, or under the warm sun at Genoa; but, alas! vast tracts of mountain and forest rob him of the sight of those pleasant regions, and the shining Ocean rolls between him and them:

> Oh ubi colles, ubi Fæsularum,
> Palladis curae, plaga, Formiæque
> Prodigae florum, Genuaeque amantes
>   Littora soles?

> Abstulit campos oculis amœnos
> Montium quantus, nemorumque tractus?
> Quot natant eheu! medii profundo
>   Marmore fluctus?

The poem entitled 'Sophonisba Massinissae Epistola' – an imaginary letter in the tradition of Ovid's 'Heroidum Epistolae' – seems to have been written in May 1742. It contains twenty-six elegiac couplets and is evidently unfinished.

Massinissa had at first been allied to Carthage, but had gone over to the Romans when Carthage had favoured his rival Syphax. Later on, he had married Sophonisba. When, however, the younger Scipio had won his final victory, he regarded Sophonisba as a prisoner of war. He demanded her surrender; or, if she preferred death to captivity, he gave her the choice of taking poison. This is the immediate occasion for her writing to her husband:

> Egregium accipio promissi Munus amoris,
>   Inque manu mortem jam fruitura fero:

[(with the phial of poison in her hand) I accept this excellent gift of promised love and, about to enjoy it, already hold death in my hand.]

She, the great glory of the daughters of Elissa, would avoid the mere appearance of indulging too ardently in a second love or of being over-terrified by her enemies –

> . . . Ne videar flammae nimis indulsisse secundae,
>   Vel nimis hostiles extimuisse manus

– which echoes 'hostiles credit adesse manus' in Ovid's *Fasti*, II, 468. She recalls the day when, after defeating Syphax, Massinissa had entered Carthage amid the plaudits of the multitude. 'How becoming were your locks flowing to your neck, a mark of royalty, how becoming the dark colour of your ardent face!'

> Jam flexi, regale decus, per colla capilli,
> Jam decet ardenti fuscus in ore color!

Here, Gray is borrowing an expression from the *Amores*, II, 440: 'et enim fusco grata colore Venus'.

And yet, she continues, how modest was your mien! Your eyes seemed to linger on me; I blushed; your gaze grew more soft, you advanced more slowly. I wondered if any woman near me might have been more worthy of attracting your gaze:

> . . . Quae poterat visus detinuisse tuos.[10]

But there was no other. That night, even when she slept, she still saw the procession, her thoughts were still of him.

The kind of poem initiated by Ovid in the *Heroides* inspired imitations even in ancient times; but Ovid's 'heroines' seem always to have been imaginary or mythological, and not historical, like Gray's. Sophonisba's 'Epistola' strikes a good judge of Latin verse as one of Gray's more original and more successful essays in the genre. For a piece of this kind, Ovid was a natural source of inspiration, and it appears that here and there, as indicated by Hendrickson, a few words or phrases are adapted from the 'Fasti', the 'Amores' and the 'Tristia'. No actual borrowings from the *Heroides* have been traced, and the reminiscences of Ovid's other poems are relatively few in number.

While in Florence in 1740 Gray had begun a poem in hexameters which he called 'De Principiis Cogitandi, Liber primus. Ad Favonium.' He added further lines in the spring of 1742, intending perhaps to complete a second book, which would develop the principles of the first. The latter contains 207 lines, in which he expounds the main principles of Locke's *Essay concerning Human Understanding* (1690). Locke had argued that our 'ideas', by which he meant concepts, derive from experience, that is, from the five senses, and from reflexion on the operations of the mind. There are, he thought, no innate 'ideas'.[11] An 'idea' is 'whatsoever is the object of the understanding when a man thinks'. This system, which Locke's own university rejected, was welcomed in Cambridge, and taken up enthusiastically by the French Philosophes, some of whom carried this kind of 'sensationalism' to the point of a mechanistic system.

In the opening lines of his poem Gray hails Locke as 'the second luminary of the English race' and calls upon God to reveal the hidden causes of things (*caecas rerum causas*). In lines 32–53 he explains the mechanism by which a kind of fluid communicates to the brain the impulses which it has received from the senses; and he illustrates this (lines 64 ff) by treating of touch, sight, sound, taste and smell. Some men's brains receive messages by only 'two entrances'. He who has been struck blind can still touch, or hear, or taste, or smell. Gray expounds Locke's *Essay* in poetical terms and with the help of classical imagery, as in lines 143–53, where he pictures a hamadryad, lying on the brink of a pool, who is amazed to see, in the mirror of the waters, another nymph moving exactly as she moves.

Just as Gray was trying to do for Locke what Lucretius had done for Epicurus, so the language he uses has been inspired by Lucretius, and also by Virgil.

The fragment of the 'Liber Secundus', in 29 lines, was written in 1742, after the death of West. It is not a continuation of the first book, but a lament for Favonius. He and his friend had planned to spend the sunny hours together, as before:

> Credulus heu longos, ut quondam, fallere Soles

But now the days are full of sorrow. He apostrophises the spirit of the departed:

> At Tu, sancta anima, et nostri non indiga luctus,
> Stellanti templo, sincerique aetheris igne,
> Unda orta es fruere; atque oh si secura, nec ultra
> Mortalis, notos olim miserata labores
> Respectes, tenuesque vacet cognoscere curas . . .
> Respice et has lacrymas, memori quas ictus amore
> Fundo; quod possum, juxta lugere sepulchrum
> Dum juvat, et mutae vana haec jactare favillae . . .

[But thou, blessed spirit, dost not need our cries of woe, while thou dost enjoy the starry realm and the fire of the pure ether which gave thee birth; but oh! if free from care, yet not from thought of mortals; if thou lookest back with pity on labours once known to thee, and hast time to think of minor cares . . . look back, I pray, on these tears which I shed, stricken with nostalgic love. All I can do is to lament by thy tomb and utter these vain words to thy silent ashes.]

These lines express a more pious grief than the sonnet in English. They are also the last of any importance that he wrote. In later years he versified in Latin a few fragments from the Greek Anthology and, as mentioned above, described various genera of insects.

Of Gray's Latin poems as a whole, the piece in Sapphics 'Ad C: Favonium Aristium', the Sophonisba 'Epistola', the Apostrophe to the Spirit of 'Favonius' – perhaps also the lines on the Grande Chartreuse – are the most personal and the least dependent on borrowings. Latin verse came to Gray more easily than English, which explains why he confided to such verse his more intimate feelings. At the same time, the practice of writing Latin verse served, as Roger Martin pointed out, as an apprenticeship to the writing of English: 'Gradus ad Parnassum'; yet one might add that Gray, in his English poems, rarely displays the inventiveness one observes in Sophonisba's 'Epistola'.

II LYRIC AND ELEGIAC POEMS: 1742–1750

The 'Ode on the Spring' was written in early June 1742, in response to a letter from West who had asked his friend to 'invocate the tardy May', and had also enclosed a poem on the subject. Gray posted his ode to West who, however, had died before it reached him. Gray's ode was communicated to Walpole in 1748 and was published anonymously in Dodsley's *Collection of Poems by Several Hands*. The scenery and the moment in the year were inspired by Gray's walks round Stoke Poges. As to the phraseology, Roger Lonsdale, in his commentary,[12] argues that Gray was aiming at richness of allusion, rather than imitating a particular model such as an ode of Horace or one of Virgil's *Eclogues*.

The 'Ode on the Spring', originally entitled 'Noontide', contains five stanzas, each of ten lines, rhyming a b a b c c d e e d. Most of the lines are octosyllabic, with a six-syllable line at irregular intervals. Gray used the same verse forms in the Eton ode and in the 'Ode on the Cat'.

The first stanza calls up a vision of spring, and is marked by the kind of diction which Gray told West was a requisite of English poetry, and should be used to distinguish it from the language of prose:

> Lo! where the rosy-bosom'd Hours,
> Fair Venus' train, appear . . .

Almost every line is reminiscent of Horace, Virgil, Lucretius, Propertius or Milton. The second stanza paints the scene:

> Where'er the oak's thick branches spread
> A broader browner shade;
> Where'er the rude and moss-grown beech
> O'er canopies the glade,
> Beside some water's rushy brink,
> With me the Muse shall sit, and think
> (At ease reclin'd in rustic state)[13]
> How vain the ardour of the Crowd,
> How low, how little are the Proud,
> How indigent the Great!

(To disparage the 'Great' became almost a literary motif for Gray in the 1740s.) In the next stanza we see the cattle at rest in the noontide warmth, while bees and butterflies enjoy the sunny hours.

> To Contemplation's sober eye
> Such is the race of Man . . .

Men, like the insects, will 'flutter thro' life's little day',

> In fortune's varying colours drest:
> Brush'd by the hand of rough Mischance,
> Or chill'd by age, their airy dance
> They leave, in dust to rest.

But the insects mock the poet, on the Horatian theme of 'Carpe diem':

> Poor moralist! and what art thou?
> A solitary fly!
> Thy joys no glittering female meets,
> No hive hast thou of hoarded sweets,
> No painted plumage to display;
> On hasty wings thy youth is flown;
> Thy sun is set, thy spring is gone –
> We frolick while 'tis May.

The parallel between the life of insects and the life of man had been drawn by Matthew Green in his verses entitled 'In the Grotto'. Gray told Walpole in 1748 that, when writing the ode, he had supposed the comparison to be his own, and realised only later that he had read it in Green. But the last two stanzas, which contain a reminiscence of Cowley's 'The Grasshopper', are more concise than the passage in 'The Grotto', and their poetic quality is superior; expressive also of Gray's slightly morbid apprehension of the future.

This preoccupation becomes more explicit in the 'Ode on a distant prospect of Eton College', which Gray wrote in August of the same year. Gray would not have to walk far from Stoke to come in sight of the Thames and Windsor Castle on the height beyond; which puts him in mind of 'Her Henry's holy shade' – Henry VI, who had founded the college:

> Ah happy hills, ah pleasing shade,
> Ah fields belov'd in vain,
> Where once my careless childhood stray'd,
> A stranger yet to pain!

Most of the boys delight in sport:

> Say, Father THAMES, for thou hast seen
> Full many a sprightly race
> Disporting on thy margent green
> The paths of pleasure trace,
> Who foremost now delight to cleave
> With pliant arm thy glassy wave?

The captive linnet which enthrall? [sic]
What idle progeny succeed
To chase the rolling circle's speed,
Or urge the flying ball?

Here are some extreme examples of the poetic diction which Wordsworth was to condemn. 'Glassy wave' is imitated from 'vitreum pontum'.[14]

Other boys, he adds, are bent 'on earnest business'; but for all of them,

> Gay hope is theirs by fancy fed
> Less pleasing when possest;
> The tear forgot as soon as shed,
> The sunshine of the breast . . .
>   Alas, regardless of their doom,
> The little victims play!
> No sense have they of ills to come,
> No care beyond to-day . . .

He foresees a fearful future for them: 'pineing Love', or Envy, or Despair, or Poverty 'And slow-consuming Age'; and continues in this strain through three more stanzas. These verses were written, one must remember, in a year of private distress. In addition to the prospect of having to return to Cambridge, which he disliked, he was haunted by the fear of poverty and death – probably a symptom of neurosis. He concludes the ode, however, on a more philosophic note:

> To each his suff'rings: all are men,
> Condemn'd alike to groan,
> The tender for another's pain;
> Th' unfeeling for his own.
> Yet ah! why should they know their fate?
> Since sorrow never comes too late,
> And happiness too swiftly flies.
> Thought would destroy their paradise.
> No more; where ignorance is bliss,
> 'Tis folly to be wise.

The concluding verse possibly comes from Lewis Theobald's 'The Invitation' (1729): 'When Wisdom grows austere, 'tis Folly

to be wise'; although the thought has been variously expressed by
many writers, from Aeschylus to Davenant.[15] The poem also
contains reminiscences of Dryden, Pope and especially of Shakespeare, whose 'fearful ecstasie' suggested[16]

> They hear a voice in every wind
> And snatch a fearful joy

– while the many abstractions (Fear, Shame, Envy, Despair and
so on) may have been inspired by Book VI of the *Aeneid*.[17]

This ode, which appeared anonymously, made no appeal to the
public, but it greatly impressed Walpole. Enthusiastically, he persuaded Gray to sit for his portrait by J. G. Eckhardt, who painted
a flattering picture of a gentle-looking young man: this portrait is
now in the National Gallery.

The 'Ode to Adversity', which also dates from August 1742,
similarly makes use of many abstract words – some of them with
very grim connotations. They are as numerous as in the Eton ode.
There are six stanzas, each of eight octosyllabic lines, with a concluding alexandrine. The tone is of dejection, and fear:

> Daughter of Jove, relentless Power,
> Thou Tamer of the human breast,
> Whose iron scourge and tort'ring hour
> The Bad affright, afflict the Best! . . .

In stanza 5 the poet pleads for himself:

> Oh, gently on thy Suppliant's head,
> Dread Goddess, lay thy chast'ning hand!
> Not in thy Gorgon terrors clad,
> Nor circled with the vengeful Band . . .

> Thy form benign, oh Goddess, wear,
> Thy milder influence impart . . .
> Teach me to love and to forgive,
> Exact my own defects to scan,
> What others are, to feel, and know myself a Man.

One could guess that this poem was written about the same time
as the Eton ode, because it ends on the same thought inspired by

Menander, according to a marginal note inserted by Gray in the Eton ode: 'I am a man, a sufficient excuse for being unhappy'.[18] The poem as a whole is full of reminiscences of Milton, Dryden and Pope; many of these had become proverbial and perhaps should not be regarded as plagiarisms. Gray's main source, however, was Horace's 'Ode to Fortune': 'O Diva, gratum . . .' (I, 35). This was pointed out by Johnson, who considered that Gray had surpassed Horace. But the tone and, to some extent, the object are different. Horace is thinking of the welfare of Rome: he begs the goddess to avert any recurrence of civil war; he laments the crimes of the Romans; let them now whet their swords, not against each other, but against the northern barbarians.

Wordsworth used Gray's ode – as he states in his note on the subject – as the model for his 'Ode to Duty';[19] but, while adhering to the form of Gray's ode, he managed to imbue his poem with a little more humanity, if one excepts the rather austere first stanza. It is curious to find Wordsworth experimenting in this more formal genre, after his earlier severe treatment of Gray's sonnet.

The final comment on the 'Ode to Adversity' is that it suffers from an excess of erudition.

The sonnet (on the death of Richard West) had probably been composed earlier in the summer of 1742:

> In vain to me the smiling Mornings shine
> And redning Phoebus lifts his golden fire:
> The Birds in vain their amorous Descant join;
> Or chearful Fields resume their green Attire . . .

Gray's model for this was obviously Petrarch's sonnet No. 310 ('In Morte di Laura'):

> Zefiro torna, e'l bel tempo rimena,
> E i fiori e l'erbe, sua dolce famiglia . . .
>
> Ma per me, lasso, tornano i più gravi
> Sospiri, che del cor profondo tragge
> Quella ch'al ciel se ne portò le chiavi:
> E canta augeletti, e fiori piagge,
> E'n belle donne oneste atti soavi,
> Sono un deserto, e fere aspre e selvagge.

'Zefiro' would at once have made Gray think of 'Favonius Zephyrinus', as he called his friend.[20] The concluding lines –

> I fruitless mourn to him, that cannot hear,
> And weep the more, because I weep in vain

– are the most moving and sincere; though it is to be regretted that Gray used Colley Cibber's words, from his adaptation of *Richard III*: 'So must we weep, because we weep in vain.'

Gray never published this sonnet, and Roger Martin was doubtless too severe when observing that it has been remembered chiefly on account of its faults. These have been sufficiently stressed by Wordsworth, who selected Gray's sonnet as an example of a composition by those (to use his own words) 'who, by their reasonings, have attempted to widen the space of separation betwixt Prose and Metrical composition'.[21] Wordsworth found only five lines of any value, by his own criterion; but Coleridge went further in suggesting that Wordsworth's selected five lines were actually less prosaic than the rest, that is 'more curiously elaborate'. He, however, handsomely conceded that this proved nothing except that 'there are sentiments which would be equally in their place both in verse and prose'.[22]

One line at least would appear incomprehensible in any context: 'To warm their little loves the birds complain.'

The death of a pet is not usually regarded as an occasion for pleasantries; yet this is how Gray treated the news that Walpole had lost one of his two cats, in February 1747. Was it, he asked, Zara or Selima? And which was the tabby and which the tortoise-shell? If he wrote an ode in condolence, he did not wish to be 'so ill-bred or so impudent as to forfeit all my interest in the survivor'. Gray did not, in fact, care for animals, and his 'ode' is not an elegy, but what Walpole would have called 'a thing of humour'. He called it 'Ode on the death of a Favourite Cat, drowned in a tub of gold fishes', and in the first three stanzas pictured Selima 'reclin'd' on the edge of a 'lofty vase', gazing at her image in the water below and then reaching down a paw to catch a fish; until, from the 'slipp'ry verge . . . she tumbled headlong in'.

> Eight times emerging from the flood
> She mew'd to ev'ry wat'ry God,

> Some speedy aid to send.
> No Dolphin came, no Nereid stirr'd:
> Nor cruel Tom, nor Susan heard.
> A Fav'rite has no friend!

Gray ends by advising young women that 'one false step is ne'er retriev'd':

> Not all that tempts your wand'ring eyes
> And heedless hearts is lawful prize;
> Nor all that glisters, gold.

In these rather unfeeling lines scholars have detected more snatches from earlier poets than seem worth mentioning: Virgil, and especially Dryden and Gay. The concluding line is a proverbial saying which could have come from Chaucer, or Middleton, or *The Merchant of Venice*; but Gray has emended it and so avoided the usual logical fallacy.

No short poem has perhaps been the subject of so many commentaries and studies as the 'Elegy written in a Country Churchyard'. Since the early nineteenth century and until recent days, schoolchildren in this country have had to learn it by heart. It has probably become better known among those who are not specially conversant with our literature than very many poems which today one would rate more highly – Keats's odes, for example. The Elegy, in the first place, appealed to the sentimentalism of readers of English and American literature. To the generality, who are neither noble nor great, and who have achieved nothing of note, it may have been gratifying to reflect that those who are noble, those who have achieved greatness, will come to the same dusty end as themselves. By abasing the great ones of the earth and seeming to ennoble the humble, Gray unintentionally ministered to envy and jealousy, two of the most unlovely of vices.

But it remains a fact that the Elegy has also been admired by poets greater than Gray: by Byron, Tennyson and Edward Fitzgerald. The ornate and studied language, the lapidary phrases, perhaps also the flavour of Miltonic diction, no doubt account for this admiration. Like many readers, they were less concerned with ideas than with language; and one suspects that it is, in the main, the beauty of the language that has made the Elegy so popular,[23] its readers not realising how little was of Gray's own invention. The most quoted line is indeed a paraphrase of a verse of his friend, Richard West – 'The paths of glory lead but to the grave'.

Gray's contemporaries were naturally not insensitive to the ideas and the sentiment. In our own days, the late Professor F. C. Green could not praise too highly the 'mellifluous and haunting melancholy' of the poem, or its author as 'the champion of oppressed humanity, the sweet mediator of divine compassion'.[24]

Nothing can be stated with certainty about the date when Gray began his poem; which stanzas were written first; or when exactly he altered what was originally a simple meditation among the tombs (like Young's *Night Thoughts* and James Hervey's *Meditations*) and turned it into an elegy. The data for any assured conclusions are lacking. In his *Memoir of Gray* (1775), William Mason wrote: 'I am inclined to believe that the *Elegy in a Country Churchyard* was begun, if not concluded, at this time also' (in the summer of 1742); that is, under the spur of poetical activity caused by the death of Richard West. On the other hand, when Gray sent the completed poem to Walpole on 12 June 1750, he wrote: 'Having put an end to a thing whose beginning you have seen long ago, I immediately send it you.' It was Walpole's impression that the poem was 'posterior to West's death at least three or four years. . . . I am sure that I had the twelve or more first lines from himself about three years after that period, and it was long before he finished it'. In response, however, to a letter from Mason, he deferred to the latter's opinion. Yet his recollection of having received 'the twelve or more first lines' some years before 1750 was probably well founded; and if so, the twelve lines may have been the 'Epitaph', and Gray may thus have written it after the shock he had received on hearing that West was dead. In that event, the bulk of the poem was written at a later date.

The Eton MS., which is regarded as the earliest, contains twenty-two stanzas, consisting of the first eighteen in the poem as finally submitted to Walpole, and four which were rejected. These began:

> The thoughtless World to Majesty may bow,
> Exalt the brave, & idolize Success . . .

and ended with the speaker (whose identity is nowhere specified) saying:

No more with Reason & thyself at strife;
Give anxious Cares & endless Wishes room
But thro' the cool sequester'd Vale of Life
Pursue the silent Tenour of thy Doom.

The punctuation is defective, and it seems that the speaker is addressing the reader. Gray replaces these four stanzas with five others, beginning: 'Far from the madding Crowd's ignoble strife', and ending:

> . . . Ev'n from the tomb the voice of Nature cries,
> Ev'n in our Ashes live their wonted Fires . . .

– verses of which the meaning is obscure.

The next stanza (verses 93–6) introduces a second person whom the speaker now addresses and yet who, surprisingly, appears to have been the speaker of all that has gone before:

> For thee, who mindful of th' unhonour'd Dead,
> Dost in these lines their artless tale relate;
> If chance, by lonely contemplation led,
> Some kindred Spirit shall inquire thy fate,
>
> Haply some hoary-headed Swain may say,
> 'Oft have we seen him at the peep of dawn
> 'Brushing with hasty steps the dews away
> 'To meet the sun upon the upland lawn.

The swain continues to recall the movements of the person in question – who turns out to be 'A Youth to Fortune and to Fame unknown' – he says that 'One morn I miss'd him on the custom'd hill', describes his burial, and concludes:

> 'Approach and read (for thou canst read) the lay,
> 'Grav'd on the stone beneath yon aged thorn.'

After this comes the 'Epitaph'. But whom is the swain addressing? Who is asked to read? It must be the 'kindred spirit' who had inquired about the youth's fate (verse 96); but he must be the same person as the one who appeared unexpectedly in verse 93, addressing whoever was speaking at this point, with the words:

> For thee, who mindful of th' unhonour'd Dead,
> Dost in these lines their artless tale relate . . .

This must be Gray himself. If this interpretation be accepted, the
first twenty-three stanzas (92 verses) should be regarded as placed
between inverted commas, since they are the words of the dead
youth. The next five lines are spoken by Gray; whilst lines 98 to
116 are spoken by the swain to Gray; and the 'Epitaph' of the dead
youth must then have been written by Gray.

This reading seems the most acceptable; and it is clear then that
the poem is a tribute to West; that the first twenty-three stanzas
are imagined as written by him;[25] that he is the strange youth,
'Mutt'ring his wayward fancies . . . Now drooping, woeful wan,
like one forlorn', and that the 'Epitaph' is for him. Another reason
for interpreting the poem in this sense is to reject the idea that
Gray, morbid though he was at times, was imagining his own last
days (in the swain's narrative) and writing his own epitaph, as
Donald Greene observes.[26]

The metrical form adopted was that which West had used in his
Monody on the death of Queen Caroline; Gray uses it only in this
poem; it is the verse form employed by West. As the poem is unlike
any other that Gray wrote, one might fancy that West contributed
more than the lines:

> Ah me! what boots us all our boasted power,
> Our golden treasure, and our purpled state?
> They cannot ward th' inevitable hour,
> Nor stay the fearful violence of Fate.

This stanza is paraphrased by Gray in

> The boast of heraldry, the pomp of pow'r,
> And all that beauty, all that wealth e'er gave,
> Awaits alike th' inevitable hour.
> The paths of glory lead but to the grave.

Nothing could have been more natural than that Gray should
make his poem a veiled tribute to West; to describe the poet (in
verses which have been, perhaps unjustly, described as theatrical)
as dying young, as West had died; but, with a certain *pudeur*, to

mingle in his description, and in the 'Epitaph', certain traits which were not specifically West's: these may have been introduced to conceal from the public the identity of the young poet.

The bulk of the Elegy, that is the first 92 lines, mingles thoughts and expressions known to be those of his friend with certain of his own; but for the most part they are borrowings from Latin, Italian and English poets – too many indeed. The principal ideas could easily have been conveyed in fewer stanzas. Gray, however, chose to include many decorative variations on his theme, and even to insert stanzas which add little to the thought, and even interrupt its development. The themes are simple enough. Here in the churchyard lie the forefathers of the hamlet; no more will they know the joys of the home and the health of country life. Some might have become great poets, statesmen or soldiers: this, however, 'their lot forbad'. Yet, if it prevented their rise to greatness, it also excluded the crimes which often accompany it. Better, perhaps, that they should have lived 'far from the madding crowd's ignoble strife'. Gray added, as an afterthought, two stanzas on the sorrow (despite the above comfortable reflection) of the 'parting soul' who leaves 'the warm precincts of the chearful day'.[27] This part of the poem was warmly praised by Dr Johnson, no doubt because it expressed his own morbid apprehension of death.[28] 'On some fond breast the parting soul relies' is no doubt true of many dying men and women. Hamlet had uttered the same wish to Horatio:

> If thou hast ever held me in thy heart,
> Absent thee from felicity awhile.

But to suppose that the old, worn out with pain and weary of life, with its bitter taste of tears, feel anything but relief in escaping from it – unless they leave those whom they love unprovided for – is probably untrue. Gray is merely expressing his own dread of the end; and Ketton-Cremer is without doubt right in saying that 'Gray told his readers more about himself in the *Elegy* than in any other poem'.[29]

The first idea of a meditation among the tombs may have come to Gray during the winter of 1734–5 in Peterhouse, which overlooks the graveyard of Little St Mary's – one of the dreariest spots in

Cambridge, except perhaps in spring when flowers and shrubs are blooming among the graves. In a letter to Walpole written from Peterhouse, he had described himself as a corpse lying among, and conversing with, other corpses. It was much later that the church-yard at Stoke Poges was assumed, no doubt rightly, to be the scene of the poem. Various details in the description point to Stoke; and by this time the macabre images of the letter to Walpole had been discarded.

Lord Lytton observed that 'ornament is less the accessory grace than the essential merit of his designs'.[30] A reading of the poem bears out this view. Compare the Elegy first with the bare sim-plicity of the sepulchral epigrams in the Greek Anthology; or, again, with Wordsworth's 'Lucy' poems which, in a few strokes, create the most poignant sense of grief; and then study the details of Gray's poem. The first six or seven stanzas are the best. The remainder are studded with literary reminiscences and para-phrases. Even the opening stanza is, on Gray's admission, deriva-tive. 'The Curfew tolls the knell of parting day' was suggested by a passage in the *Purgatorio* –

> . . . la squilla di lontano
> che paia 'l giorno pianger, che si muore

– the beauty of which is lost in the paraphrase. 'The plowman homeward plods his weary way' sounds like a personal observation, but in fact comes from Roscommon's version of Horace's Ode 6 in Book II. In Book IV of the *Aeneid*[31] an owl 'complains'; and so in Gray's third stanza we read:

> Save that from yonder ivy-mantled tow'r
> The mopeing owl does to the moon complain . . .

Gray should have known that in the twilight hour owls do not mope: they are singularly alert to scare small birds and mice into movement with their fearsome cry. Verses 31 and 32 also provoke surprise. If Gray thought of the village[32] he is describing as at all typical, a recent study of the history of Foxton,[33] a village half-way between Cambridge and Royston, and very old like most English villages, shows that the 'annals of the poor' are neither short nor simple (it is significant that the author refers more than once to

Gray's Elegy). In the Middle Ages the dwellers in Foxton were not the Arcadian peasants of Gray's imagination. Penury did not freeze the 'current of [their] soul', nor were their wishes particularly 'sober'. The Abbess, who before the Dissolution of the Monasteries, was Lord of the Manor, punished one of them for ploughing 'a public way to the width of half a foot' – a heinous offence which cost 2d – and another for committing adultery, which cost 6d. Prior to about the mid-fifteenth century they were, most of them, tied to the land; but after that, it was not difficult to escape. England has never had a caste system. The commercial middle-classes are mainly of peasant origin, and the landed aristocracy has constantly been recruited from below.

The stanza adapted from West's poem, and which was so much admired by General Wolfe –

> The boast of heraldry, the pomp of pow'r,
> And all that beauty, all that wealth e'er gave,
> Awaits alike th' inevitable hour.[34]
> The paths of glory lead but to the grave

– expresses a commonplace which occurs again and again in seventeenth-century verse, both French and Italian. Malherbe had treated it in one of his best known pieces. West might have found it in an 'Epitaffo' by Chiabrera, that gifted and versatile poet, some of whose epigrams were later to be translated by Wordsworth:

> In van speme mortal sorge superba;
> Forza di tempo ogni valor consuma;
> Appunto è l'uom come nel prato l'erba,
> E gli onor suoi, come nel mar la spuma.[35]

This could not be bettered. Later poets might compose variations by changing the imagery. Thus 'the boast of heraldry' was probably suggested to Gray by the many coats of arms at the base of the windows in King's College Chapel;[36] while the next stanza –

> If Mem'ry to their Tomb no Trophies raise,
> Where thro' the long-drawn isle [sic] and fretted vault
> The pealing anthem swells the note of praise

– evokes a memory of King's College Chapel and the fan-tracery

of its 'vault', or possibly of St George's Chapel at Windsor. In
stanza 13 –

> But Knowledge to their eyes her ample page
> Rich with the spoils of time did ne'er unroll . . .

– Gray has taken 'rich with the spoils of time' textually from Sir
Thomas Browne's *Religio Medici*.[37]

A possible source of stanza 14 –

> Full many a gem of purest ray serene
> The dark unfathom'd caves of ocean bear:
> Full many a flower is born to blush unseen,
> And waste its sweetness on the desert air

– has been traced by American scholars[38] to verses by Celio Magno
(1536–1602), who belonged to the generation preceding Chiabrera's:

> Ma (qual in parte ignota
> Ben ricca *gemma* altrui cela il suo pregio,
> O *fior*, ch'alta virtu ha in se riposta
> *Visse in sen di castita nascosta*) . . .

One may fairly assume that Gray was adapting these lines; but if
so, he made two mistakes. Gems are not found on the ocean-bed,
and flowers do not waste their sweetness. They have their own
functional *raison d'être* as well as providing honey for bees and
fragrance for humans. Roger Lonsdale explains the first error by
citing from the *Works* of Joseph Hall: 'There is many a rich stone
laid up in the bowels of the earth, many a fair *pearl* in the bowels
of the *sea*, that never was seen, nor never shall be.' Gray seems to
have confused the gem which Celio Magno describes with the
'fair pearl' of Hall's description.

'Far from the madding crowd's ignoble strife' embodies a
platitude which can be traced far back in Italian poetry. The most
recent use of the expression occurred in Drummond of Hawthorn-
den's Sonnet 49: 'Far from the madding worldling's hoarse dis-
cords'.[39] But Gray, and before him, Drummond, must have been
familiar with Petrarch's sonnet –

> Solo e pensoso i più deserti campi
> Vo misurando a passi tardi e lenti . . .

– in which he watches for any 'vestige' of human presence and is ready to flee at the first sign of it. In another sonnet he writes:

> Povera e nuda, vai, Filosofia,
> *Dice la turba al vil guadagno intesa* . . .

Here indeed is the crowd, intent on 'filthy lucre'. Maurice Scève, the Lyonnese poet, had clearly echoed these lines in Dizain 414 of *Délie*:

> Aussi j'y vis loing de l'Ambition
> Et du sot Peuple au vil gaing intentif.[40]

Neither Gray nor his commentators refer to these lines, but they seem the most likely source, the more so as he elsewhere deprecates ambition.[41]

Stanza 21 is probably the weakest in the Elegy:

> Their name, their years, spelt by th' unletter'd muse,
> The place of fame and elegy supply:
> And many a holy text around she strews,
> That *teach* the rustic *moralist to die.*

The 'unletter'd muse' is the stonemason who engraves texts on tombstones. He cannot properly be said to 'strew' them (but 'strews' is to rhyme with 'muse'); 'many a holy text' is singular (cf. 'Full many a flower is born', etc.) and line 24 should therefore read: 'That *teaches . . . how* to die'; and why 'teaches the rustic *moralist*'? Gray's editors have not commented on these defects, whether because they have not noticed them or because the text of the Elegy is too 'sacred' to be questioned.

Stanza 22 (lines 85–8) is reminiscent of Belial's speech in the 'Infernal Council', described in Book I of *Paradise Lost*:[42]

> . . . For who would lose,
> Though full of pain, this intellectual *being*, [my italics]
> Those thoughts that wander through eternity . . .

Gray adapts the thought in the lines:

> For who to dumb Forgetfulness a prey,
> This pleasing anxious *being*[43] e'er resign'd,
> Left the warm precincts of the chearful day,
> Nor cast one longing ling'ring look behind?

In the lines

> On some fond breast the parting soul relies,
> Some pious drops the closing eye requires . . .

Gray appears to be inspired by Ovid's *Tristia*. But the two verses that follow are far from clear:

> Ev'n from the tomb the voice of Nature cries,
> Ev'n in our Ashes live their wonted Fires.

In adding a few annotations to the 1768 edition of his *Poems*, Gray pointed to Petrarch's Sonnet 170 as his source:

> Ch'i veggio nel pensier, dolce mio fuoco,
> Fredda una lingua, e due begli occhi chiusi
> Rimaner doppo noi pien di faville.

> [I see in thought . . . two fair eyes, now closed, remaining after us, full of fires.]

One suspects, however, that Gray was diverting attention from his real source, which was surely Chaucer's 'Yet in our ashes cold is fire yreken'.[44] Similarly, with reference to the verse in the 'Epitaph' – 'There they alike in trembling hope repose' – he calls attention to the 'paventosa speme' in Petrarch's Sonnet 115. He had been annoyed and disappointed that few readers had understood the many allusions in the Pindaric odes, and in response to Walpole's urging he agreed to annotate them, and also the Elegy. Cultured readers, the *Sunetoi*, as he called them, should have been able to recognise the many choice phrases he had taken from Latin and English poets, on a range of subjects which did honour to his learning.

As indicated above, Gray appears to have thought that an

English poem should be treated like a Latin one. The poet should select a subject, decide on the line of development, and fit into his verses appropriate expressions from well-known authors. This was not to be regarded as plagiarism.

In the copy of the poem which appears in Gray's Commonplace Book, and in the first edition, he had inserted just before the 'Epitaph' a stanza as beautiful as some that were retained:

> There scatter'd oft, the earliest of the Year,
> By Hands unseen, are Show'rs of Violets found:
> The Red-breast loves to build, & warble there,
> And little Footsteps lightly print the Ground.

But he omitted this in subsequent editions, perhaps because it was too literally reminiscent of Herbert or Collins.[45]

It will be recalled that, owing to Walpole's indiscretion, Gray made it appear that he was obliged reluctantly to publish these stanzas under his own name. Mason persuaded him to re-entitle them an 'Elegy'. They won immediate and lasting celebrity, and nothing he wrote in later years contributed so much to the prestige which he was to enjoy. He became famous in spite of himself. However, as the years went by, he found his fame a useful asset; although he had never wished to be popular with the public at large, and would gladly have repeated after Horace: 'Odi profanum vulgus'. He did not regard the Elegy as his best poem, and was irritated when complimented about it. He rated the Pindaric odes much more highly. His tart rejoinder to Dr Gregory in Edinburgh, when Gregory innocently reminded him of verses he wished to forget,[46] illustrates this attitude. It is not unusual for a poet to be annoyed when the public insists on applauding a production which he knows to be inferior. In France Leconte de Lisle and Sully Prudhomme both found themselves subject to this kind of vexation: they treated it good-humouredly in public, and in private, rather wryly, as a joke.

The Elegy had appealed to those eighteenth-century readers who, living in a comfortable and prosperous age, with servants to wait upon them, had time to indulge in the luxury of tears. Melancholy was fashionable,[47] as was sententious verse, and Gray wrote exactly the kind of poetry which the public expected; only, he wrote it better than anyone previously. He had followed Boileau's precept: 'Polissez donc vos vers, et les repolissez.' He worked over the stanzas again and again, annexing other men's thoughts in memorable lines. The modern reader probably prefers a more astringent pessimism; or, by contrast, the simple gaiety which is his defence against the tragic realities of life.

III LYRIC AND ELEGIAC POEMS (continued)

The year 1752 marks the end of Gray's first poetic period. During the twenty years of life that remained to him, apart from a few humorous or satirical pieces, he composed mainly learned poems and verses written to order. Taken all together, they would fill a very slender volume. Matthew Arnold in a famous essay ascribed the sparseness of Gray's output to the fact that he was living in an age of prose, and lacked the stimulus which was to animate the Romantic poets. Had Gray been born between 1770 and 1800, the mighty events of the French Revolution would have inspired a more abundant response. A new era had suddenly opened, with

> France standing in the top of golden hours,
> And human nature seeming born again.

One might hail it, or abhor it; one could not be indifferent. More recent critics have disagreed with Arnold. Given Gray's character and indolence, it is argued, he would have written no more in 1800 or 1810 than in 1750. When Walpole urged him to write, he replied that, if he did not write more, it was because he could not. He was referring to poetry. Had he been obliged to work for his living, and had he remained invincibly averse to the Law, he would have had to rely on his pen, as Goldsmith was obliged to do; and would then have probably become a journalist, translator and compiler, like Goldsmith. His education and wide, miscellaneous reading would have well equipped him for such work; and in that event his prose writings would have resembled Goldsmith's, although his prose was not in the same category. As it was, an independent income, which increased from time to time, enabled him to avoid any such toilsome occupation.

Between 1742 and 1752 Gray appears to have written nothing

except the Elegy, the 'Ode on the Cat', the short 'Alliance of
Education and Government', which he left unfinished, and 'A
Long Story'. In 1752 Walpole persuaded him to have six of his
poems in English illustrated with designs by Richard Bentley.
Bentley designed a frontispiece for each poem, and also head-
pieces and tail-pieces; and Gray was so delighted with the results
that he insisted on the little quarto volume's being entitled:
Designs by Mr R. Bentley for Six poems by Mr T. Gray. He
addressed to the artist seven stanzas which are among the most
spontaneous, if not the best, he ever wrote. Even if the parallel
between poetry and pictorial art can be traced back to Horace, and
a model found in Dryden's 'Epistle to Kneller', Gray's stanzas
(which Mason printed continuously) seem to be among his most
original:

> In silent gaze the tuneful choir among,
>   Half pleas'd, half blushing, let the muse admire,
> While Bentley leads her sister-art along,
>   And bids the pencil answer to the lyre.
>
> The tardy rhymes that used to linger on,
>   To censure cold, and negligent of fame,
> In swifter measures animated run,
>   And catch a lustre from his genuine flame . . .
>
> . . . .
>
> But not to one in this benighted age
>   Is that diviner inspiration giv'n,
> That burns in Shakespear's or in Milton's page,
>   The pomp and prodigality of heav'n.
>
> Enough for me, if to some feeling breast
>   My lines a secret sympathy *impart*;
> And as their pleasing influence *flows confest*,
>   A sigh of soft reflection *heave the heart*.

As a corner of Gray's manuscript had been torn off, the words in
italics were supplied by Mason, who first printed the poem.
    As mentioned earlier, the fame of the churchyard Elegy had
caused Lady Cobham, who was living in the Manor House at
Stoke Poges, to ask Lady Schaub and Miss Speed to call on Mrs

Gray and make her son's acquaintance. A little later, to amuse them,
Gray composed 'A Long Story'. It appears that Henrietta Speed,
who had been attracted to Gray, asked him for some verses 'on the
subject of love'. He responded in 1761 with two short 'Songs', of
which the first is more humorous than amatory:

> Midst Beauty & Pleasures gay triumphs to languish
> And droop without knowing the source of my anguish
> To start from short slumbers & look for the morning –
> Yet close my dull eyes when I see it returning.

> Sighs sudden & frequent, Looks ever dejected,
> Sounds that steal from my tongue by no meaning connected.
> Ah say Fellow-swains, how these symptoms befell me.
> They smile, but reply not: sure Delia will tell me.

The second song, in two six-verse stanzas, is too slight to be worth
quoting. These verses alone would confirm what his life already
makes clear, that Gray was not a man to commit himself without
a great deal of reflexion.

The years between 1742 and 1752 Gray had filled in, when not
writing the verses mentioned above, by reading all the Greek
authors he found available and copying out extracts from them. In
July 1752 he wrote to Walpole: 'I may send . . . a high Pindarick
upon stilts, which one must be a better scholar than [Dodsley] is
to understand a line of, and the very best scholars will understand
but a little matter here and there.' This was 'The Progress of
Poesy'. He completed it in 1754 and it was to be printed, with 'The
Bard', by Walpole in 1757.

Gray was not the first to try his hand at this kind of verse. Ronsard, a brilliant Hellenist, had written Pindaric odes, but without
much success with the public. Cowley had composed what he
considered Pindarics: they had irregular rhymes and no regular
pattern.[11] Gray saw that any serious adaptation of Pindar would
require a strict division into strophe, antistrophe and epode, the
epodes being in a different metre from that of the strophes and
antistrophes. Since a genuine imitation of Greek and Latin verse
is impossible in a modern language, the lines would have to conform to English prosody, both as to metre and rhyme. 'The
Progress of Poesy' and 'The Bard' were both composed on this

pattern, strophe, antistrophe and epode being repeated twice. The formal elements are fairly regular. In the strophes the lines are octosyllabic and decasyllabic with one seven-syllable line and the concluding line an alexandrine. The rhyme scheme is a b b a c c d d e e f f. The epodes are in a lighter measure, as designed to accompany a dance.

Both odes were difficult in that they demanded much knowledge and understanding on the reader's part; even more so for 'The Bard' than for 'The Progress of Poesy'. Gray's argument, in the latter, is that poetry was given us by heaven to soothe our cares, calm our passions, and inspire us with joy. Poetry was invented in ancient Greece; from there it passed to Italy, and from Italy to England – or so Gray imagined. The strophes and epodes were composed as though designed to be sung to the accompaniment of music and dancing:

> Awake, Aeolian lyre, awake
> And give to rapture all thy trembling strings
> From Helicon's harmonious springs
> A thousand rills their mazy progress take . . .

> Perching on the scept'red hand
> Of Jove, thy magic lulls the feather'd king
> With ruffled plumes, and flagging wing:
> Quench'd in dark clouds of slumber lie
> The terror of his beak, and light'nings of his eye.

The first strophe and antistrophe contain reminiscences of Pindar, and the passage about the eagle is imitated from the first 'Pythian'. The first epode begins:

> Thee the voice, the dance, obey.
> Temper'd to thy warbled lay

and contains the lines (34, 35):

> To brisk notes in cadence beating
> Glance their many-twinkling feet

which puzzled some readers.[49]

The second strophe enumerates the ills which afflict mankind; but

> The fond complaint, my Song, disprove,
> And justify the laws of Jove.

Gray's 'song' is to justify what Milton had failed to do – 'the ways of God to man'. The muses have brought comfort even in 'climes beyond the solar road', as, for example, among 'Chili's boundless forests'. But chiefly (Epode II) they flourished in Delphi and Attica and the isles of the Aegean:

> Till the sad Nine in Greece's evil hour
> Left their Parnassus for the Latian plains . . .
> When Latium had her lofty spirit lost,
> They sought, O Albion! next thy sea-encircled coast.

The following strophe pays tribute to 'Nature's Darling':

> What time, where lucid Avon stray'd,
> To Him the mighty Mother did unveil
> Her aweful face . . .

The antistrophe celebrates Milton in a similar rhetorical style:

> He pass'd the flaming bounds of Place and Time:[50]
> The living Throne, the sapphire blaze,
> Where Angels tremble, while they gaze,
> He saw; but blasted with excess of light,
> Closed his eyes in endless night . . .

Next:

> Behold, where Dryden's less presumptuous car
> Wide o'er the fields of glory bear
> Two coursers of ethereal race,
> With necks in thunder cloath'd, and long-resounding pace.

That Gray should introduce here the image of a chariot-race, often celebrated by Pindar, is unexpected; and it is out of accord with the next verse – in Epode III:

> Hark, his hands the lyre explore!

He could hardly explore the lyre and handle two coursers at the same time. The 'coursers' may represent satiric verse and dramatic poetry. But when one reads: 'But ah! 'tis heard no more', Gray is referring, it seems, to Dryden's 'Ode on St Cecilia's Day'; because, as he explains in the abundant annotations to the poem in the 1768 edition, he wrote: 'We have had in our language no other odes of the sublime kind' since this one. Cowley's, though not without merit, were definitely inferior.

In the third epode, he continues:

> Oh! Lyre divine, what daring Spirit
> Wakes thee now? tho' he inherit
> Nor the pride, nor ample pinion,
> That the Theban Eagle bear . . .
> Yet oft before his infant eyes would run
> Such forms as glitter in the Muse's ray
> With orient hues, unborrow'd of the Sun . . .

Gray is here describing himself and his own ambition to be ranked among the great English poets.

The ode, as might be expected, is full of allusions and imitations. The opening verse, 'Awake, Aeolian lyre, awake' had been understood by the *Critical Review* to refer to an Aeolian harp.[51] The first antistrophe is an imitation of Pindar's first 'Pythian' ode, and Gray acknowledged that line 20, in which the lyre, 'Perching on the scepter'd hand/Of Jove', lulls the eagle by its magic, 'is a weak imitation of some incomparable lines in the same Ode'. It seems unnecessary to enumerate the many other reminiscences, if one may so call them. Gray explained most of them, with quotations from Greek, Latin and Italian authors, in the 1768 edition. In 1757 he had protested that he had too much respect for the understanding of his readers to explain passages which he knew were in fact very obscure. But none but a learned classical scholar could have identified all the authors whom he was recalling.

The ode contains, as one would expect, a number of abstractions – penury, disease, sorrow, death and so on; many studied periphrases and metaphors. The 'argument', simple in itself, is covered with as many ornaments of style as the 'argument' of the Elegy; but 'The Progress of Poesy' would have been more pleasing if there had been fewer; if the language had been more simple and natural; and, finally, if the argument had been historically exact.

For it was not from Italy that poetry came first to England. Even if one ignores Anglo-Saxon poetry, and the possible influence of the Welsh, poetry seems first to have come to England from the Anglo-Norman *trouvères*, from Béroul and Thomas, and Marie de France, who lived in London; and, in the time of Richard I, from the Provençaux. It was only later that Chaucer drew abundantly, though by no means exclusively, from the Italians.

'The Bard' was begun in 1754, but was put aside, unfinished, the year after. It was the visit of a Welsh harper to Cambridge in 1757 that incited Gray to complete it. The idea had come to him from a passage in Thomas Carte's *A General History of England* (1750), founded on a manuscript of Sir John Wynn's *History of the Gwedir Family*. Gray noted this under the heading of 'Cambri' in his Commonplace Book. The versification is strongly marked by techniques of Welsh poetry, which Gray carefully studied, and also by an image borrowed from Icelandic verse. The plan of the ode was sketched out in prose, whether before or after he had written it, is not known:

> The army of Edward I, as they march through a deep valley, are suddenly stopped by the appearance of a venerable figure seated on the summit of an inaccessible rock, who, with a voice more than human, reproaches the King with all the misery and desolation which he had brought on his country; foretells the misfortunes of the Norman race, and with prophetic spirit declares, that all his cruelty shall never extinguish the noble ardour of poetic genius in this island; and that man shall never be wanting to celebrate true virtue and valour in immortal strains, to expose vice and infamous pleasure, and boldly censure tyranny and oppression. His song ended, [the Bard] precipitates himself from the mountain, and is swallowed up by the river that rolls at its foot.

The poem, as first published in 1757, was simply headed by an 'Advertisement: The following Ode is founded on a Tradition current in Wales, that EDWARD THE FIRST, when he compleated the Conquest of that country, ordered all the Bards, that fell into his hands, to be put to death'.

The strophes and antistrophes contain fourteen lines rhyming a b a b c c d d e f e f d d; the epodes contain twenty lines of irregular length, 6-syllable, 10-syllable, 8-syllable, 7-syllable, and 12, and rhymes recurring at long intervals.

In the first strophe, the one surviving Bard menaces King Edward and his army. The scene is then described and, in the last lines of the antistrophe, he continues his threats. In the following epode he invokes the ghosts of his murdered brethren:

> Dear as the ruddy drops that warm my heart,[52]
> Ye died amidst your dying country's cries —
> No more I weep. They do not sleep.
> On yonder cliffs, a griesly band,
> I see them sit, they linger yet,
> Avengers of their native land:
> With me in dreadful harmony they join,
> And weave with bloody hands the tissue of thy line.

In the second strophe, antistrophe and epode, and in the first four lines of the third strophe, the ghosts of the slain bards foretell the disasters that will befall the Plantagenets. Like the Fatal Sisters of Norse Mythology, they weave the destinies of men: 'weave the warp, and weave the woof'; and conclude, in Strophe 3, 'The web is wove. The work is done.' The Bard begs them not to leave him, but is now consoled by a vision of the return of 'long-lost Arthur' in the person of Henry VII, and cries (third strophe): 'All hail, ye genuine Kings, Britannia's Issue, hail!' In the third antistrophe, he celebrates in grandiloquent language the age of the Tudors:

> In the midst a Form divine!
> Her eye proclaims her of the Briton-line;
> Her lyon-port, her awe commanding face,
> Attemper'd sweet to virgin-grace . . .'

The third epode describes the poets who adorned the age of Elizabeth, and their successors.

Many of the persons named in the prophecy of the bards' ghosts would be obscure to readers not fairly familiar with medieval history. Thus the verses:

> Mark the year, and mark the night,
> When Severn shall re-echo with affright
> The shrieks of death, thro' Berkley's roofs that ring,
> Shrieks of an agonizing King!

foretell the murder of Edward II; while the 'She-Wolf of France'
is Queen Isabelle.

'Is the sable Warrior fled?' refers to the Black Prince. The lines

> Fair laughs the Morn, and soft the Zephyr blows . . .
> In gallant trim the gilded vessel goes;
> Youth on the prow, and Pleasure at the helm . . .

recall Richard II in his days of prosperity; while the first six lines
of the second epode evoke a dreadful image of his death by
starvation. The following verses describe the Wars of the Roses.
One might guess that

> Ye Towers of Julius . . .
> Revere his Consort's faith, his Father's fame,
> And spare the meek Usurper's holy head

refers to Margaret of Anjou and her husband, Henry VI. Similarly,

> The bristled Boar in infant gore
> Wallows beneath the thorny shade

pictures Richard III, allegedly murderer of the little princes,[53]
lying dead on Bosworth field.

The 'Visions of Glory' which now appear, the 'genuine Kings',
are Henry VII and Henry VIII: one, the meanest of our kings, the
other, one of the most brutal. The 'Form divine' with the 'lyon-
port' is obviously Elizabeth I. The last epode evokes Spenser and
especially Shakespeare:

> In buskin'd measures move
> Pale Grief, and pleasing Pain,
> With Horrour, Tyrant of the throbbing breast.

The Bard next foresees Milton: 'A Voice as of the Cherub-Choir';
while the expression: 'And distant, warblings lessen on my ear'
refers to Dryden and his successors. The Bard concludes his
prophecy – and the poem:

> To triumph, and to die, are mine!
> He spoke, and headlong from the mountain's height
> Deep in the roaring tide he plung'd to endless night.

The great number of allusions to unnamed historical figures are so veiled that even educated readers were mystified. Gray explained them in the 1768 edition.

Whatever may be thought of the matter of this ode, the versification appears to be original. The notion of prophets weaving the woof of men's destinies was, as already observed, taken from Norse mythology, in which this is done by the Valkyries. Of more immediate interest are the techniques of Welsh prosody which Gray had studied in J. H. Rhys's *Cambrobrytannicae Cymraecaeve linguae institutiones*.[54] These included a constant use of alliteration of consonants and vowels, and the repetition of a word in the same line, as in the following passages:

> Ruin seize thee, ruthless King!
> . . . Conquest's crimson wing . . .
> Helen, nor Hauberk's twisted mail . . .

or again in Epode I:

> Ye died amid your dying country's cries.
> No more I weep. They do not sleep.

In the second strophe occurs the line: 'Weave the warp, and weave the woof . . .' and the reference to Shakespeare in the third Epode has

> In buskin'd measures move
> Pale Grief, and pleasing pain . . .

Alliteration could hardly be carried further; but this and other features were appropriate in a poem relating to the Welsh, in which the Bard (with whom Gray said that he had identified himself) cries out:

> Hear from the grave, great Taliessin, hear . . .

Gray's own explanatory notes did not exhaust the reminiscences in which the ode abounds. When the Bard sees the ghosts of his erstwhile fellows 'on yonder cliffs', Gray may have been recalling that, on his first ride up the gorge of the Guier Mort to the Grande Chartreuse, he had imagined he saw West's image on the opposite

cliffs saying words which he could not hear. Expressions reminiscent
of Virgil, Horace and Dryden are such as one would expect. 'Dear,
as the ruddy drops that warm my heart' (line 41) is taken from
Julius Caesar:

> As dear to me as are the ruddy drops,
> That sadden my sad heart.

Less expected, however, is the imagery in Antistrophe II of 'Youth
on the prow, and Pleasure at the helm'. This – one of the best lines
in the poem – was suggested by a line in Ovid's *Heroides*, XV:

> Ipse gubernabit residens in puppe Cupido.[55]

In a short but valuable commentary, Roger Lonsdale observes that
the massacre attributed to Edward I is not historically accurate;
the king merely issued an edict against vagrants,[56] the bards being
men of that kind. History here has been sadly distorted. Gray, who
had lavished more learning and more care on the Pindaric odes
than on any of his other poems, was deeply annoyed that even his
most sympathetic friends found them difficult and obscure.
Curiously, Mrs Garrick declared that Gray's verses were the only
ones that really set one dancing. But she was an Austrian and
perhaps knew little about English poetry; she had probably not
read Sir John Suckling's verses:

> Her feet beneath her petticoat
> Like little mice ran in and out;
> But oh, she dances such a way,
> No sun upon an Easter Day
> Is half so fine a sight.

Walpole declared the odes to be truly 'sublime'. Gray had
already sold the copyright to Dodsley, and wished to have the odes
published quietly; Walpole, however, intervened to persuade Gray
to let him print them on his press at Strawberry Hill, Dodsley
being named simply as the publisher. Finally, Walpole pointed out
that some explanatory notes really were called for. This was a
further source of vexation to Gray. In preparing the 1768 edition
of his collected poems, he deliberately avoided mentioning the fact

to Walpole. He inserted abundant explanations – over thirty notes alone to 'The Bard' – and wrote to Beattie: 'As to the notes I do it out of spite, because the Publick did not understand the two Odes . . . the second ['The Bard'] alluded to a few common facts to be found in any six-penny History of England.'

Dr Johnson's criticism of the odes in 1782 was resented by the *Gentleman's Magazine* and other periodicals. His remarks were construed as due to the personal antagonism which he was known to feel for Gray; he was at the same time charged with flouting the taste of those readers who wanted a change from the conventional poetry of the age, and who relished a taste for the mysterious, and especially for the 'sublime'.[57] In this matter Johnson found himself virtually isolated; but he stood to his arms. Although he had been a little unfair in criticising the use of alliteration in 'The Bard', it is now felt that on the whole he had been justified. His strictures, in his study of Gray in *The Lives of the Poets*, could have been applied to others of Gray's pieces, though in a lesser degree. 'Gray', he wrote, 'thought his language more poetical as it was more remote from the common use.' He was attacking the very personal theory of poetic diction which Gray had laid down in the letter to West, in which he had said: 'The language of the age is never the language of poetry; except among the French, whose verse where the thought or image does not support it, differs in nothing from prose.' Here, and generally in his remarks on Gray, Johnson was closely anticipating Wordsworth's objections in the 1802 Preface to the *Lyrical Ballads*: 'It may be safely affirmed that there neither is, nor can be, any *essential* difference between the language of prose and metrical composition.' Only, as Wordsworth hastened to point out, the poet must *select*, from the vocabulary of ordinary people, the words most appropriate to the thought or feeling which he wishes to convey.[58]

As to French practice in this matter, French poets as diverse as Racine, La Fontaine and Baudelaire all use, but select, the language in 'common use'. What they, and some of the best English poets have done, in addition, is to make the language musical and incantatory. Gray did not understand French poetry well enough to see that one of the principal beauties of Racine's style is its music: it *sings*, whether in joy or sadness. He did not foresee – and indeed no one in Gray's time could possibly have done so – that the sublime may be attained in poetry by the selection of words normally used in prose as, for example, in Wordsworth's 'The passage of the Simplon'; or that the same means – the barest simplicity of language – can immediately awaken in us a sense of what is most poignant and tragic in man's destiny, as Housman's poetry does.

On the other hand, it can be urged in defence of Gray that he was so much steeped in Milton, whose poetic diction was certainly not the language of 'common use' in Milton's day, that he could not but try to employ a similar diction; whereas it required an uncommon genius to do this with success. It has not been pointed out that there is a specific poetic vocabulary in much Italian verse, which may also account for Gray's practice. And, finally, two of Gray's admirers among Victorian poets, Tennyson, and, to some extent, Matthew Arnold, also make use at times of a kind of poetic diction; but with them it does not seem artificial; it is highly moving and successful. Here again, as in the case of Milton, uncommon genius enabled them to triumph over too rigid theory.

In assessing Gray's experiments, most critics today agree that he misjudged his ability in attempting to adapt Pindar's pattern and manner to modern poetry. Where Ronsard had failed, Gray could hardly succeed. The odes are overloaded with erudition, they are too studied; and, in 'The Bard' particularly, the tone is too strident. Gray's chief title to greatness may be to have discouraged the prevalent taste for the rhymed couplet. Even so, he was more happily inspired when he dashed off a poem quickly, with less of study and 'anguish', as in the 'Ode on the Pleasure arising from Vicissitude'.

This is an unfinished fragment, 'found amongst Mr Gray's papers after his decease', according to Mason, who added four stanzas in order to complete it, and publish it in 1775. It contains twelve stanzas, including Mason's, each of eight lines which rhyme a b a b c c d d. The lines are of lengths varying from six to eight syllables, and with no regular pattern in each stanza, except that the fourth line has six syllables. There is more freedom and spontaneity in this ode than in Gray's other serious poems; one has the impression that he wrote it more quickly than was his habit, corrected it rapidly, and then laid it aside.

The first stanza evokes early spring, when April '. . . o'er the living scene/Scatters his freshest, tenderest green'. Then:

New-born flocks, in rustic dance,
Frisking ply their feeble feet;
Forgetful of their wintry trance,
The birds his presence greet:
But chief, the Sky-lark warbles high
His trembling, thrilling extacy;[59]
And, lessening from the dazzled sight,
Melts into air and liquid light.

Yesterday the sullen year
Saw the snowy whirlwind fly;
Mute was the music of the air,
The herd stood drooping by:
Their raptures now that wildly flow
No yesterday, nor morrow know;
'Tis Man alone that joy descries
With forward and reverted eyes.

Still, where rosy Pleasure leads,
See a kindred grief pursue;
Behind the steps that Misery treads
Approaching Comfort view . . .
See the Wretch, that long has tost
On the thorny bed of pain,
At length repair his vigour lost,
And breathe, and walk again:
The meanest floweret of the vale,
The simplest note that swells the gale,
The common sun, the air, the skies,
To him are opening Paradise.[60]

The next stanza contrasts 'humble Quiet' with the futile turbulence
of the crowd; while in the concluding stanzas Mason, imitating
Gray's style and love of abstractions, points to the miseries
attendant on 'Ambition'; whilst the peasant, free from the passions
of ambition, envy and spleen, is far happier in his 'rugged Penury'
than the man who strives for worldly greatness (a variation on the
theme of the Elegy).

He, unconscious whence the bliss.
Feels, and owns in carols rude,
That all the circling joys are his,
Of dear Vicissitude.

While the poem is not free from the artificial diction which has been deprecated, there are several lines of a freshness which seems to have influenced Wordsworth and perhaps also Shelley, whose line 'He looks before and after' seems to point to Gray's 'forward and reverted eyes.' According to Mason, Gray had told him that Gresset's 'Épître à ma Soeur' (1748) had given him 'the first idea of this Ode'. Gresset was 'a great master', in Gray's opinion. The most striking of his stanzas ('See the Wretch, that long has tost . . .') turns out to be a paraphrase, in a more concentrated form and in fresher language, of the following verses:

> O jours de la Convalescence!
> Jours d'une pure volupté!
> C'est une nouvelle naissance,
> Un rayon d'immortalité.
> Quel feu! tous les plaisirs ont volé dans mon âme,
> J'adore avec transport le céleste flambeau;
> Tout m'intéresse, tout m'enflamme,
> Pour moi l'univers est nouveau . . .

It is as though God has endowed man with new senses when he recovers from sickness; as when Spring returns to deck the woods with green, to summon the violets to flower and the warbler to sing.

Gray seems not to have reflected, before he read Gresset, that man would experience no great joys, if it were not for life's ups and downs. His was not an inventive mind. He had known two great sorrows. The loss of West had inspired his first outburst of poetry; as a great personal loss has this effect, to rescue from oblivion 'ce que jamais on ne verra deux fois'. But subsequently, those first outpourings, the springs of poetry, had seemed to run dry. When, in 1753, his mother died, he began 'The Bard' a year later and wrote the 'Vicissitude' ode. But even now he was not inventing. The subjects were suggested by his reading. As he grew older, his inspiration became more and more *literary* until, in the Norse and Welsh poems, he was simply paraphrasing, and adding nothing of himself.

IV THE NORSE AND WELSH ADAPTATIONS: 1759–1761

From the preceding pages it emerges that Gray's sparse production after 1757 is not to be ascribed only to his disappointment at the public response to his work. The Pindaric odes had been fairly well received. A clique of devoted admirers had formed itself and was to increase, in defiance of the criticism of the Grand Cham; but their appreciation was not enlightened enough to please Gray. He was also physically unwell: the deterioration in his health can be followed from the careful records which he kept. He suffered periodical attacks of gout, but the malady which was to cause his death – a disease of the kidneys, it seems – must have been troubling him already in the 1760s.

Still dreaming of the *History of English Poetry* which he had planned, and of those little-known languages which he believed had had some influence on its prosody, he now turned to a study of Norse and Welsh poetry. He had 'gone mad about' Macpherson's first book when it appeared in 1760; he was 'extasié' with the 'infinite beauty' of these so-called 'Fragments of Ancient Poetry'. Next, under the heading 'Cambri', he copied into his Commonplace Book a Latin translation of three Welsh poems by the Rev. Evan Evans, a distinguished scholar who had communicated them to one of his friends. Evans had written his *De Bardis Dissertatio* in 1759, but it did not appear until 1764. Works on Icelandic, that is, Old Norse poetry were, however, available, and while Gray was able to follow the meaning of the poems from the Latin versions he could, without knowing much Icelandic, make out the principal features of the prosody, from a study of the texts.[61]

'The Fatal Sisters' commemorates the expedition undertaken by Sigurd, Earl of the Orkneys, to support Sictryg, who was at war with Brian, King of Dublin. The ensuing battle, in Ireland, had been fought in 1014; and the lay which Gray paraphrased – 'The Web of War' – dating from the eleventh century, was incorporated in the thirteenth-century *Njáls Saga*. Gray found this in Thormodus Torfaeus's *The Orcades* (1697). The Fatal Sisters are the Valkyries who weave on their loom[62] the destinies of warriors. The original poem was written in lines of irregular length, some very short. Gray adapted this in seven-syllable lines in quatrains rhyming a b a b.

Here is the Valkyries' Song:

> Now the storm begins to lower,
> (Haste, the loom of hell prepare)
> Iron-sleet of arrowy shower
> Hurtles in the darken'd air.
>   Glitt'ring lances are the loem,
> Where the dusky warp we strain,
> Weaving many a Soldier's doom,
> *Orkney's* woe, & *Randver's* bane.

'Orkney' refers to Earl Sigurd. 'Randver' appears to designate any warrior doomed to perish. The Valkyries continue their song, increasing in horror.

> *Mista* black, terrific Maid,
> *Sangrida*, & *Hilda* see
> Join the weyward work to aid:
> 'Tis the woof of victory.
>   E'er the ruddy sun be set,
> Pikes must shiver, javelins sing,
> Blade with clattering buckler meet,
> Hauberk crash, & helmet ring.
>
> . . . .
>
> Sisters, hence with spurs of speed:
> Each her thundering faulchion wield,
> Each bestride her sable steed,
> Hurry, hurry to the field.

Since the battle took place near Dublin, one might wonder why the song should be known in Scotland. Gray had read that 'a native of Caithness . . . saw at a distance a number of Persons on horseback riding . . . towards a hill, & seeming to enter into it'. He followed them and, looking in, saw 'gigantic figures resembling Women: they were all employ'd about a loom . . .' This appears to explain why the fate of a battle in Ireland had been decided by the Valkyries in Caithness. It is interesting to read a passage quoted[63] from Lockhart's *Life of Scott*, according to which a clergyman, about 1769, took a copy of Gray's paraphrase to North Ronaldsha and 'read it to some of the old people as referring to the ancient history of their islands. But so soon as he had proceeded a little way, they exclaimed they knew it very well in the original'. If Gray knew of this episode, it would probably have confirmed him in his belief in the authenticity of the Ossianic poems.

'The Descent of Odin' is a free translation of Bartholin's version of 'Baldrs Draumar'. It describes Odin's visit to hell, to seek from the Prophetess the meaning of the dream which Balder has had, that he is doomed to perish. The original text is in lines like those of the *Njáls Saga*, of irregular length. Gray adapted it in eight-syllable and seven-syllable lines in rhymed couplets.

> Uprose the King of Men with speed,
> And saddled strait his coal-black steed
> Sleipner was his horse: he had eight legs.
> Down the yawning steep he rode
> That leads to Hela's dread abode.
> Him the Dog of darkness spied:
> His shaggy throat he open'd wide
>
> Hoarse he bays with hideous din,
> Eyes that glow, & fangs that grin,
> And long pursues with fruitless yell
> The Father of the powerful spell.
> Onward still his way he takes,
> (The groaning earth beneath him shakes)
> Till before his fearless eyes
> The portals nine of hell arise.
>   Right against the eastern gate
> By the moss-grown gate he sate
> Thrice he traced the runic rhyme,
> Thrice pronounc'd in accents dread
> The thrilling verse, that wakes the Dead,
> Till from out the hollow ground
> Slowly breath'd a sullen sound.

> Prophetess: What call unknown, what charms presume
>   To break the quiet of the tomb?

The remaining forty-one lines contain the dialogue between Odin and the Prophetess. She tells him of Rinda's 'wond'rous Boy' who was to slay Hoder and thus avenge Balder – when he was only one night old! – an exploit similar to that of the infant

Heracles. The Virgins 'in speechless woe' appear to be the three Nornes, who in spite of Odin's reproaches wish good to gods and men. Lok (Loki) is a sort of Scandinavian Satan. After the death of Balder, the gods had chained him to a rock, and there he remained 'till the Twilight of the Gods approaches, when he shall break his bonds', and the whole world shall perish – as Gray explains in his annotations to the 1768 edition.

It seems possible that Matthew Arnold knew this poem when he composed his 'Balder Dead'; which relates the next episode but one in the *Edda*.

As ignorant of Welsh as of Icelandic, Gray relied on the Rev. Evan Evans's Latin version of Gwalchmai's 'Ode to Owain Gwynedd'. Owain was Prince of North Wales (Gwynedd), and the battle commemorated, in which Owain defeats a simultaneous attack of fleets from Ireland, Norway and Denmark, took place in 1157. In the 'Advertisement' to his paraphrase Gray acknowledged his debt to 'Mr Evans's Specimens of the Welch poetry. Lond: 1764.' Evans had apparently communicated the manuscript in advance to Gray, because the latter's poem probably dates from 1761.[64] It was published in 1768, as 'The Triumphs of Owen: A Fragment'.

It follows Evans's translation in the first thirty lines, which are in seven-syllable verse, in couplets. The remaining ten lines are mainly Gray's own:

> Owen's praise demands my song,
> Owen swift, & Owen strong,
> Fairest flower of Roderic's stem,
> *Gwyneth's* shield, & Britain's gem.

The next lines celebrate his prudence and liberality, and describe the simultaneous attack by Danes and Norsemen. But:

> Dauntless on his native sands
> The Dragon-Son of Mona stands;
> In glitt'ring arms & glory drest
> High he rears his ruby crest.
> There the thund'ring strokes begin,
> There the press, & there the din,
> Talymalfra's rocky shore

> Echoing to the battle's roar.
> Check'd by the torrent-tide of blood
> Backward Meinai rolls his flood:
> While heap'd his Master's feet around
> Prostrate Warriors gnaw the ground.

'Mona' is Anglesey. The remaining ten lines describe the mêlée in language rather like that of 'The Fatal Sisters'.

For 'The Death of Hoël' Gray was indebted to Evan Evans for the Latin translation of a poem in the Gododin by Aneurin, a bard of the sixth and seventh centuries of our era. Aneurin seems to have died soon after the battle in which Prince Hoël was defeated and killed by the Angles[65] of Deira. Gray's paraphrase is in octosyllabic couplets:

> Had I but the torrent's might,
> With headlong rage & wild affright
> Upon Deira's squadrons hurl'd,
> To rush, & sweep them from the world!

The next three couplets relate the death of Hoël, and recall his virtues.

> To Cattraeth's vale in glitt'ring row
> Twice two hundred warriors goe;
>
> . . . .
>
> Wreath'd in many a golden link:
> From the golden cup they drink
> Nectar, that the bees produce,
> Or the grape's extatic juice.
> Flush'd with mirth & hope they burn:
> But none from Cattraeth's vale return,
> Save Aeron brave, & Conan strong,
> (Bursting thro' the bloody throng)
> And I, the meanest of them all,
> That live to weep, & sing their fall.

Deira was the southern of the two English kingdoms, afterwards united as Northumbria; and it included the modern Yorkshire; Cattraeth was probably Catterick.

The next fragment compares Caradoc to the 'tusky Boar', or the Bull; and the last, on Conan, probably relates to the same battle, in which he slew many of the Angles.

To sum up: to a reader with no knowledge of Icelandic, the Norse poems would have the impression of something very rude and primitive, written in a prosody many centuries anterior in development to that of the Homeric epics. The Welsh poems, on the other hand, offer examples of a prosody more advanced, and exacting, for successful translation, an uncommon virtuosity. Gray's paraphrases may mark an improvement on the original Norse, but do less than justice to the best qualities of the Welsh originals.

On the other hand, Gray merits praise for having used his art to make better known the old Welsh and Nordic poetry, although he depended on translators, to whom the prime credit is due. It is a mistake to give him, as does J. R. Green (in his chapter on the Conquest of Wales in *A Short History of England*) the chief credit. (Green does go on to demolish the fable of the alleged massacre of the bards.)

V   ENGLISH POEMS: 1748–1769

Gray had tried his hand, many years before, at dramatic and philosophical verse. The example of Racine's *Britannicus*, which had impressed him in Paris, inspired an attempt to write a sequel in blank verse on the last days and death of Agrippina, Nero's mother. West had pointed out that the speeches were too long and that the language, suggestive of Shakespeare, was too archaic. The criticism was just, and Gray, after composing twelve lines of Scene 2, abandoned his drama. The versification is in fact imitated from Shakespeare, and the best lines –

> . . . things, that but whisper'd
> Have arch'd the hearer's brow, and riveted
> His eyes in fearful extasy . . .

– repeat Shakespeare's 'fearful extasie', which, in the Eton ode, he changed to 'fearful joy'. It might have been better, as West argued, to employ a language like Otway's; or at least one in more common use. This defect, however, would have mattered less if

Gray had had more dramatic sense. He did not understand how to make use of the clash of personalities, or the intervention of contingency. Aceronia, the Empress's confidante, is as meditative and long-winded as her mistress. Gray had no more feeling for the dramatic than Johnson, whose *Irene*, in spite of Garrick's loyal support, had been a disastrous failure.

But for the exposition of philosophic ideas he lacked the understanding which makes the *Vanity of Human Wishes* so memorable. In 1748 he began a poem, of which the subject, he told Wharton, was 'the Alliance of Education & Government; I mean they must necessarily concur to produce great & useful Men'. The synopsis, which Mason afterwards found among Gray's papers, shows that he had wished to study the effect of soil and climate on the character of nations; that a southern climate, like that of the Mediterranean, promotes contemplation, intelligence and the arts of peace, but tends to make men effeminate. The severities of a northern climate make men hardy and warlike. 'Those invasions of effeminate Southern nations by the warlike Northern people, seem . . . to be necessary evils.' The aim of education, therefore, should be 'to make men *think* in the Northern climates, and *act* in the Southern'. Roger Lonsdale suggests that Gray may have known Bodin's *Livres de la République* (1577) and Chardin's *Travels in the Orient* (1686 and 1711). The latter seems likely; but with equal probability, Gray may have known the *Réflexions critiques sur la poésie et la peinture* (1719 and 1733), in which the Abbé Dubos had also studied the influence of soil and climate on a people's character.

Gray's argument, a familiar one, seems to have been based on the supposed cause of the fall of the Roman Empire in the West (lines 50–3 of the poem). There may be some ground for this view; but a comparison of the northern and southern peoples of today does not make it self-evident. Are the Spaniards effeminate but intelligent, and the Norwegians warlike but unintellectual? and so on. The poem is written in decasyllabic rhymed couplets, and in a style similar to Johnson's or Goldsmith's, but with more of simile and metaphor. The first thirty-seven lines are lacking in clarity. Here is an example of the diction to which this kind of poetry is apt to succumb:

> This spacious animated Scene survey,
> From where the rolling Orb, that gives the Day,

His sable Sons with nearer Course surrounds
To either Pole, & Life's remotest Bounds.

The following verses were said to have been admired and repeated by C. J. Fox:

What wonder, in the sultry Climes, that spread
Where Nile redundant o'er his summer-bed
From his broad bosom life & verdure flings,
And broods o'er Egypt with his wat'ry wings . . .

Gray abandoned the piece, after writing 107 lines.

Matthew Arnold states that Goldsmith probably borrowed the theme of 'The Traveller' from Gray's poem, but the dates of publication do not support his view, tempting as it is; Goldsmith could have taken the idea from a variety of other sources.

In June 1758 Dr Wharton wrote from Old Park to tell Gray that he had lost his son Robin, then aged about five, and asked him for an epitaph. Gray replied, with expressions of sympathy, that he was 'little qualified' to give satisfaction in that respect, since inspiration was by no means voluntary. He sent the following:

Here free'd from pain, secure from misery, lies
A Child, the Darling of his Parent's eyes:
A gentler Lamb ne'er sported on the plain,
A fairer Flower will never bloom again!
Few were the days allotted to his breath;
Here let him sleep in peace his night of death.

Gray's editors indicate no source for this, but it sounds very much like an adaptation of an epigram in the *Greek Anthology*,[66] which has been paraphrased as follows by A. C. Benson:

Five years I lived, and knew no grief;
What need of tears for such as those?
For if my span of life was brief,
Small was my share of all its woes.[67]

Gray might have found this in Planudes' selection of Greek epigrams, in Henri Estienne's edition of 1566, to which he is known to have had access. One notices that both children were five years of age. Gray expanded and adorned the simplicity of the Greek by inserting two verses, of which the first is imitated from *Richard II*, II, 1: 'In peace was never gentle lamb more mild.'

Gray wrote two or three other epitaphs at the request of friends or of the bereaved. Of these, the one on Mrs Clerke, wife of a former Fellow of Pembroke, is the best (1757). The epitaph on Sir William Williams, a young officer who was killed in the attack on Belle Ile in 1761, contains too much of convention and rhetoric.

To the composition of the 'Ode for Music', written to honour the Duke of Grafton on his installation as Chancellor of the University in 1769, Gray devoted much time and thought. The poem is divided into airs, choruses and recitatives, each in lines of varying lengths and rhyme schemes. Gray had realised by this time how much he was indebted to Cambridge, and he set out to praise the University and, as gratitude required, to compliment the Chancellor. The opening air begins: 'Hence, avaunt, ('tis holy ground) . . .', for Cambridge is no place for ignorance, sloth, sedition or flattery; and the first chorus ends: 'Hence, away, 'tis holy Ground!' The words 'Hence, avaunt' are taken from *Henry IV, Part II*. The first recitative evokes the figures of Henry VI and Milton, and it is Milton who is imagined as singing the next air, while

> Meek *Newton's* self bends from his state sublime,
> And nods his hoary head and listens to the rhyme.

In the following air, which Milton is supposed to recite, Gray uses the metre which Milton employs in the 'Hymn' in the 'Nativity Ode':[68]

> 'Ye brown o'er-arching Groves,
> 'That Contemplation loves,
> 'Where willowy *Camus* lingers with delight!
> 'Oft at the blush of dawn
> 'I trod your level lawn,
> 'Oft woo'd the gleam of *Cynthia* silver-bright
> 'In cloisters dim, far from the haunts of Folly,
> 'With Freedom by my side, and soft-ey'd Melancholy.'

Through the following recitative moves a procession of kings, 'Royal Dames' and noble ladies –

> All that on Granta's fruitful plain
> Rich streams of regal bounty pour'd,
> And bad these aweful fanes and turrets rise,
> To hail their *Fitzroy's* festal morning come . . .

Personal gratitude required Gray to compliment the Duke, but hardly to suggest that the shades of the great departed should be assembled to hail a man whose cynical disregard of the domestic virtues, and mediocre political ability, had mobilised London opinion against him. It was even more injudicious in the next recitative to picture the 'venerable Marg'ret', that is the Countess of Richmond, mother of Henry VII, as tracing in Fitzroy's 'lineaments' 'A *Tudor's* fire, a *Beaufort's* grace'. Since Beaufort had been an illegitimate son of John of Gaunt, the Tudors' claim to the throne was through him. He had been legitimated, but only on condition of renouncing the right of succession. The Duke of Grafton was an illegitimate descendant of Charles II through the Duchess of Castlemaine. All this lent a handle to the Wilkesites. Gray had feared he would be ridiculed. 'Junius', in one of his attacks on Grafton, sneered at the poet's 'venal' pen, while a satirist in *The London Chronicle* of 27–29 July remarked:

> As a certain Church-yard Poet has deviated from the principles he once profest, it is very fitting that the necessary alterations should be made in his epitaph. – *Marcus.*

EPITAPH

> Here rests his head upon the lap of earth,
> 　One nor to fortune nor to fame unknown;
> Fair science frown'd not on his humble birth,
> 　And smooth-tongued flatt'ry mark'd him for her own.
>
> Large was his wish – in this he was sincere –
> 　Fate did a recompence as largely send,
> Gave the poor C – r four hundred pounds a year,
> 　And made a d – – – y Minister his friend.

No further seek his deeds to bring to light,
    For ah! he offer'd at Corruption's shrine;
And basely strove to wash an Ethiop white,
    While Truth and Honour bled in ev'ry line.[69]

The 'Ode to Music' was the last of Gray's poems. He sent a copy to Beattie, while admitting that it hardly deserved to survive.

VI THE HUMOROUS POEMS

Gray wrote more spontaneously, and often more effectively, when in humorous vein. The first of his humorous pieces, 'Lines spoken by the ghost of John Dennis at the Devil Tavern', was composed at the end of his first year at Eton, and addressed to 'Céladon' (Walpole). A severe critic of Pope, Dennis had died early in 1734. Gray supposes that at Céladon's command Dennis has risen from the nether world and described his experiences down there:

> That little, naked, melancholy thing
> My Soul, when first she tryed her flight to wing;
> Began with speed new Regions to explore,
> And blunder'd thro' a narrow Postern door . . .

After threading sordid passages,

> It came into a mead of Asphodel:
> Betwixt the Confines of ye light & dark
> It lies, of 'Lyzium ye St James's park:
> Here Spirit-Beaux flutter along the Mall,
> And Shadows in disguise scate o'er ye Iced Canal:

In a PS, he describes the diversions enjoyed in the nether world:

> Plays, which were hiss'd above, below revive;
> When dead applauded, that were damn'd alive:
> The People, as in life, still keep their Passions,
> But differ something from the world in Fashions.
> Queen Artemisia breakfasts on Bohea,
> And Alexander wears a Ramilie.

'That little, naked, melancholy thing' is imitated from Hadrian's address to his soul as 'Animula vagula blandula', etc. Artemisia built the famous Mausoleum in commemoration of the husband she had adored. The last line satirises the custom of dressing the heroes of plays, evoking the ancient world in modern costumes, with full-bottomed wigs.

The manuscript of these verses, which is in Pembroke College, was first published in 1915.

'A Long Story' was written late in 1750 for the amusement of Lady Cobham and her friends. Gray afterwards told Beattie that it 'was never meant for the publick, & only suffer'd to appear in that pompous edition because of Mr Bentley's designs . . .'.

> In Britain's Isle, no matter where,
> An ancient pile of building stands:
> The Huntingdons & Hattons there
> Employ'd the power of Fairy hands
>
> To raise the cieling's fretted height,
> Each panel in achievements cloathing,
> Rich windows that exclude the light,
> And passages that lead to nothing.

From the house now issues

> A brace of warriors, not in buff,
> But rustling in their silks & tissues.
> The first came cap-a-pee from France
> Her conqu'ring destiny fulfilling,
> Whom meaner Beauties eye askance,
> And vainly ape her art of killing.
>
> The other Amazon kind Heaven
> Had arm'd with spirit, wit & satire:
> But COBHAM had the polish given,
> And tip'd her arrows with good nature.

Having learned that 'a wicked Imp they call a Poet' is living near them, the heroines called at his home,

> Rap'd at the door, nor stay'd to ask,
> But bounce into the parlour enter'd.

The trembling family they daunt,
They flirt, they sing, they laugh, they tattle,
Rummage his Mother, pinch his Aunt,
And upstairs in a whirlwind rattle.

A thorough search fails to discover the culprit, because

On the first marching of the troops
The Muses hopeless of his pardon,
Convey'd him underneath their hoops
To a small closet in the garden.

But the visitors had 'left a spell upon the table':

So cunning was the Apparatus,
The powerful pothooks did so move him,
That, will he, nill he, to the Great-house
He went, as if the Devil drove him.

'He once or twice [only once] had penn'd a sonnet;
'Yet hoped, that he might save his bacon:
'Numbers would give their oaths upon it,
'He ne'er was for a conj'rer[70] taken.'

'The ghostly Prudes . . . had condemn'd the sinner', but

My Lady rose, and with a grace . . .
She smiled, & bid him come to dinner.

To the great scandal of the Prudes.

(Here 500 stanzas are lost)

And so God save our noble King,
And guard us from long-winded Lubbers
That to eternity would sing,
And keep my Lady from her Rubbers.

The metre, suitable only for humorous verse, may have been
imitated from Matthew Prior. The first and third lines in each
stanza are octosyllabic, the second and fourth sometimes have
eight, sometimes nine syllables, in which case the last two are
required to rhyme, e.g. Imbroglio/folio. As for the rhyme system,

Gray manages the double rhymes fairly well, but there are many imperfect rhymes, such as satire/nature. Other examples are: daunt/Aunt; Apparatus/Great-house; old-tree/poultry.

'William Shakespeare to Mrs Anne, Regular Servant
to the Rev^d Mr Precentor of York.'

When staying with Mason in York in June 1765, Gray discovered that his friend was engaged on an edition of Shakespeare with a commentary. From Old Park on 8 July he sent these verses to dissuade Mason from pursuing a task for which he deemed he was not fitted.

> A moment's patience, gentle Mistress Anne!
> (But stint your clack for sweet St Charitie)
> 'Tis Willy begs, once a right proper Man,
> Tho' now a Book, & interleav'd you see.
>
> Much have I borne from canker'd Critick's spite,
> From fumbling Baronets and Poets small,
> Pert Barristers, & Parsons nothing bright:
> But, what awaits me now, is worst of all!
>
> 'Tis true, our Master's temper natural
> Was fashion'd fair in meek & dovelike guise:
> But may not honey's self be turned to gall
> By residence, by marriage, & sore eyes?

So he begs Mrs Anne to 'Steal to his closet at the hour of prayer' and tear up all that Mason has written.

> Better to bottom tarts & cheesecakes nice,
> Better the roast-meat from the fire to save,
> Better be twisted into caps for spice,
> Than thus be patch'd, & cobbled in one's grave!
>
> So York shall taste, what Clouët never knew;
> So from *our* works sublimer fumes shall rise:
> While Nancy earns the praise to Shakespear due
> For glorious puddings, & immortal pies.

Sir Thomas Hanmer had edited Shakespeare in 1743–4, and several barristers and clergymen had also published editions. Mason's gentleness had exposed him more than once to Gray's raillery. The poet had derided him, not very kindly, for seeking advancement through the patronage of Lord Holdernesse and the Archbishop, although this was the only means of obtaining a living: 'A whore's dreams are a sure sign of church preferment.'[71] Mason had endured a good deal. He naturally did not appreciate the poem; he laid it aside, and of course did not publish it.

Monsieur de St Clouët was the Duke of Newcastle's chef, a talented French cook. He recalls the Duc de Condé's chef, who, when the fish did not arrive for an important banquet, felt so much humiliated that he fell on his sword. Clouët was well aware of his prestige. A contemporary caricature depicts him in his kitchen, complaining to the Duke that he objected to being called a Papist, and shows him being besought by the Duke not to leave him.

The last line but one is obviously imitated from *The Rape of the Lock*: 'And Betty's praised for labours not her own.'[72]

VII THE SATIRES

Gray took far more readily to satire than to serious verse: the degree of antipathy which he felt, often for people who had done him no harm, surprises in one outwardly so gentle.

The 'Hymn to Ignorance' which he wrote on returning to Cambridge in 1741, has already been discussed. It merely expresses the contempt he felt at the time for both the town and the university. This attitude, it is fair to say, was replaced by something akin to gratitude in the course of years.

'Tophet' is more pointed. The Reverend Henry Etough, who had a living in Hertfordshire, occasionally visited Cambridge, but only to make mischief. In 1749 Gray, who had been, perhaps jestingly, accused of being a sort of atheist, feared that Etough would do him further harm. When Mason drew a caricature of this disagreeable parson, Gray composed eight lines to be inscribed under it.

> Such Tophet; so looked the grinning Fiend
> Whom many a frightened Prelate call'd his friend;
> I saw them bow & while they wish'd him dead

With servile simper nod the mitred head
Hosannas rang thro' Hell's tremendous borders
And Satan's self had thoughts of taking orders.

'Tophet' was probably intended as an anagram, roughly speaking,
of Etough.

The 'Sketch of his own Character', dating probably from the
1760s, is more humorous than satirical:

Too poor for a bribe, and too proud to importune;
He had not the method of making a fortune:
Could love, and could hate, so was thought somewhat odd;
No very great wit, he believ'd in a God . . .

The 'Satire on the Heads of Houses' was probably written
towards 1750. Gray had regarded the Masters as alike in being too
docile in conforming to the Chancellor's wishes; and he himself,
as previously mentioned, had conceived a violent dislike for the
Duke of Newcastle. This piece is more contemptuous than anything he would have written after 1760, and its only interest lies
in the ingenuity of the rhymes as, for example, in verses 5–10:

Know the Master of Jesus
Does hugely displease us;
The Master of Maudlin
In the same dirt is dawdling;
The Master of Sidney
Is of the same kidney

– and so on to the PS.

As to Trinity Hall
We say nothing at all.

There is no absolute proof that Gray wrote 'The Candidate' and
one would prefer to think him guiltless of it. Walpole, however,
had a copy of it in Gray's hand, which he sent to Mason. According
to the American editors of the poems, Mason wrote in October
1774: 'I remember when he repeated [the verses] to me . . .'
(p. 78); but on p. 238 they state that Walpole wrote to Mason in
September 1774 that he 'had heard Gray recite the poem much

earlier, found a copy in Gray's hand and at some later date may have printed it.'

Lord Hardwicke, the High Steward of the University, had fallen ill in 1763; it was not thought he would live very long; and in consequence there was a contest for the succession between the Newcastle faction or 'party', to which Hardwicke belonged, and the Grenville Ministry, supported by the King. In this juncture, the Earl of Sandwich offered himself as candidate for the court 'party'. He had offended public opinion by turning against Wilkes, formerly a friend, and even more by his reputation for profligacy. His private life seems to have been as shameful as the Duke of Newcastle's was blameless. In spite of this, a large number of the clergy, including such leading figures as the Bishop of Chester and the Lady Margaret Professor of Divinity at Cambridge, were supporting Sandwich, apparently in hope of further preferment from the Crown. This explains why, in the satire, 'Divinity' treats 'Jemmy Twitcher's'[73] 'peccadillos' as trifles and offers to marry him, while 'Physic' and 'Law' reject his courtship.

> When sly Jemmy Twitcher had smugg'd up his face
> With a lick of court white-wash, and pious grimace,
> A wooing he went, where three Sisters of old
> In harmless society guttle and scold.

Physic says to Law:

> Not I, for the Indies! you know I'm no prude;
> But his nose is a shame, and his eyes are so lewd . . .

This is not the only clear allusion to the disease he had caught – like his ancestor, Lord Rochester, whom Law now refers to. But it is his character, 'his swearing and roaring,/His lying, and filching . . .', that decide Law to reject him. Divinity, however, is favourable:

> What a pother is here about wenching and roaring!
> Why David loved catches, and Solomon whoring.

> The prophet of Bethel, we read, told a lie:
> He drinks; so did Noah: he swears; so do I.
> To refuse him for such peccadillos were odd;

Besides, he repents, and he talks about G – – .
Never hang down your head, you poor penitent elf!
Come, buss me, I'll be Mrs Twitcher myself.
D – – n ye both for a couple of Puritan bitches!
He's Christian enough, that repents, and that – – – – – – – – .

In the copy of the satire which Walpole sent, with a covering letter to Mason, the last word was 'stitches', meaning 'fornicates'. Walpole deleted this, and said he wished that Mason 'could alter the end of the last line, which is too gross to be read by any females, but such cock-bawds as the three dames in the verses!'. He suggested:

Damn you both! I know each for a Puritan punk.
He is Christian enough that repents when he's drunk.

Mason proposed other alternatives, but in the end the concluding couplet did not appear in print. Some scholars, loath to accept 'stitches', have thought that Gray wrote 'twitches', but this does not make much sense. The verses as a whole are so indecent that one is driven to conclude that Gray did write this word, as it appears, scored through, in the copy which Walpole sent to Mason.

Gray's verses cannot be excused on the ground that other satirists wrote as indecently. Churchill's attack on Sandwich in 'The Candidate',[74] and earlier, in 'The Duellist', is pointed and effective, without being gross or indecent. Two or three other satires by Gray, including one on the Duke of Newcastle's visit to Hanover, were destroyed by Mason.

'On Lord Holland's Seat near Margate, Kent' is in language so different that, but for the evidence that both Walpole and Mason believed 'The Candidate' to be by Gray, one would still be incredulous. In 1768, while staying with Robinson at Denton, Gray visited the eccentric villa and sham ruins which Henry Fox, Lord Holland, had built, probably to console himself for his political downfall. He was so much detested that his former associates, Shelburne, first Marquis of Lansdowne, Rigby and Calcraft, all turned against him. In 1767 he retaliated in verses entitled 'Lord Holland returning from Italy'. Gray does not seem to have intended his own verses to be printed; or, at least, he acted as if he did not intend it. The satire opens and closes as follows:

Old and abandon'd by each venal friend
　　Here H —— took the pious resolution
To smuggle some few years and strive to mend
　　A broken character and constitution.

. . . .

Ah, said the sighing Peer, had Bute been true,
　　Nor Shelburne's, Rigby's, Calcraft's friendship vain,
Far other scenes than these had bless'd our view
　　And realis'd the ruins that we feign.
Purg'd by the sword and beautifyed by fire,
　　Then had we seen proud London's hated walls,
Owls might have hooted in St Peter's Quire,
　　And foxes stunk and litter'd in St Paul's.

CHAPTER 2

The Translator[1]

Gray occupied part of his leisure in translating a few Italian poems, one English poem and some thirteen Greek epigrams into Latin. The version of an anonymous English ode certainly belongs to his earliest period. He later made English versions of extracts from Propertius, Statius, Dante and Tasso. The translations into Latin are of no interest to the general reader; while the translations into English have scarcely enough merit to interest him.

Gray probably began by making a version in Latin elegiacs of a mediocre anonymous ode which had appeared in *Miscellaneous Poems by several Hands* in 1726.

The version of a sonnet by Petrarch (*Canzoniere*, 170) in elegiacs must have been made a few years later. The sonnet begins: '*Lasso ch'i ardo, ed altri non me'l crede . . .*', and Gray renders the fourteen lines in sixteen.

A clever poem in eight lines by the Abbate G.-M. Buondelmonti, a contemporary of Gray's, suggested to the latter a poem in six lines which, whatever their merit, are neither a translation of, nor an improvement on, the original Italian.

The notion of translating Greek epigrams into Latin could have occurred to no one but a young man with a great deal of time on his hands. None of the epigrams he selected are of particular interest or merit, except a very amusing one by Agathias Scholasticus, a witty professor of the age of Justinian. In this epigram Agathias relates how a farmer once consulted Aristophanes as to whether the fates had foretold a plentiful harvest, and how Aristophanes told him exactly what climatic and other conditions would be needed if the harvest were to be good – not a difficult forecast.

Of more interest are the translations from Latin and Italian into English. Gray seems to have begun by rendering three extracts from the *Thebaid* in rhymed couplets. The first is from Book VI, lines 646–88; the second from lines 704–24; the third from Book IX, lines 319–26. The style is hardly distinguishable from that of any imitator of Pope, and is inferior to Johnson's or Goldsmith's.

The version of a passage from Canto XIV of the *Gerusalemme liberata* was probably made in 1738. One might have thought that Gray would have imitated the rhymed octaves of the original, or used the Spenserian stanza, instead of rhymed couplets. It is instructive to compare Gray's rendering of Stanza 32 with the version which W. H. Biffen published in 1824. Gray writes:

> Dismiss'd at length they break thro' all delay
> To tempt the dangers of the doubtful way;
> And first to Ascalon *their steps they bend*,[1]
> Whose walls along the neighbouring sea extend:
> Nor yet in prospect rose the distant shore,
> Scarce the hoarse waves from far were heard to roar;
> When thwart the road a River roll'd its flood
> Tempestuous, and all further course withstood.

Gray is here describing them as travelling by land, whereas a glance at Stanza 30 would have shown him that they had been instructed to go by sea, as indeed is clear from Stanza 32 itself. Biffen translates the text more closely. While using a more difficult verse-form, he makes an accurate translation and makes it in better English.

The version of the episode in the *Inferno*, Canto 33, where Count Ugolino tells Dante how he and his sons were imprisoned and left to die of hunger, probably also dates from 1738. In default of the rhymed couplet, which would have been unfitting for an episode so grisly, Gray fell back on blank verse:

> Where are thy Tears? too soon they [the children] had arous'd them,
> Sad with fears of Sleep, & now the Hour
> Of timely food approach'd: when at the gate
> Below I heard the dreadful Clank of bars,
> And fastning bolts; then on my Children's eyes
> Speechless my Sight I fix'd, nor wept, for all
> Within was Stone: they wept, unhappy boys!
> They wept, & first my little dear Anselmo
> Cried, 'Father, why, why do you gaze so sternly?
> What would you have?....

Matthew Arnold selected the original of this passage as an example of the grand manner in poetry:

> I wept not, but all stone I turned within;
> They wept.

– 'Piangevan elli'. Gray, by diluting the language and inserting 'unhappy boys', failed to bring out the tragic contrast. Shelley's cousin, Medwin, who translated lines 22 to 75 in *terza rima* – the metre of the original – produced a better version. Medwin failed to carry over the rhyme between two of the tercets, but he did not mar the contrast by adding useless words.

The last of the translations into English were sent to West in 1742. These were versions of Propertius, Book IV, Elegy 1 (to Maecaenas) in 108 lines and most of Book III, Elegy 5, in 58 lines of rhymed couplets. Whatever may be thought of Propertius's style, there is little to be said for his matter, as Maecaenas appears to have told him. Gray, for his part, had certainly by now acquired greater facility. Speaking of his mistress 'Cynthia', who obsesses his thoughts, Propertius concludes (in Gray's version):

> In brief, whate'er she do, or say, or look,
> 'Tis ample Matter for a Lover's Book:
> And many a copious Narrative you'll see
> Big with the important Nothing's History.

It will be remembered that, apart from the lines ascribed to the ghost of John Dennis (1734), Gray wrote no original poems in English before 1742. A study of the translations shows that, prior to that date, he possessed no marked facility for versifying in English, and never attempted anything as difficult as *ottava rima* or *terza rima*. Translators so much less famous than he, as Biffen and Medwin, have displayed more ability in English verse. One wonders, indeed, whether Gray intended to write English poems before West gave him an example and urged him to write. Furthermore, one wonders whether he did not, like Andrew Marvell,[2] first write some of his poems in Latin and then translate them. At all events, he found great difficulty in composing an English poem, if it were not comic or satirical. The Elegy took over five years to complete. The conclusion imposes itself that, in verse as in other fields, he was a dilettante.

CHAPTER 3

The Letter Writer[1]

Gray's letters contain much of his biography and tell the reader a great deal about his character. They are exceptionally abundant, not because he was a born letter writer but, as he confessed to Mason, because he wrote '*pour me désennuyer*, tho' I have little enough to say'. Unfortunately he sometimes said too much. The tone of the letters he sent to Walpole, when he heard that his portrait was to appear as the frontispiece to the *Six Poems*, suggests no ordinary mental disorder; and three at least of his letters to Mason should never have been printed. Critics of Gray have generally ignored these aberrations. Dr Johnson, after an avowedly 'slight inspection' of that part of the correspondence which Mason had thought suitable for publication, considered that Gray's 'curiosity was unlimited and his judgement cultivated'. That Walpole should have declared 'His letters were the best I ever saw' makes one doubt his sincerity. They were not nearly as good as his own, and not to be mentioned in the same breath with Madame de Sévigné's. If Gray foresaw that his correspondence would one day be published, he would probably have been indifferent; and yet, had he wished to preserve the image of himself as the gentlemanly scholar, he would scarcely have written to Mason in the deplorable language he used, for example, about the latter's proposal to marry. But no doubt he did not care what posterity might think of him. 'What has it ever done to oblige me?' he once asked.

After reading the three volumes of his letters, one is led to inquire whether they in any respect deserve the high opinion of men as intelligent as Walpole.

They are usually adapted to his correspondents. As a young man, he wrote admiringly, sometimes wittily, to Walpole; a little later, more intimately and affectionately to West. The letters belonging to this period (1734–42) are in general more readable and agreeable

than those which belong to the last twenty years of his life. The
letters to Dr Wharton, his most regular correspondent, are jocular
and gossipy. To Wharton he sent, in instalments, the record of his
tour of the English Lakes.

There is a great difference in tone between the youthful letters
to Walpole, his 'dear dimidium meae', and those written after the
quarrel and reconciliation, which begin 'My dear Sir'. Nevertheless he assists his benefactor by looking up in the British Museum
and other libraries material for the *Anecdotes of Painting* and the
Historic Doubts. He discusses these at length: the superior tone of
his remarks does not seem to have annoyed Walpole. On the other
hand, his solicitude on account of Walpole's health and his advice
as to a suitable regime indicate that much of the old intimacy had
been recovered. But Walpole's description of the intellectual life of
Paris in 1765, of the salons and of Madame du Deffand, met with
no sympathetic response: Gray abandoned himself to diatribes
against the French in general and Voltaire in particular. These
outbursts, however, did not disturb the amicable relations which
now prevailed between the old friends.

In the 1760s an increasing number of letters were written to
such new acquaintances as Nicholls and Beattie. They regarded
Gray as an oracle, and he accepted the part.

No letter writer among poets, except Byron, and Swinburne,
would benefit more from a selection. A 'Selected Letters of Thomas
Gray' would be a great deal more readable than the complete
Correspondence which we have, although it would convey only a
very partial impression of the man. Since his characteristic letters
have been quoted or referred to in Part One of this work, it is
proposed here to cite, with one exception, only extracts from those
letters which are studied, literary, compositions. He was not at his
best, as Walpole was, when writing spontaneously. Thus, in the
very first of his letters in the *Gray–Walpole–West–Ashton Correspondence*, dated 16 April 1734, when he is urging Walpole to
write at greater length, he quotes Congreve and adds:

. . . why I, that am in the country could give you a full & true
account of half a dozen Intrigues, nay, I have an amour carried
on almost under my window between a boar and a sow,[2] people
of very good fashion, that come to an assignation, & squeak like
ten masquerades; I have a great mind to make you hear the

whole progress of the affair, together with the humours of Miss Pigsnies, the lady's Confidente [sic] . . .

He continues to urge Walpole to write:

> . . . for I find by your excuses you are brought to your dernière Chemise; & as you stand guilty. I adjudge you to be drawn to the place of execution, your chamber; where taking pen in hand, you shall write a letter as long as this, to him, who is nothing, when not
>
> your sincere friend
> & most devoted Servt
> T: Gray.

The expression 'you are brought to your dernière Chemise' is a reference to the French mistranslation of Cibber's play, *Love's Last Shift*, which had appeared in French as *La dernière chemise de l'amour*![3]

When, in the autumn of 1739, Walpole and Gray made their pilgrimage to the Grande Chartreuse, the former wrote at the time and more than once to West, now amusingly, now lyrically: 'Yesterday I was a shepherd of Dauphiné; to-day an Alpine savage; tomorrow a Carthusian monk; and Friday a Swiss Calvinist.'

West was so much struck with Walpole's description of the gorge of the Guier Mort that he wrote (15 October):

> Nay, there is a couple of verses which perhaps you did not take notice of . . . –
>
> Others all shagg'd with hanging woods,
> Obscur'd in pines, or lost in clouds.[4]

Gray wrote far less often at this time. It was only after reaching Turin, some six weeks later, that he described the ride up the gorge to the Grande Chartreuse:

> I do not remember to have gone ten paces without an exclamation . . . Not a precipice, not a torrent, not a cliff, but is pregnant

with religion and poetry. There are certain scenes that would
awe an atheist into belief . . . You have Death perpetually before
your eyes . . . If I do not mistake, I saw you . . . every now and
then at a distance among the trees . . . You seemed to call to me
from the other side of the precipice, but the noise of the river
below was so great that I really could not distinguish what you
said; it seemed to have a cadence like verse . . .[5]

The whole passage appears to have been carefully thought out and
composed. A few days later, on the 21st, he sent West an enthusiastic description of Genoa. At a service in the church of the Madonna
delle Vigne, he and Walpole had seen the Doge and the members
of the Senate.

During his stay in Italy he gave especial care to his letters to
West, entertaining him now with a description of the Falls of the
Anio, now by pretending facetiously that he has been back in
ancient Rome, dining at Pompey's villa: 'we made an admirable
meal. We had the dugs of a pregnant sow, a peacock, a dish of
thrushes, a noble scarus just fresh from the Tyrrhene, and some
conchylia of the Lake (Lake Albano) with garum sauce: For my
part I never eat better at Lucullus's table . . .'

No doubt; but he was more happily inspired when describing
scenery, especially that of the Grampians and the Lake District.
A feeling for wild scenery grew on him with the passage of time,
a symptom of the changing sensibility of the age. While staying at
Glamis Castle in September 1765, he was taken by Major Lyon
into the Highlands, and he sent Wharton a long account of the
tour. If in 1739 the peaks above the Mont Cenis had repelled
him[6] he was now enthralled by the peaks visible from Loch Tay:

. . . it was one of the most pleasing days I have pass'd these
many years . . . to the East is that monstrous creature of God,
She-hallian . . . spiring above the clouds. directly West (beyond
the end of the Lake) Beni-More (the Great Mountain) rises to
a most aweful height, & looks down on the tomb of Fingal . . .[7]

More studied, and more often quoted, is the *Journal* of his tour
of the Lakes, which he sent in instalments to Wharton between
30 September and 9 October 1769. Between Penrith and Keswick,
he 'pass'd through *Pendradock* & *Threlcot*[8] at the feet of *Saddle-*

back, whose furrow'd sides were gilt by the noon-day Sun, while its brow appear'd of a sad purple from the shadow of the clouds, as they sail'd slowly by it . . .'.

On his way to Borrowdale next day (3 October) he paused under Walla Crag to gaze across Derwentwater:

> . . . to the left the jaws of *Borodale*, with that turbulent Chaos of mountain behind mountain roll'd in confusion; beneath you, & stretching far away to the right, the shining purity of the *Lake*, just ruffled by the breeze enough to shew it is alive, reflecting rocks, woods, fields, & inverted tops of mountains, with the white buildings of *Keswick* . . . & *Skiddaw* for a background . . .[9]

His description of Lodore, of Gowder Crag (from which some rocks had recently fallen across the road) and of his entertainment by a farmer at Grange, has already been touched on. He and his guide returned in a leisurely way. To expand a passage already quoted above, Gray continues:

> In the evening walk'd alone down to the Lake by the side of *Crow-Park* after sunset & saw the solemn colouring of night draw on, the last gleam of sunshine fading away on the hill-tops, the deep serene of the waters, & the long shadows of the mountains thrown across them, till they nearly touch'd the hithermost shore. at distance heard the murmur of many waterfalls not audible in the day-time. wish'd for the Moon but, she was *dark to me & silent, hid in her vacant interlunar cave.*[10]

If the shift in Gray's attitude to mountain scenery was a symptom of a new sensibility, there is no evidence that he did much to promote it.[11]

To the feeling for mountains in general Gray contributed virtually nothing. In 1739 the sight of the Alps above the Mont Cenis and Susa had appalled him.

Others, in contrast to Gray and Madame de Sévigné, had pointed the way to their wonders, beginning with Windham's visit to the Montenvers and his book on *The Ice-Alps of Savoy* (1741). After about 1760 more and more Englishmen made the pilgrimage to Chamonix; French men and women went to the valley of Lauterbrunnen.[12] Gibbon, on his return to Lausanne in 1783, wrote that 'the fashion of viewing the mountains and Glaciers has opened us on all sides to the incursions of foreigners'.[13]

One sees an author in better focus by comparing him with other authors. Dr Ian Jack, who doubts whether Gray would have liked to be described as 'the greatest poet of [his] generation', considers his letters in juxtaposition with Keats's, and also with Gibbon's *Memoirs*. The contrasts are striking. Poetry is the very stuff of Keats's letters; poems come to him 'as naturally as Leaves to a tree'.[14] Gray, on the contrary, rarely writes about poetry. When he sends poems to Walpole, he speaks of them as 'things' which he has promised or which have taken him some time to complete. The truth is, as Dr Jack observes, that 'Gray did not devote his life to poetry; he devoted it to learning'.[15] And while Gibbon's learning enabled him to produce an historical masterpiece, Gray communicated only fragments of his own, in an occasional letter to Walpole or Nicholls.

The eighteenth century abounded in good letter writers, especially in France. The letters of such well-known figures as the Président de Brosses, Voltaire, J.-J. Rousseau and others – even of writers with no literary pretensions, such as Madame du Deffand – are often works of art in their own right.[16] In England, the letters of Lady Mary Wortley Montagu (*Selected Letters*, 1763) are among the wittiest of the age; those of Walpole are not only witty but amusing, tolerant and historically important. The most one can say of Gray's letters is that he has 'left us the best and fullest first-hand account we have of the life of a scholar during the most distinguished period in the history of our prose'.[17]

Unfortunately, it is a diffuse and depressing account. To be a good letter writer, one needs a certain zest for life, a keen interest in men and affairs; and preferably, though not necessarily, a genuine affection for one's correspondent, as Madame du Deffand felt for Horace Walpole. The small number of Gray's letters which have literary value are, with one or two exceptions, those which he wrote to West and, in later life, to Wharton. These have been palpably thought out and worked up, with a view to giving pleasure. It was not Gray's fault, it was his misfortune, that he lacked the warmth of feeling that is needed for friendship; and that, in consequence, life was burdensome to him. In all that really matters he was an introvert, who – as Bonstetten perceived –

suffered from a 'misère du coeur', an aridity of the affections; and this, more than anything else, probably explains why his correspondence is so disappointing.

CHAPTER 4

The Scholar[1]

Gray regarded himself primarily not as a writer but as a scholar. Reading very widely, making extracts from the Greek and Latin classics, and from medieval historians, studying Linnaeus and other naturalists – such were his principal occupations. Having begun to collect a library at Eton, he added to it steadily in later years. In Pembroke Hall it occupied the wall space in his living-room and overflowed into a room on the floor above.

There is no catalogue of his library. He bequeathed it to Mason, who bequeathed it to Stonhewer. From the latter it passed to a Mr Bright, of Skeffington Hall, and, after his death, a part of it was sold by auction; while some of the more interesting items were reserved and sold later.

At Eton, Gray had a copy of Pope's *Iliad*, and Pope's own copy of Dryden's Virgil in three volumes, with Pope's book-plate; Waller's poems; and Plutarch's *Lives*, with notes by Dacier.[2] But he had very many other books as a young man, certainly all of Virgil and Horace; most, if not all, of Ovid; and a number of French works, such as Honoré d'Urfé's *Astrée* and Madame de Sévigné's *Letters*. He appears to have learned Greek (and French) at Eton, and one discovers from his letters and notebooks of later years that he read all the Greek authors then available. He copied extracts from Sophocles, Thucydides, Xenophon and Isocrates. He read Aeschylus through twice. His copy of Euripides, in the 1694 edition by Joshua Barnes, Regius Professor of Greek at Cambridge, is marked to emphasise what interested him. He preferred Menander's comedies, as he supposed them to be – judging from Terence's adaptations – superior to what he read of Aristophanes. But of all Greek authors Plato was his favourite.

Of the great numbers, probably hundreds, of English, French and Italian books of which he must have had copies, it is difficult to discover the precise details. In an auctioneer's catalogue Austin

Dobson found that Gray had Clarendon's *History of the Great Rebellion*, four volumes, in-folio, and the 1730–8 edition of Milton in two volumes. A London edition of Boccaccio's *Decameron* was actually interleaved and annotated with indications of the sources and of the subsequent influence of the work:[3] all this, and much more, inserted merely for his own edification.

His library also contained the copies he had made, while staying in Florence, of musical scores of works by Zamparelli, Pergolesi (one of his favourites), Arrigoni and Galuppi, with a copy of 'the rules for the accompaniment'.

Fortunately, a guide to his library towards 1738 is provided by the 'Dialogue of Books'[4] which he sent in a letter to West and which is the wittiest of his compositions. While sitting in his room, he says, he was 'suddenly alarmed with a great hubbub of Tongues'. Madame de Sévigné complains that she is being jostled by Aristotle, who replies that he has as much right to be there as she. When she appeals for help to her cousin, Bussy-Rabutin, he also is in difficulties. 'Voici un Diable de Strabon qui me tue,' he complains; there is no one 'worth conversing with but Catullus.' Locke is annoyed because his neighbours are Ovid and the naturalist John Ray. Virgil can be heard reciting one of his own verses. Henry More, the neo-Platonist, asserts that no speculation is 'of greater moment' than that of the immortality of the soul. Euclid begins to define a point: 'Punctum est, cujus nulla est,' whereupon Boileau and Swift interrupt him 'to call for the banishment of Mathematicians'.[5]

This shows that, while still an undergraduate, Gray possessed a wide variety of standard works, most of which were of a scholarly kind; it shows too that he could turn his reading to good account when he wished. He could have produced equally happy effects from other sources. Setting aside the greater Greek authors, one might single out, as particularly entertaining, the major work of Athenaeus, which Gray himself speaks of studying. *The Deipnosophistai*,[6] which has already been alluded to, contains information about daily life among the Greeks and Romans, of a kind which no other writer furnishes. From this work alone Gray could have popularised material for a book of more general interest than is provided by any of the great classics.

It is supposed to have been written between AD 225 and 230, and it relates, in the form of a dialogue between the author and his friend Timocrates, the conversation at a dinner-party given by the distinguished Roman, Laurentius. The host and his guests, who included Plutarch, were interested in good food and, equally, in good books. They describe the eating habits of the Greeks and Romans, and quote passages from writers of whom we have no other knowledge.

There are many fascinating and informative things to be found in the *Deipnosophistai*. Gray, if he had taken the trouble, could have made of them and other details a book which eighteenth-century readers – and not simply classical scholars – would have welcomed. Similarly, his knowledge of the French chroniclers of the Middle Ages, whom he recommended Nicholls to study,[7] would have enabled him to write interesting works on, for example, medieval historiography, or, again, on the history of the Fourth Crusade, as described by Villehardouin, or of the Fifth, which was chronicled by Joinville.

With regard to Gray's classical scholarship, it is clear that most English poets have been Latinists. Milton and Arnold, perhaps Coleridge and Shelley, are among the few who have been imbued with the Greek spirit. Our seventeenth century produced no great Hellenists before the time of Joshua Barnes and Richard Bentley, who belong to the turn of the century. And these two had no important successors before Tyrwhitt and Porson some seventy years later. Many scholars and writers understood Greek; Gray, as already mentioned, seems to have read the Greek authors then in print. But what effect did they have? How far, if at all, was his mind permeated by the Greek spirit? And was his scholarship such that he can properly be called a Hellenist?

The two Pindaric odes have been cited in support of the view that he was a true Hellenist; but the Greek colouring in these poems is entirely superficial, as Goldsmith perceived. Pindar had spoken to the whole of the Greek world; Gray spoke only to a small minority,[8] and even they found him difficult to understand. He was not interested in studying the people, to use Goldsmith's expression.[9] He set great store by Plato, and rightly, though one looks in vain for any influence. The Greeks did not teach him to know himself or to moderate his passions. His real masters were Virgil and Horace; he remained always at heart a Latinist. Even so, the Latin influence was more linguistic than moral; he did not learn urbanity from Horace.

The statement, often repeated, that he 'was perhaps the most learned man of his age' cannot be substantiated. He had a fair knowledge of French, though it is doubtful if he could write it correctly; he did not *know* French as Gibbon and Walpole knew and wrote it. He made no attempt to write Italian. He was not, in short, a linguist of the stature of Tyrwhitt, who had an expert knowledge of several languages and who produced the first good editions of Chaucer and of Aristotle's *Poetics*.[10] Nor was he as careful a scholar as Malone. A number of Englishmen were more learned than he; and the same could be said of many Frenchmen, such as Voltaire and Diderot.

Gray's learning, as Dr Jack observes, 'did not result in a single published book, or edition, or pamphlet, or review'.[11]

CHAPTER 5

The Critic[1]

Gray seems to have read more books, ancient, medieval and modern, than any other Englishman of his time. His letters, and the conversations recorded by Norton Nicholls, contain a certain number of critical observations on books and authors, but they do not show him obsessed with an interest in poetry as do Keats's letters.

He never wrote a treatise on style, or on prosody, or an Art of Poetry, though he was well equipped to write on all three. He planned a *History of English Poetry*, but handed over the synopsis to Thomas Warton, who was later to produce the work.

Literary criticism as a genre did not appeal to him; thus he deprecated commentaries on Shakespeare. From his own scattered observations it is possible to disengage only two or three principles of criticism.

1   The Rules

Prior to about 1780 the weight of critical opinion, supported by the authority of Johnson and the enduring popularity of Boileau's *Art poétique*, favoured an observance of the neo-classic rules as laid down by Castelvetro and Scaligero. The poet should 'follow Reason' and 'imitate Nature'. This meant in practice that he could not do better than imitate Virgil and Horace, and observe, in tragedy and comedy, the unities of action, time and place; especially action and time. There was nothing arbitrary about this because, as Pope had written:

> Those Rules of old discover'd, not devis'd,
> Are Nature still, but Nature methodis'd . . .
> Learn hence for ancient rules a just esteem;
> To copy Nature is to copy them.

Gray would have agreed with Boileau, and Pope, that observance of the rules alone could not produce a good poem. There was also needed inspiration, or something akin to genius. In a letter of December 1751 to Mason, he denies 'that the excellencies of the French writers are measured by the verisimilitude, or the regularities of their Dramas *only* . . .; other beauties may indeed be heightened' by means of 'regularity', but 'of itself it hardly pleases at all'. Drama therefore should give pleasure. There was nothing original here. Molière had said it all better and more clearly. It was only in his admiration of the Norse poems and Ossian that Gray departed from Boileau's opinion of the 'merveilleux' (always excepting Greek Polytheism). But by the 1760s European opinion, influenced by Shakespeare's use of the supernatural as well as by Macpherson, was accepting this more liberal aesthetic.

In a letter to Beattie of 8 March 1771, Gray wrote: 'Rules are but chains, good for little, except when you can break through them.' This shift in attitude enabled him to admire Shakespeare unreservedly, whereas in 1752 he had admitted to Wharton that Shakespeare was 'more open to criticism of all kinds' than Racine. One 'kind' of criticism which can still be directed against Shakespeare is that he put scenes of violence, murder or maiming, on the stage. Who can view without a shudder the blinding of Kent or the smothering of Desdemona?[2] Aeschylus and Sophocles had been right in excluding acts of violence from the stage. The audience is aware of what is happening, but is spared the physical horror of seeing it.

Gray does not state what he thinks a modern tragedy should be like, in respect of subject, propriety or verisimilitude, but it seems that Voltaire's practice appeared to him the best. One suspects that he ranked Voltaire above Racine, because the former had put more action on the stage, though not action as horrifying as Shakespeare's. Gray's conception of comedy, however, is much clearer. 'Comedy', he said, 'contrived to be an odd sort of Farce . . . till the Chorus was dismissed, when Nature and Menander brought it into that beautiful form which we find in Terence'. This implies that he disliked Aristophanes and that, in his view, comedy should aim, not so much at making us laugh as at holding up the mirror to Nature. 'He thought the Comedies of Cibber excellent', according to Nicholls; but there is no record of what he thought of Molière, or Congreve, or of such contemporary comedies as

The Clandestine Marriage and *The Good-Natured Man*; which is strange.[3]

2   Relativity In Criticism

If Gray's views on drama lack precision, he seems definitely to have accepted the principle of relativity in literary criticism. On this question, the French critics, especially the abbé Dubos in the *Réflexions critiques sur la poésie et la peinture*, were forty years or more in advance of the English. It was only after about 1750 that Gray, Warton and Malone justified the view that medieval poets were far from being 'barbarous', as most people had supposed. Thus Gray was able to rehabilitate Chaucer, whose prosody no one seemed to have yet understood.[4] Even such Renaissance poets as Spenser had to be defended.

As a young man Gray had accepted unquestioningly the neo-classic creed. But after about 1750 he saw how far it was inadequate. It needed to be modified in the light of Longinus's treatise on the Sublime; and this opened a way to the belief that imagination transcended reason and even judgement. Gray's enthusiasm for Welsh poetry prepared him to welcome what may be called Macpherson's 'happy forgeries'. 'Our great Augustan Gray', as Smart had called him, had ceased to be an Augustan.

Apart from judgements based on general principles – such as the value of the 'Rules', or their uselessness; or again, the principle of relativity in criticism – Gray's criticial observations were impressionistic. He held that one's personal dislike of an author should not affect one's judgement of his writings – a sound principle which, however, he did not always follow.

He had the opportunity of steeping himself in Greek Literature, mainly after leaving Eton. Nicholls, in his *Reminiscences*, wrote: 'It is . . . truth to say that the minds of those are best cultivated who have cultivated them by Greek Literature; more rigorous writers have written in that language than in any other.' Gray devoted much time to the study of Plato, admiring 'his excellent Sense, sublime morality, and the perfect dramatic propriety of his dialogues'. He considered Thucydides 'the greatest of historians'. Isocrates filled him with enthusiasm.

But Gray's silences are sometimes as informative as his remarks.

There is no indication that he valued Homer as highly as Virgil, or that he set much store by the *Anthology*, or that he had any preference among the great Attic tragedians. From his praise of Menander, one guesses that Aristophanes' boisterous humour probably repelled him, while the exquisite poetry in the choruses – a poetry absent from Menander – was insufficient compensation. Pindar he tried to imitate – the sincerest form of flattery. He read and copied extracts from Athenaeus's *Deipnosophistai*, which has been alluded to in a previous chapter.

Whatever Gray may have said or thought about Greek literature, it is evident that he was more deeply influenced by Latin. Even his English verses are full of reminiscences of Virgil, Horace and others. While ranking Shakespeare above Virgil as a poet, he thought that Shakespeare was open to criticism; Virgil was 'faultless'. Among Latin prosateurs he especially admired Tacitus, who united 'the brilliant in wit' and concision 'with the truth and gravity of better times, and the deep reflection and good sense of the best moderns'.[5]

Gray's admiration of the Welsh poets has already been noted; but his principal contribution to criticism and to the history of poetry lay in the field of English literature. He was reputed to know more about our fourteenth-century poets than any other writer of his time, and he seems to have been amongst the first critics to appreciate Chaucer. It is true that he wrote at greater length on Lydgate, while recognising that Chaucer far surpassed him in 'a certain terrible greatness'. Gray's contemporaries were more familiar with Chaucer's bawdy tales than with the Knight's, the Squire's or the Prioress's; of *Troilus and Creiseyde* they probably knew nothing; and they regarded his prosody as crude. In their view he misplaced the tonic accent: hence they could not scan him. Gray saw the mistake and noted that a large part of Chaucer's vocabulary was taken from French or Anglo-Norman, and – what was more important – that it was pronounced and accented much as in French. Chaucer's decasyllabic couplet, the source of our heroic couplet, was imitated from the French decasyllabic verse which, until towards 1550, remained more popular in France than the alexandrine. In Chaucer the so-called mute e's inside the verse were to be sounded before a consonant, as in French, but need not be sounded at the end of a line, though they could be, as in singing today. Finally, whereas in the eighteenth century and today the accent in English is pushed forward, in Chaucer's time words were accented, as in French, on the last syllable; and this applied to words of Saxon as well as of French origin.

As soon as these principles were grasped, it was seen that Chaucer was a master of versification. The first few lines of the Prologue to the *Canterbury Tales*, which had appeared grossly inaccurate to Urry and other students, were now seen to scan perfectly:

> Whan that Aprille with his shoures soot(e)
> The droght(e) of March(e) hath perced to the root(e),
> And bathed ev(e)rich veyn(e) in swich licour
> Of whose vertu engendred is the flour . . .

Thus 'Aprille', 'licour' and 'vertu' are all accented on the second syllable, and the e-mutes followed by a consonant, except 'h', are sounded as unaccented syllables. The metre is generally iambic, although the first foot is a trochee.

Spenser had appealed to Gray while he was still a young man, and he stated, amusingly, that the *Faerie Queene* should be judged as a 'Gothic' poem, and not as a classical one. According to Nicholls, he 'placed *Shakespeare* high above all poets of all countries & all ages; & said that the justest idea of the historical characters he treated might be taken from his plays'. Shakespeare had been well inspired, he thought, in inventing words; but he admitted to Walpole that 'the affectation of imitating Shakespeare may doubtless be carried too far'. His own imitation of Shakespeare's language in 'Agrippina' had certainly gone too far. Donne offended his taste and the 'Metaphysicals' generally meant nothing to him. For Milton, however, his admiration was unbounded. He disliked blank verse, but not Milton's. The influence on Gray of this last of the Renaissance poets cannot be gauged simply from his many borrowings. For instance, Gray's feeling for the 'romantic' in mountain scenery (so often quoted from his letter to West describing the visit to the Grande Chartreuse)[5] has been attributed to a new attitude to Nature; but it seems more likely to have arisen from the Miltonic cosmogony taken over from Galileo and involving the conception of infinite space. As long as time and space were limited, as they had been by orthodox theology, imagination was fettered: the scientific revolution set it free to conceive the sublime. It was the presence of the sublime that Gray appears to have felt when riding up the gorge of the Guier Mort. Hence his appreciation of mountain scenery was probably of literary origin and not original.

It has been argued that appreciation of mountain scenery, which developed slowly in the eighteenth century, was due more often to painters than to poets, and notably to Salvator Rosa. His was the name which immediately occurred to Walpole on that visit to the Grande Chartreuse. Whether the feeling was of literary or pictorial origin, it can scarcely have been intuitive.

Of the three great figures evoked on the 'Progress of Poesy', Dryden's immediately follows Milton's. Writing to Beattie in October 1765, Gray adds in a postscript: 'Remember Dryden & be blind to all his faults.' Gray regarded himself as having taken up the mantle left by Milton and Dryden.

This implied that he thought less highly of Pope. He did, however, admire him both as man and poet. To quote Nicholls again: '. . . when he heard [Pope's translation of the *Iliad*] criticised as wanting the simplicity of the original . . and not giving a just idea of the poet's style & manner, he always said "there would never be another translation of the same poem equal to it".' Gray was making a risky forecast and, moreover, he was not answering the criticisms.

His opinions of contemporary writers are uneven and capricious. He thought little of the poets. Warton and Collins 'deserve to last two years, but will not'. Nicholls recalls that he 'was with him at Malvern when he read "The Deserted Village" . . . he exclaimed: "That man is a poet." ' Ten years earlier, in a letter to Wharton about Macpherson, we read: 'in short this Man is the very Demon of Poetry, or he has lighted on a treasure hid for ages'. Richardson's *Clarissa* met with his approval, as did the character-drawing in Fielding's *Joseph Andrews*, and the 'good fun' in *Tristram Shandy*. Sterne's sermons 'are the style I think most proper for the Pulpit, & shew a very strong imagination & a sensible heart'. No such indulgence was extended to Samuel Johnson; Gray 'disapproved his style, & thought it turgid & vicious'. (Johnson, in his *Life of Gray*, was to be more fair and judicious.) David Hume fared even worse at Gray's hands, probably because he was 'an enemy to religion'. 'A pernicious writer . . . [he] had continued all his days an infant, but one that has . . . been taught to read & write.'

Gray was more indulgent to his personal friends; but he is amusing when he condescends to Walpole, an original author and witty letter writer. There is some ground for Roger Martin's severity here in his *Essai sur Thomas Gray*. Only the great writers of the past deserved his esteem: 'Le jeu de son orgueil, de sa défiance, de son esprit critique lui interdit tout rapport avec le monde littéraire du jour'. This implies that Gray held aloof from other literary critics of the time; but he advised his friends on their writings, and devoted much time to correcting them, if always on the assumption that he was the supreme arbiter.

Gray's comments on French and Italian writers are of much the same order. He advised Nicholls to read the French chroniclers of the Middle Ages, Villehardouin, Joinville and Froissart, whose work 'is a favourite book of mine'. On the other hand, he makes no mention of the *Chansons de geste*, or of Thomas, or Béroul, or Chrétien de Troyes. The only French poets he admired were La Fontaine and Gresset; and Racine in *Britannicus*. He had seen a production of *Phèdre* which, however, had not greatly impressed him. There is no indication that he had read Descartes, or Pascal, or Molière, or La Rochefoucauld. He admired La Bruyère, perhaps because La Bruyère had adapted the *Characters* of Theophrastus. Like Walpole and other young men, he eagerly read the instalments of Marivaux's *Vie de Marianne* as they appeared. It was his enduring taste for Marivaux and the younger Crébillon which made it difficult for him in later years to appreciate J.-J. Rousseau. Oddly enough, he never mentions Marivaux's journals of moral observation, which had won great popularity in England; or any of the brilliant comedies, which are his surest title to fame. The abbé Prévost had been a guest, with Walpole and Gray, at a dinner in Paris, yet Gray nowhere speaks of *Manon Lescaut*. He knew about *Cleveland*, though he had probably not read it. In June 1748 he tells Wharton that he has seen a new comedy from Paris, Gresset's *Le Mechant*, one of the best dramas I ever met with'. Gresset's *Ver-Vert* pleased him 'extremely', says Nicholls; while we know from a letter to Wharton that he admired the 'Ode au Roi', and from Mason that the inspiration for the 'Vicissitude' ode came from the 'Epître à ma soeur'. Gresset was only a minor figure. The literary giants provoked Gray more often to outbursts of indignation.

Nicholls, dutifully recalling what he had been told, says that

Gray's aversion to the moral character of Voltaire 'did not prevent his paying the full tribute of admiration due to his Genius.' Did Gray know that Voltaire, who could be mean and spiteful on occasion, had treated Marivaux outrageously and Rousseau with gratuitous unkindness? There is no evidence that he was aware of this. It was apparently Voltaire's mockery of any ardent religious faith that seemed to him immoral. 'Atheism is a vile dish', he wrote to Walpole in March, 1771; '. . . as to the Soul, perhaps they have none on the Continent; but I do think we have such things in England.' Gray had forgotten that Voltaire was not an atheist; that Walpole himself had told him how a Parisian infidel had reproached Voltaire for being a deist. (Voltaire did in fact feel an intellectual need for God to account for the world and for man, and to preside inscrutably over Providence; there was, after that, no further need of Him.) As to the works of that 'inexhaustible, eternal, entertaining Scribbler', Gray 'placed his tragedies next in rank to those of Shakespeare', Nicholls recalled. Gray had spoken to Walpole of *Micromégas* when it appeared, but he nowhere mentions *Zadig or Candide*.

Jean-Jacques Rousseau, who had broken noisily with the Philosophes, those 'ardent missionaries of atheism and most imperious dogmatists' (as he called them), was much admired in England towards 1760, for the paradoxes of his character and the brilliance of his style – or rather styles, for he had one style in the *Contrat social* and another in the *Nouvelle Héloïse*. It was unfortunate that Gray waded through the six volumes of the *Héloïse* when he was confined to Mason's house by a bad cold. The composition he thought 'absurd and improbable. If all the characters had been hanged at the end of Vol. 3, no one would have cared'. According to Nicholls, he regarded the characters as 'unnatural, & vicious, & the tendency immoral'. The 'tendency' of the *Confessions*, a later work, could be considered immoral, but not the tendency of the *Héloïse*. To our modern taste the novel is far too diffuse; no one today reads it through; but it is difficult to be insensitive to the thought, the feeling and the style of certain passages, such as the so-called 'Promenade sur le lac' in Volume IV, Letter 17. The admiration it inspired in England, as in France, went on increasing into the following century. It was on account of this passage that Shelley and Byron made the pilgrimage to Meillerie and Clarens.[6]

Gray may have read more Italian poets than he mentions in his letters. In March 1737 he wrote to tell West that he was learning Italian 'like any dragon, and in two months am got through the 16th book of Tasso'. There is another reference to the *Gerusalemme liberata* in his appreciation of *Paradise Lost*. He revered Dante, and was a 'zealous admirer of Petrarca', Nicholls recalled. He must have heard of Metastasio,[7] perhaps a greater poet than any of the eighteenth-century Frenchmen; yet he nowhere mentions him; nor does he seem to have read any of the Italian prose-writers of the age, except Algarotti—not even Baretti, who lived for some time in London.

Gray made no claim to be a literary critic. His observations are, for the most part, those of a cultured dilettante. On three matters only he made definite contributions to criticism. Dryden and Dubos, extending the sense of Horace's 'Ut pictura poesis . . .' beyond Horace's intention, associated poetry with painting. Gray associated it more often with music. Under the heading 'Metrum' in the Commonplace Book he made a careful study of English versification from the fourteenth century onwards. In the age of Chaucer rhyming was much easier than it later became, because 'words of two or three syllables', derived from a foreign language, 'did still retain their original accent' and that accent, derived mostly from the French, fell on the last syllable. It now falls generally on the first, with the result that, except, for example, in humorous verse in nine-syllable lines, it is difficult to rhyme more than one syllable.[8]

Puttenham had wished to fix the caesura after the fourth syllable in a decasyllabic verse; but Milton had varied its position at will, and had also used verses of seven and eight syllables, and mixed trochees and spondees with iambs.[9] Gray himself followed this practice in the Elegy and still more in the Pindaric odes.

The synopsis he drew up for a projected *History of English Poetry* gives him a title to a place in the history of criticism. It was briefly as follows:

Part I   School of Provence, which arose about AD 1100. This inspired the first French School, and the first Italian School which attained perfection in Dante, Petrarch and Boccaccio.

Part II   Chaucer, who introduced the manner of the Provençaux, improved by the Italians.

Part III   A second Italian School, represented by Ariosto (and later by Tasso). Surrey and Wyatt were the first to find inspiration here; Spenser at a later time.

Part IV   A third Italian School, marked by a taste for *concetti* (conceits). This affected Donne and Crashaw, and persisted to some extent in Cowley.

Part V   A second School of France, which triumphed at the Restoration in Waller and Dryden, and persisted in Addison, Prior and Pope.

This was the first serious attempt to trace the genealogy of English verse. Gray somewhat underestimated the French influence; he also failed to see that in the sixteenth century French poetry often served as an intermediary for Italian. By not writing a book on the subject, he missed a great opportunity. Here, as on other occasions, he showed his indolent character.

On the other hand, his practice in versification is more important than all his theories, because it almost certainly affected the Romantic poets. In the first odes, the metre is fairly regularly iambic, with an occasional trochee in the first foot, especially in the 'Ode to Adversity'. The Elegy opened on a regular iambic measure, and this partly accounted for its popularity: readers of Pope and Johnson were not accustomed to much else. However, as the poem progressed, Gray once at least introduced a spondee in 'Chill Penury/ . . .', while lines 73, 91, 92, 97 and others begin with trochees. 'A Long Story' contains other irregularities, including the use of rich rhymes, which are not always suitable in serious verse.

In 'The Progress of Poesy' he went further, to avoid monotony, by varying the length of the lines and the arrangement of the rhymes, and also by the frequent use of dactyls, as in line 43:

Labour and / Penury / the racks / of Pain.

'The Bard' contains still greater variety. One could scan the first line in two ways: first by making the first foot a monosyllable, followed by three iambs:

Ru / in seize / thee ruth / less King /

but, better, by scanning it as three trochees followed by an accented monosyllable:

Rūı̆n / seīze thĕe / rūthlĕss / Kīng.[10]

Line 57,

Shē-Wōlf / ōf France / wı̆th ŭn / rĕlēn / tı̆ng fāngs,

opens with a spondee, followed by four iambs; but trochees frequently occur in the first foot of a line, and the best-known line is also the most irregular,

Yōuth ŏn thĕ / prōw ănd / Plēasŭre ăt / thĕ hēlm,

involving a dactyl, a trochee, a dactyl and an iamb.

In the seven-syllable verses of 'The Fatal Sisters' trochees predominate, with dactyls and iambs, varying the metre. The octosyllabic metre of 'The Descent of Odin' occasions a more frequent use of iambic feet, varied, however, with trochees and dactyls.

It is clear from this analysis that Gray broke with the regular decasyllabic rhymed couplet, as practised by Pope, Johnson and Goldsmith, and prepared the way for later poets, more by his experiments in prosody than by the subjects and tone of his verse.

CHAPTER 6

The Student of Natural History[1]

Gray seems to have had no knowledge of natural history when he was young or even before the age of thirty-six. City-bred, he was not interested in watching wild birds and animals. The landscape of Stoke Poges he saw through the eyes of Virgil; the insects which he speaks of, without however mentioning a single species, in the 'Ode on the Spring', were suggested by Matthew Green. All this was very bookish, as were all his poems. No one with any knowledge of the country would have described an owl as 'moping' at nightfall.

But it is significant that on his return from Durham in the autumn of 1753 he wrote to Wharton describing in some detail the scenery he had passed through; the ripening grapes which he had seen near Darlington; and various trees which he names. In a PS he speaks of the song of the 'Wood-Lark, & the Robin'. All this is a novelty in Gray's correspondence, and it points to the conclusion that, during his first visit to Durham, Dr Wharton had taught him the names of trees and flowers, and shown him how much of interest he could find in observing the sights and sounds of the countryside. After this, and increasingly in later years, his letters to Wharton are full of observations about flowers and crops, the first appearance of migrating birds, the dates of their departure. From a letter of 21 July 1759, when Gray was staying in Wharton's former lodgings in Southampton Row, it is clear that they were exchanging notes on the temperature in certain months; and because, in that July, Gray was not in a country place, he sent Wharton a detailed list of the various flowers, wild or cultivated, which he had observed at Stoke in 1754; with the dates of their blooming and their 'going off'. Thus, on 31 January 1761 Gray wrote to Wharton: 'I send you a Swedish & English Calendar. the first column is by Berger, a Disciple of Linnaeus; the 2nd by Mr Stillingfleet, the 3d . . . by me. you are to observe how the Spring advances in the North, & whether Old Park most resembles Upsal or Stratton.'[2]

It may have been in 1762, when he spent the late summer and autumn at Old Park, that he first made a collection of butterflies and other insects; he probably botanised, too. The Wharton children were still very young at this time; Mary, the eldest, was about fourteen, and Deborah, who was to be Gray's special favourite, about seven. He saw them all again in 1765. On this occasion he stayed at Old Park from about 12 June to 19 August. Deborah was then breeding butterflies, and Gray speaks of her and of her sister Betty tending 'their chrysalises'.[3] But Deborah was even more interested in botany, and made a very fine *hortus siccus*, which was preserved until about 1915 in the Durham University Museum.[4] During Gray's visit to the Whartons in 1765 he and his host went twice to Hartlepool to study the sea-birds, fishes and marine plants. By encouraging these interests in Gray at a time when poetic inspiration had deserted him, Wharton proved a real benefactor.

Towards 1760 Gray had acquired a copy of the tenth edition of Linnaeus's *Systema Naturae* (1758) in three volumes. Gray had these interleaved, and filled most of the blank pages with the relevant information which he had collected on his own account. In Volume I, which dealt with mammals, amphibians, birds and fishes, his personal observations, mostly in Latin, were naturally not those of a specialist. He padded them out by giving the names of various creatures in twenty-one different languages, on occasion. For example, he described the habits and character of the domestic cat in seventeen Latin words, and its name in ten foreign languages.[5] For Part 2 of Volume I, which treats of insects, Gray was better informed. He had collected a considerable number and studied their life-cycles, and he now described them and made drawings of them. This occupation he justified by quoting Aristotle, who had written: 'Wherefore one ought not to feel a childish dislike at inspecting the lowest animals, for in every object of nature dwells something marvellous.' Volume II of the *Systema* was devoted to plants. Gray may have known as much about botany as about insects, but his notes are fewer.[6]

These interests then, rather than literary studies, were his principal occupation in later years. 'The favourite study of Mr Gray for the last ten years of his life was Natural History . . . It led him more frequently out into the fields and, by making his life less sedentary, improved the general course of his health and spirits' –

so wrote Mason in 1775. If these walks did not improve his health, they at least obviated a more rapid deterioration. He could have quoted Dryden to himself:

> Better to hunt in fields for health unbought
> Than fee the doctor for a nauseous draught:
> The wise for cure on exercise depend;
> God never made his work for man to mend.

A picture of Mr Gray, armed with a net and collecting-bottle, stalking butterflies on Coe Fen or Sheep's Green, would convey a more pleasing picture of his activities in the 1760s than the portrait made after his death by Benjamin Wilson, from earlier drawings, which represents a stout and rather florid man in middle age. If he felt too indolent to write, he proved himself a fairly industrious and competent draughtsman. It seems that he had brought back from his expeditions a large number of insects and shellfish; possibly even of dead birds. It has been observed that he drew the heads of 24 birds; made 172 pictures of insects and 28 of molluscs – all in pen and ink.[7] The birds do not appear sufficiently differentiated: it would be difficult to identify them all, if they were not named. The pictures of insects, on the other hand, are more accurately drawn.

Here again, as in his knowledge of Greek writers and daily life in ancient Greece, one regrets that the reading public never profited from his labours. He might have written, on the natural history of the Cambridge countryside, a book perhaps as interesting as White's *Natural History of Selborne*.

But it would have been the work of an observant amateur, not a real naturalist. He was obviously not a Linnaeus, or a Willoughby or a Pennant. His work was simply descriptive; beyond this he did not go far, either in botany or entomology. Wild animals abounded in the country round Cambridge, and probably north of Stoke: foxes, badgers, hares, stoats and weasels, and others; yet there is no sign that he observed them or took any interest in them – perhaps because they did not smell nice.[8] And it seems strange that his visits to the Derbyshire Peaks, to the Highlands and Lake District should have aroused no curiosity as to their geological or other physical features. In short, his interest in science amounted to little more than that of a tepid dilettante.

CHAPTER 7

Conclusion: The Man and the Writer

Gray had enjoyed few opportunities of real happiness after his schooldays at Eton and his European tour. Settling in Cambridge in 1741, he sank into a state of what he called 'leucocholy', alternating with melancholy. He escaped from this for a few months at a time, in later life, by visiting his friend Wharton near Durham, and by exploring various parts of the country. But he had always in due course to return to 'dirty, ugly' Cambridge, and live through the long, slow months. 'To be occupied is to be happy',[1] he told a friend, and often repeated the maxim in other words. His harpsichord, and later a piano-forte, afforded an occupation for an hour or two in the evening; but his principal escape from ennui lay in reading for pleasure. He may not have been, as one admirer declared, the most learned man in Europe, but he certainly amassed an exceptional amount of knowledge, mostly literary and historical. The collecting of it acted, according to Edmund Gosse, as a sort of narcotic.

Constitutionally indolent, he made no attempt to correct the fault. Possessed at an early age of an independent income, he was under no compulsion to adopt a profession. Had he been penniless, like Johnson and Goldsmith, he would have been compelled to work, probably as a journalist, and this might have made him happier.[2]

A delicate child, he avoided playing outdoor games, which would have strengthened his system and improved his digestion. When staying at Burnham in August 1736 with his aunt and her husband, Jonathan Rogers, he complained to Walpole that his uncle's dogs 'take up every chair in the house . . . he holds me mighty cheap I perceive for walking, when I should ride, & reading, when I should hunt'. But there was something to be said for Rogers's criticism. Gray could have learned to ride, which is not difficult. In 1739 when he visited the Grande Chartreuse,

someone must have hoisted him onto a mule. Even as a walker he
was indolent: Christopher Smart depicted him as moving along
with short, mincing steps.

He lived a virtuous life in the sense that he committed no sins of
the flesh. Norton Nicholls relates that Gray regarded genius and
knowledge as 'of little account compared with *virtue*', which was
'the exercise of right reason'. 'I remember in the early part of my
acquaintance with him saying that some person was a "clever
man" – he cut me short & said "Tell me if he is good for anything" '.
True virtue includes 'spiritual sweetness', in Pater's words. Gray's
dislike of Dr Long, and antipathy to the Duke of Newcastle, neither
of whom had done him harm, were so extravagant as to appear
psychopathic. The contemptuous, even salacious, letters which he
wrote on occasion to Mason are disturbing. He was neither
charitable nor modest. It appears to have been not simply personal
dignity, but wounded pride, that explains why he refused Walpole's
offer of reconciliation in 1741; and again why, in the autumn of
1745, Walpole found it so difficult to bring him round. The
reputation he acquired as a poet, after 1750, did little to modify
this self-importance – on the contrary. From Durham, on the
occasion of the first visit, he wrote to James Brown, the senior
Fellow of Pembroke, giving orders as to a servant. There is no
evidence that the prestige he enjoyed rested on anything but his
poems, and the attitude of superiority he affected.

Walpole admitted that in conversation Gray was 'the worst
company in the world'. Dining at the Thrales on 28 March 1775,
Boswell said: 'I understand [Gray] was reserved, and might appear
dull in company.' Johnson: 'Sir, he was dull in company, dull in
his closet, dull every where. He was dull in a new way, and that
made many people think him GREAT.'[3]

There was some truth in this. One imagines that at High
Table[4] and in the Fellows' Parlour his reserved attitude inspired
awe. In short, his reputation was such by 1762, that, when Norton
Nicholls was introduced to him in June of that year, Nicholls
wrote to Temple: 'That I should be acquainted with one of the
greatest men who ever existed in the World! That he should (as
it is probable he may) visit me in my Room!' Temple received a
similar impression – the exact opposite to Walpole's. Gray was for
him 'the best-bred man and the most agreeable companion in the
world'. Was there an element of the snobbish lion-hunter in these

reports? Taking all the evidence into account, one concludes that he was diffident and tongue-tied in company and even with men of his own age, but amiable and talkative with admiring youngsters.

His relations with Johnson, whom he never met, throw his character into clearer relief. The two men instinctively disliked each other. They had this in common, that both were physically handicapped from childhood, and both had a neurotic fear of death. In other respects they were poles apart: Johnson massive in body, dirty in person, careless in the matter of clothes, coarse in eating habits, overbearing in argument; but also a very sociable or, as he said, 'clubbable' man; Gray, small and delicate in body, cleanly in his habits, the dandy of Pembroke Hall; reserved in conversation. Writing to West from Florence in April 1741, he confessed to 'a want of love for general society, indeed! an inability to it'. He and Johnson were divided also by their theories of literature, and by their practice. Gray thought Johnson's style 'turgid and vicious'. Johnson admired the Elegy, but not the Pindaric odes. Whatever the verdict on them today, they undoubtedly broke with the old versification; and Johnson, a zealous defender of tradition, was bound to treat them as dangerous. This does not mean that in his *Life of Gray* he is as unjust as might be supposed.

In the final count, one cannot but feel compassion for the man Thomas Gray. Roger Martin ascribed his difficult character, and even the nature of his work and the slenderness of his output, to heredity. The son of a man subject to periodical fits of insanity and senseless violence could hardly have been normal. The very privileges he enjoyed throughout life worked, paradoxically, to his disadvantage. Was it good for this son of a bourgeois to be educated with gentlemen like West and Walpole? One wonders whether their society did not give him an unconscious sense of his disadvantages, for which he sought compensation by assuming an air of superiority, and in the end, coming to believe in it. He had never, as far as one can judge, been forced to do anything for himself; he had never had to face the battle of life. In Cambridge, the college servants prepared his meals and waited on him. His young cousin, the daughter of the postmistress, made his ruffles and laundered his linen. He was frequently entertained by Walpole, Chute and other gentlemen, especially by Wharton; and never apparently returned their hospitality. (He probably gave gratuities to the servants.) His personal income rose, at intervals, until by

1768 he must have been in receipt of at least £1000 a year, equivalent in purchasing power to very many times that figure in the currency of today. He had no one to care for or to worry about but himself; and, consequently, was full of worry. Subject as he was to attacks of gout, fits of dizziness and severe headaches, he developed the habit of recording his symptoms, and came near to becoming a professional hypochondriac.

As a linguist Gray had an excellent knowledge of Latin and of Latin literature. He was regarded, justly or unjustly, as having known Greek better than any other Cambridge scholar in the period between Bentley and Porson. At Eton he had learned enough French to read the *Astrée* and other seventeenth-century works; he improved his knowledge in later years, read many French books as they appeared, and frequently used French expressions in his letters. But he never tried to write in French, as Gibbon did, with any success; for Gibbon, French was 'a second native language'.[5] Gray neither knew nor spoke French with the perfect mastery and fluency of Walpole; for Walpole was one of the only three foreigners whom Sainte-Beuve names as having written and spoken French like a native.[6] Gray learned Italian from Signor Piazza at Cambridge. He worked hard at this language and, Nicholls tells us, greatly admired Dante, Petrarch and Tasso. Nicholls does not mention Boccaccio or other Italian writers. Gray corresponded with Algarotti, but in English. Of modern languages, in short, he knew all that was usual at that time, namely French and some Italian. Today a knowledge of German may be considered of more practical, if less cultural advantage. It is piquant in this matter to notice that it was probably Gibbon's ignorance of German which prevented his writing that History of the Swiss Confederation of which he had composed the Introduction.[7]

His most evident failing was a deficiency of heart. He appears to have felt no love for any one person after the death of West, and of Mrs Gray (which latter he felt less keenly), except possibly Dr Wharton and his family. Even before his mother's death, he had begun to suffer a desiccation of the spirit. Bonstetten put his finger on this moral malady, this 'misère du coeur', which was due, he supposed, to Gray's never having been in love. It was certainly part of the truth, though the trouble lay deeper. His cold-blooded account of the trial of the Scottish Lords contrasts strikingly with

Walpole's more generous attitude. Cole was shocked, in 1770, by his indifference to the indecency of Dr Long's burial. It throws light on this aspect of Gray's character to record that he appears to have felt no obligation to society, or to his fellow men in general. Pembroke Hall and its servants might have existed for his sole convenience. It is difficult for a reader of his letters to avoid comparing them with those of his lifelong benefactor, Horace Walpole. To Walpole much certainly had been given by nature; but how much did he give in return! Unfailing generosity, and wit, and good humour; untiring activity in politics, in literature, in versatile accomplishments, in encouragement to Gray. Gray's attitude is hardly expressed by fancying that it was simply one of detachment. His intense dislike of persons who had done him no injury, as, for example, the Duke of Newcastle – a man of exemplary personal character[8] – has already been mentioned. His vitriolic attacks on Lord Sandwich and Lord Holland appear symptomatic of some mental, as well as moral, disorder.

Finally, it does not seem that he obtained much, if any, comfort from religion. Most of his friends were in holy orders; some were country parsons. When staying with Mason in York, he attended service in the Minster, but the motive was probably social. Walpole can be believed when he states that Gray was a deist – like so many Anglicans of his time. But there were widely differing varieties of deism. Voltaire's sort was intellectual, J.-J. Rousseau's intuitive, probably pantheistic. One can hardly picture Gray, even among the Lakeland mountains, raising his arms to heaven and murmuring 'O grand Être! O grand Être!' as Rousseau did. It is curious to read that his friend Bonfoy's mother had 'taught him to pray',[9] as though he had not previously been in the habit of praying, even in compulsory chapel at Peterhouse! On the other hand, as Nicholls recorded, 'he had an aversion to Hume' because 'he thought him irreligious, that is, *an enemy to religion*; which he never pardoned in any one, because he said it was taking away the best consolation of man without substituting any thing of equal value in its place'.[10] One would like to suppose that religion consoled him in the end. When he knew he was dying, he directed James Brown's attention to the place where he kept his will, but it does not appear that he asked for the sacrament.

Sainte-Beuve held that knowledge of a writer's life gives the key to an understanding of his work: 'Je dirais volontiers: "Tel l'homme, telle l'oeuvre." ' This may not always be the case, but it is certainly true of Gray. His work is limited and indecisive, like his life. Particularly instructive in this matter is the comparison which Dr Ian Jack draws between Gray and Gibbon. Gibbon could look back on his writings and feel that he had used his talents to advantage; he could review his life, and feel that it was complete. 'I must acknowledge', he wrote, 'that I have drawn a high prize in the lottery of life'.[11] This judgement was hardly fair to himself. He had won the prize by devotion to literature, by hard work, and the steady pursuit of a great enterprise. Gray could not have written so contentedly about himself, or his achievement.

An appraisal in detail of his published work has been attempted above. A general review seems now appropriate.

A competent Latinist, he expressed his feelings more easily in Latin verse than in English. The last section of the 'De Principiis Cogitandi' expresses a more natural and more moving tribute to West than does his sonnet. The habit of writing Latin prose and verse persisted into the last decade of his life, when, as Mason admitted, his Latin was growing a little rusty.

With regard to his poems in English, he confessed to being incapable of writing a long poem. Thus he told Nicholls 'that he had been used to write only Lyric poetry in which the poems being short, he had accustomed himself, & was able to polish every part; that this having become a habit, he could not write otherwise'.[12] That he had no talent for didactic or philosophical verse is evident from 'The Alliance of Education and Government', which is marred by the worst kind of extravagant language, and was left unfinished. He confessed, justly, that he found it hard to finish more than a short poem. The Elegy appears to have taken four or five years to complete; 'The Bard' remained unfinished until Parry's recital on the harp rekindled the spark of inspiration. Gray had the gift, however, of identifying himself with his subject. When asked how he had composed 'The Bard', he said: 'Why, I felt myself the bard.' He likewise seems to have identified himself with the 'Fatal Sisters' and with 'Odin'.

As so often stated, nearly all his poetry, except perhaps the stanzas to Bentley, is derivative. Admittedly, this was very much in the manner of the age, which did not expect novelty. (It is significant that Christopher Smart's two best poems, the 'Song to David' and the 'Jubilate Agno', so entirely original, have been acclaimed only in recent years.) On the other hand, Gray was an innovator in prosody, notably in the Pindaric odes. Yet for most readers, Gray has been the poet of the Elegy. Tennyson would rather have written the Elegy than the whole of Wordsworth.[13] Bagehot thought it probably the most admired of his pieces, for example by such critics as Hazlitt, Leigh Hunt and Gosse. For Gosse, it was 'unquestionable that the *Churchyard Elegy* stands first' among his poems. Palgrave, who included most of Gray's English verses in *The Golden Treasury*, went further. He declared that the Elegy was the noblest poem in the language; which means that he thought it nobler than Wordsworth's 'Lines written above Tintern Abbey' or Keats's 'Ode on a Grecian Urn'. It may well have been, in the past, more popular; but this was because the generality of readers prefer the conventional and sentimental to anything original and thoughtful.

Some of Gray's most distinguished contemporaries considered the Pindaric odes truly sublime. Boswell was enraptured by them. Discussing Gray with Goldsmith, he said: 'Well, I admire Gray prodigiously. I have read his odes till I was almost mad.' Goldsmith replied: 'They are terribly obscure. We must be historians and learned men before we can understand them.' Johnson was more severe: 'Sir, I do not think Gray a superior sort of person. He has not a bold imagination, nor much command of words. The obscurity in which he has involved himself will not make us think him sublime.'[14] Newman, a century later, refers to 'The Bard' as 'exalted and splendid'. To Coleridge the Pindaric odes seemed frigid; he spoke contemptuously of Gray to Hazlitt. Even for Hazlitt, who was more indulgent, most of Gray's poems were 'too scholastic and elaborate . . . too visibly the result of laborious and anxious study'.[15] Wordsworth's criticism of Gray's poetic diction has already been discussed.

The schoolboy practice of inserting in his Latin poems many choice expressions from the Latin classics seems to have led him to compose English poems in the same way. He inserted at frequent intervals fine phrases, even standard quotations, from all manner of poets, English and foreign, precisely as if they were his own. He clearly regarded this practice as not only legitimate, but normal.

Gray had a gift for paraphrasing universally accepted truths in memorable form, usually in couplets. It was this ability, rather than any original thought – notably in the Elegy – which brought him the fame he enjoyed. Unhappily, many of these expressions are imitations. He was actually handicapped by the sheer bulk of his specialised knowledge. He had read and memorised so much poetry that it came naturally into his compositions without his always realising that the ideas, and often the forms, were not his.

He had aimed, he said, at 'extreme conciseness of expression' in lyric poetry, while confessing that he 'never could attain' it. For he did not put into practice what Pater calls 'the art of omission'.[16] The Elegy is 'loaded with epithets', to use Goldsmith's expression. A great many could, with advantage, have been dispensed with. To take only one stanza:

> For who to dumb Forgetfulness a prey,
> This pleasing anxious being e'er resigned,
> Left the warm precincts of the chearful day,
> Nor cast one longing ling'ring look behind?

Here there is a surfeit of adjectives. Lord Lytton observed that 'ornament is less the accessory grace than the essential merit of [Gray's] designs'. But, as Walter Pater notes, 'the true artist . . . will remember that, as the very word ornament indicates what is in itself non-essential, so the "one beauty" of all literary style is of its very essence, and independent . . . of all removable decoration'. This was also Arnold's view. He gave importance to subject matter rather than to ornate asides and fanciful expressions. In this respect the Elegy is so full of ornamental passages that, as Pater says, they act as a narcotic. The stanzas beginning

> Can storied urn or animated bust
> Back to its mansion call the fleeting breath? . . .

and

> Full many a gem of purest ray serene
> The dark unfathom'd caves of ocean bear . . .

are largely decorative and divert the reader's mind from the essential thought.

No great loss or notable event inspired in Gray verses as simple as Wordsworth's 'Lucy' poems, or Arnold's 'Marguerite' series. He unfortunately lacked the advantage of having any such lyrical models. In prose, he had not the example of the perfectly bare style of Stendhal and Flaubert. But he might have learned the art of omission from the epigrams in the *Greek Anthology*, or from the *Maximes*, in which La Rochefoucauld usually dispenses with epithets, or uses only those which are essential.

To conclude: there has been no unanimity, among the major critics of our literature, in their judgements on Gray. All have been concerned with the slenderness of his output, but they have offered widely differing explanations. Matthew Arnold, in his sympathetic essay, ascribed it to an atmosphere unfavourable to poetry. 'An east wind was blowing', and this discouraged him. But a poet truly inspired triumphs over environment. Pindar's heavy-witted countrymen did not prevent his becoming one of the greatest of all lyric poets. Sir Leslie Stephen, in his fair and appreciative study, 'Gray and his Friends', reprinted in *Hours in a Library*,[17] had certain reservations. Like Arnold, he thought that the environment, 'Gray being shut up in a small scholastic clique', dragged him down almost as soon as inspiration had lifted him from the earth: 'Even the Elegy flags a little towards the end.' 'The Bard' comes near to collapsing, since the facts did not fit the prophecy. The view that the atmosphere of eighteenth-century Cambridge was unfavourable to inspiration is largely unfounded. The university, as stated earlier, produced active teachers and original minds. There is no evidence to suggest that, if Gray had lived in London or elsewhere (and in fact he often stayed in London and travelled far and wide in the country), he would have written more or better poetry. The reason that he did not lay not in the environment but in Gray himself.

Finally, Stephen excused the extent to which Gray interwove his poems with 'any quantity of previously manufactured material', on the ground that it was 'perfectly allowable' by the habits, even the principles, of the age.

George Saintsbury[18] is less indulgent. Gray's 'poetical inspiration' was less original than Collins's; but he was a better scholar. While agreeing with Arnold 'that Gray's small original production was due to the times being out of joint with him', he added that it was not easy 'to think that in others Gray would have done much more that was original'. Gray 'was still in verse a slave . . . to a certain classical and literary convention. His poems are careful mosaics of previous literary expression; he delighted in that feeble personification which is really worse . . . than the older imagery of the *Rose*'. The 'rosy-bosomed hours', 'the toiling hand of Care', etc., 'jostle tags from Virgil, Milton, Shakespeare'. The Elegy has great merits, 'but the expression never quite reaches the poignant suggestiveness, that endless circling of new and ever new music, which distinguishes the greatest poetry'. Arnold, by extending James Brown's remark that Gray 'never spoke out' to his work as a whole, implied that he had in him treasures of poetry which he kept to himself. Saintsbury suggests that no such treasures existed. He concludes that what is good and new in Gray's later poems is 'jumbled up with the tawdry, the artificial and the stale'.

These defects would have mattered less if Gray's poems had been animated by a genuine quality of heart. The Eton ode and the Elegy remained popular, not simply for their ornate and memorable diction, but because of the warmth of feeling which they communicated. In the Elegy Gray was grieving over West. The greater part of the poem seems to be spoken by the dead poet, that is by West: here, and not in any deep pity for 'the rude forefathers of the hamlet', lay the source of the poet's emotion.

The public as a whole has not been mistaken in feeling little more than curiosity in Gray's subsequent verses. 'The Progress of Poesy' – an amusing metrical experiment – is little more than a short *précis* in verse of that *History of Poetry* which he had outlined but could not trouble to write. The emotion in 'The Bard' is a feeling experienced at second hand, expressed in a too strident rhetoric, and hardly communicable to the reader; while the 'history' lacks even the merit of being true. Gray's poetry is wanting in that plainness and simplicity of diction which are among the merits of poets as diverse as Homer and Sappho in the ancient world, and Wordsworth in the modern.

It has been said by one of Gray's admirers that 'few men have published so little to so much effect; few have attained to fame with so little ambition'.[19]

The best stanzas of the Elegy were plagiarised from Latin, Italian and English poets. When Gray tried to be original, his language and grammar collapsed. He depicted a graveyard where 'heaves the turf in many a mouldering heap' – a fearsome spectacle. He meant 'lies'. Elsewhere he refers to a stonemason ('th'unletter'd Muse') who 'strews around' 'many a sacred text'. Gray set greater store by the Pindaric odes; but in these the allusions were so obscure that even his warmest admirers were mystified. If a personal opinion be permitted, the 'Sophonisba Massinissae Epistola' and the lines 'Ad C: Favonium Aristium' are his best poems; and, for the English ones, the 'Stanzas to Bentley' and the ode 'On the Pleasure arising from Vicissitude'.

Gray's prose writings, which are confined to his correspondence and Commonplace Books, have been discussed in earlier chapters. As regards the Journal descriptive of the Lakeland Fells, Leslie Stephen pointed out that this neither promoted a feeling for mountain scenery nor accounted for the flow of tourists to Westmorland and Cumberland. The fashion for visiting the Lake District had begun before the publication of the Journal, which was virtually unknown at the time to the general public.

One cannot therefore allow that Gray can claim any credit for the new interest in mountain scenery, soon to be reflected in literature. His only tour on the Continent was highlighted by the two visits to the Grande Chartreuse; but Nab Scar in the 'Jaws of Borrowdale' seems to have impressed him as much. (One may compare Dr Thomas Arnold's preference of Fairfield to the Alps.) In this more stolidly traditional attitude, once again Gray must be denied a significant place among the pre-romantics.

APPENDIX

Gray's Poetic Diction
by Iris Lytton Sells

Notes and References

Bibliography

Index

APPENDIX

Gray's Poetic Diction

by Iris Lytton Sells

Any appreciation of Gray's poems must take into account his views on poetic diction, which are here considered separately from his critical views in general; and his own practice, which was not always in accord.

'The language of the age is never the language of poetry, except among the French,' he wrote to West on 8 April 1742. His fondness for the classics, and for the diction of the older Italian poets, and also of Shakespeare, Milton and Dryden, may have accounted for this attitude. His poems are full of archaic terms, neo-classic periphrases, and rather artificial expressions. 'The rosy-bosomed hours, fair Venus' train', 'redd'ning Phoebus', 'Full many a gem', etc., and 'Nature's darling' (to designate Shakespeare) – these and other expressions are examples of the application of a theory which Dr Johnson deplored, and to which Wordsworth reacted, after his first admiration of Gray, by overstressing the need to employ the language of ordinary people.[1]

Gray seems generally to have favoured a poetic language which should be constantly enriched 'with foreign idioms and derivatives', as he told West in the letter quoted above. 'Shakespeare and Milton', he added, 'have been great creators in this way . . . in truth Shakespeare's language is one of his principal beauties.'[2] Only much later, and perhaps too late, does he seem to have realised the danger of inventing new words, and, for example, imitating too closely the language of Shakespeare.[3]

West had understood this danger as early as the winter of 1741–2, when Gray had sent him the manuscript of Act I, Scene i of 'Agrippina'. He had then pointed out that Gray would do better to employ in his tragedy a vocabulary more like Otway's.

Gray's views on poetic diction, as expressed in 1742, seem to belie his practice in certain respects. Writing again to West on 23 April, he praises the concision of Tacitus, adding: 'The English tongue is too diffuse and daily grows more and more enervate'; 'Too many new words have been introduced'; and so on. Gray's observation might seem tantamount to saying that England needed grammarians like those of early seventeenth-century France, a Malherbe or a Vaugelas, to restrict the vocabulary and to lay down severe rules for composition. But his own practice, particularly in his poetry, is at variance with this pronouncement.

In the view of Wordsworth, as stated earlier, the poet is constrained to use the language of prose, subject to the discipline of metre which is of primitive origin; and in this view Wordsworth appears to agree with the French, whose methods Gray had deprecated in his letter to West. One may note, as an example, La Fontaine's vocabulary, which is very near that of everyday speech. According to the experts, in the youth of the world all language was poetry; Mallarmé held that to write at all, with style, is to write poetry. (Admittedly Mallarmé's poetry is a *genre* of its own.)

Gray's practice far departs from any such theory. Thus, one important feature which differentiates his poetry clearly from the language of prose is his constant use of inversions; generally allowed in poetry, but not to the exaggerated extent in which Gray indulges. In Gray it often involves ambiguities, and even syntactical errors. In such a line as 'No hive hast thou of hoarded sweets' (from the 'Ode on the Spring') the sense is clear enough, in spite of the inversions (object, verb and subject). But 'Thy Joys no glittering female meets' is objectionable on another ground, which would have been immediately perceived if the normal order had obtained. 'Female', a concrete noun, is made the subject of a verb governing the pluralised abstract noun 'Joys'. This is a confusion of terms, not acceptable in good style, unless Gray fancied he could personify 'Joys' on the analogy of 'Loves' (as in 'The Progress of Poesy'), or 'Cupids', in which sense it would be a neologism.

More flagrant is the departure from the natural order in these lines from the 'Adversity' ode:

> When first thy Sire to send on earth
> Virtue, his darling child, designed . . .

The separation of the verb from the infinitive it governs is a construction inadmissible in prose, disagreeable in verse. Equally eccentric are the lines:

> But Knowledge [History?] to their eyes her ample page,
> Rich with the spoils of time, did ne'er unroll.

In the normal order, one would have felt surprise at the idea of unrolling a page, which is evidently confused with a parchment roll. Also in the Elegy, one of the most striking examples of this eccentric order seems to have no justification at all:

> All that beauty, all that wealth e'er gave
> Awaits alike th'inevitable hour . . .

The gratuitous inversion does not seem to improve either the sound or the sense ('the inevitable hour awaits . . .').

Actual obscurity is the result of an inversion in the Eton ode, which again serves to mask a stylistic abuse, in this case tautology:

> Say, Father Thames,
> Who foremost now delight to cleave
> With pliant oar thy glassy wave,
> The captive linnet which enthrall?

That is to say, which boys enthrall [sic], i.e. put in thrall or catch, the captive linnet? The linnet is already captive, as stated.

The editors of the *Complete Poems* do not seem to have troubled to note these near-improprieties; and yet examples are many. In 'The Progress of Poesy', lines 63-4, the expression is again obscure, and the syntax very questionable, with the two subjects separated by their plural verb:

> Her track, where'er the Goddess roves
> Glory pursue [i.e. follow on], and generous shame.

A poem should give delight, and not perplex the reader; one is inclined to take Leigh Hunt's side in this argument, rather than Gray's, when the latter goes to extremes, as in the following four lines of the 'Vicissitude' ode:

> Whilst Hope prolongs our happier hour
> Or deepest shades that daily lower
> And blacken round our weary way
> Gilds with a gleam of distant day.

Apparently he means to say that hope prolongs our happier hour, or gilds with a gleam of distant day deepest shades, etc. . . . . 'Gilds' has here strayed three lines from the normal order: an impossible construction in ordinary English. In Latin such constructions are valid; inflections are there to clarify the meaning. There is an amusing quotation to illustrate this point: 'Brutus et Cassius Caesarem interfecerunt.' The same five words, translated without reference to their Latin inflections, will give six different senses in English: Brutus slew Cassius and Caesar; Caesar slew Brutus and Cassius, etc. An example of this sort of ambiguity occurs in Pope's: 'And thus the son the fervent sire addressed'. But here the context makes the meaning fairly clear.

Gray seems to have thought it more poetical to torture the language in this way, aping Latin,[4] than to conform to the English order of proximity. Obscurity he may almost have considered to be a distinguishing mark of poetry; since, as Cardinal Newman observed, by the feebleness of ordinary words to express the 'eternal forms of beauty and perfection', language must fall back on figures of speech, such as metaphor, etc. But one doubts if he would have considered Gray's perverted syntax as necessary for the imparting of these otherwise incommunicable sentiments. One is reminded of Monsieur Jourdain's desire to give a more gallant turn to the words: 'Belle marquise, vox beaux yeux me font mourir d'amour'. After considering the various alternatives (in this case, fortunately, the question of ambiguity did not arise): as, 'D'amour mourir me font, belle marquise, vox beaux yeux', or 'Mourir vos beaux yeux, belle marquise, d'amour me font', his *maître de philosophie* assures him that the order of his original statement is the best.[5]

Perhaps Gray's oddest sentence occurs in 'A Long Story':

> The words too eager to unriddle
> The poet felt a strange disorder

[i.e. the poet, too eager to unriddle the words, felt . . .]

Gray was not obviously singular in another practice, which, however, he did abuse, and it clearly marks his lack of inventiveness; this is his habit of repeating himself, often the result of over-borrowing. His use of the phrase 'the lap of earth' is an example. In the Epitaph at the end of the Elegy he makes his youth rest his head upon the lap of earth; in 'The Progress of Poesy' he writes: 'In thy green lap was Nature's darling laid'; and again in 'Agrippina' one finds the expression amplified into 'the flowery lap'.

Gray had apparently found the phrase in Lucretius, I, 250–1:

> Postremo pereunt imbres, ubi eos pater aether
> In gremium matris terrai [an archaic genitive in three syllables]
> praecipitavit . . .

In II, 375, Lucretius refers similarly to 'telluris gremium'. Subsequently the image reappears in the *Aeneid* (III, 509), the *Thebaid* (IV, 793), and also in various prose works. In Apuleius one reads 'florentis caespitis gremio' (literally, 'in the lap of the flowery turf').[6] Gray probably had this last passage in mind when writing 'Agrippina'. Matthew Arnold's use of the lines in 'Memorial Verses' is better known, when he says of Wordsworth:

> He laid us as we lay at birth
> On the cool flowery lap of earth.

Here Arnold may simply have been repeating the phrase in 'Agrippina', although he must almost certainly have known its original in Apuleius.

Gray in his poetry does in fact repeat himself often enough to support the view that the spring of poetry in him was very near at times to drying up. However, in 'The Ode for Music', he speaks of the 'flower unheeded and the latent gem', and here he is clearly meaning to recall the well-known stanza on this subject in the Elegy (perhaps naturally wishing to draw attention to this poem, on which his greatest title to fame then reposed). His oft-repeated remarks in his letters to Walpole, running down his poems, do not ring very sincere. This mock-modesty may have disarmed Walpole, but it does not strike the reader today as altogether artless. He pretended to belittle the Elegy, but the above images, repeated from it, do seem designed to recall the attention of his admirers to the poem.

On the other hand, the phrase 'to chase the rolling circle's speed' in the 'Eton' ode appears in the Commonplace Book as 'to chase the hoop's elusive speed', and this is reminiscent of 'with more elusive speed' which occurs in 'Agrippina'. In this example he may have been conscious of, and trying to escape from, repeating himself. One could cite many more examples.

All this is not to say that, despite a certain poverty of style, he did not put together[7] many memorable lines and phrases. Apart from the numerous quotable passages in the Elegy, there are others, less well known, which have even inspired imitations. Thus his lines in the 'Eton College' ode:

> . . . all are men
> Condemn'd alike to groan
> The tender for another's pain,
> Th'unfeeling for his own

may perhaps be the source of Francis Thompson's

> For we are born in other's pain
> And perish in our own.

Wordsworth's 'meanest flower that blows' is certainly taken from Gray's perhaps loveliest stanza in the 'Vicissitude' ode:

> . . . The meanest floweret of the vale . . .
> To him are opening Paradise.[8]

A legitimate poetic device of which Gray avails himself at times is the use of the transferred epithet, as in 'drowsy tinklings' (the Elegy) and 'conscious tail' ('Favourite Cat'). (There is also a sly ellipsis in the latter example, as 'conscious' could mean either 'self-conscious' or 'with a guilty conscience'.)

Gray's use of alliteration is an aid to much mellifluous verse, but tends to become monotonous, perhaps excusably when he is attempting to reproduce something of the tone of the ancient Bardic poetry; to this end, he even inserts occasional internal or 'leonine' rhyme. Examples of this occur in 'The Bard': 'No more I weep, they do not sleep', 'The bristled Boar, in infant gore', and 'Be thine Despair, and sceptr'd Care'.

He makes little impressive use of simile, unlike Milton, whom he so much admired and whose practice must have inspired many of Matthew Arnold's most beautiful specimens. One has only to recall Keats's use of this device in the sonnet in which he compares himself to 'Stout Cortez . . . Silent upon a peak in Darien' to recognise Gray's inferior handling of the same figure. The eight first rather dreary lines of the 'Alliance' fragment, beginning 'As sickly plants betray a niggard earth', are pertinent here.

His metaphors are at times too strained to be effective and are often associated with personification.[9] They are frequently mixed, as in the opening lines of 'The Progress of Poesy', severely criticised by Johnson. Gray has, in this form, nothing to compare with Shelley's reference in 'Adonais' to the 'shaft that flies in darkness' (i.e. Death), recalling the Psalmist's 'arrow that flieth by day'. (Shelley was, of course, alluding to the anonymous review which he supposed had dealt Keats his death-blow.)

Wit is not a feature of pure poetry, and is certainly not one of Gray's most regarded qualities, although he occasionally hits off a successful epigram, as in 'A favourite has no friend' ('Favourite Cat'). In spite of his many so-called humorous poems his verse lacks the real humorous play of thought, and its innocent gaiety. His humour tends to satire or even burlesque. These effects are often achieved by neat antitheses, as in 'Plays which were hiss'd above, below revive' ('Ghost of John Dennis'); but sometimes are the unintended result of circumlocution, as 'the attic warbler' ('Spring Ode') for nightingale. The burlesque element in 'A Long Story',[10] however, is intentional. Mason, his editor, usually indulgent, refers to the imagery of this 'poem' as 'grotesque','ludicrous', and as being often 'unintelligible'. 'It is only to be relished', he says, 'by those who are conversant with the old romance-writers'.

The many involved expressions match the mood of this particular phantasy; but elsewhere his poetic figures add an archaic sound to his verse. Thus, 'enchanting shell'[11] ('Progress of Poesy') is an instance; this metonymy, or, strictly, synecdoche, he uses to designate the lyre, with 'bowl-shaped body' (the one made by Hermes for Apollo was of tortoise-shell,[12] in contrast to the cithara which had a box-like body). To play this instrument, the left hand is bound to it by a sling, leaving the left fingers free to damp the chords (guts) required to remain silent as they are plucked by a plectrum swept across on the other side.

It is difficult to see how Dryden, in the poem, managed this instrument whilst his 'presumptuous car' was being swept along by two 'coursers', however 'etherial'. Gray was very impatient with the reviewer who fancied his Aeolian lyre was an Aeolian harp. The 'kinnor' (harp) which David used to suspend above his bed, and which made sweet music of itself when the breezes stirred it, would have been hardly more inappropriate for Dryden's drive over the 'fields of glory'.[13] Gray's objection was, however, directed to the point that the 'harp is a very bad instrument to dance to'.[14]

As the 'Progress of Poesy' is subtitled a Pindaric ode, he took the trouble to note, in the 1768 edition, that Pindar describes his odes as being accompanied by Aeolian song, Aeolian strings [that is, the lyre], and the breath of the Aeolian flutes[15] – 'Αιολιδων πνοαί αυλων'. (The *aulos* is the flute, the primitive flute of antiquity, played in pairs. Theocritus at a later date refers to four pipes: the *syrinx; aulos; plagi-aulos*, a transverse flute; and *donax*, perhaps the double pipe.)

Thus Gray fittingly invokes the Aeolian lyre in his opening line as a synonym for the spirit of lyric poetry; but after this address, and a reference to it as the accompaniment of the song and 'frolic measures'[15] of the 'rosy-crowned Loves', the poetry of Shakespeare and Milton is symbolised in other ways. It is only Dryden, and Gray himself, who use the lyre. The savage 'Youth of Chili' uses recitation; Shakespeare is given a pencil and paints, as well as some golden keys, to express his art; and Milton rides 'on seraph wings', to be blasted with blindness in the empyrean (a reference to the 'welcome minstrel' from whom the muse took away his sight). He does later, in 'The Ode for Music', 'strike the deep-toned shell', which is here made to accompany choral music. There is a confusing reference to a 'pictur'd urn' in the lines devoted to Dryden's achievements. But he is earlier described as using his hands 'to explore the lyre'. Gray depicts himself as awakening its strings; but apparently he employs the lyre, not so much as a musical instrument, but as a means to mount 'far above the Great' (although still, according to his modest disclaimer, 'far beneath the Good').

Owing to its allusiveness, for Gray cites many borrowings from Pindar and even from an ode by Cowley, 'The Progress of Poesy' is a too exuberant mixture of poetic figures. Gray himself refers to the 'simile' of the first strophe, – a misnomer. 'The rich stream of music' which follows the evocation of the lyre is at most an implied simile, that is, a metaphor. Johnson's criticism of these lines seems a just one; and Mason's Gilbertian diatribe in Gray's defence rather ridiculous, when he stigmatises Johnson's remarks as 'those acid eructations of vituperative criticism which are generated by uncocted taste and intellectual indigestion'. This is out-Johnsoning Johnson!

The apostrophe to poetry is, however, classic compared with other instances of this device used by Gray. Too often his apostrophes are vehement in expression, marring the serenity of otherwise effective verses. In this connection, the invocation 'Hail, Horrors, hail!' ('Hymn to Ignorance') comes to mind. An amusing anecdote connects itself with the opening words of the 'Ode for Music', 'Hence, avaunt . . .', hurled at Nicholls when the latter inadvertently burst into Gray's room where Gray was beginning to recite to himself his poem, in preparation for the Chancellor's Installation.

Bombast, alas! is also too often present in Gray's verse; a mild example is the line 'When Nile *redundant* [meaning 'superabundant' or 'overflowing', not 'superfluous'] o'er his summer-bed . . .'.

A fondness for obsolete words and phrases also contributes to the air of singularity which distinguishes his poetry. There are too many of these; as for example 'full many a gem',[16] for 'very many gems', or simply 'many a gem'; 'haply', 'swain', 'poesy', the owl's 'bower' – did Gray's owl have the sanctuary of the bower-bird? – and so on.

Tautology is another device, sagely used, to enhance some desirable effect; but it seems jejune to say: 'The ploughman homeward plods his weary way', the idea of weariness being implicit in the verb 'to plod'. But perhaps the attractive alliteration was Gray's motive for inserting 'weary' before 'way' and following 'homeward'.[17] 'The captive linnet which enthrall' has been discussed above, in another context.

Striking also is Gray's use of uncommon words, and inconsistencies in spelling which seem deliberate. 'Parting day' is a gallicism, preserved in the phrase 'to speed the parting guest'; here Gray evidently wished to avoid the literal translation of Dante's 'il giorno chè si muore'. (But he gave a different reason.) So he altered 'dying' to 'parting', as 'departing' would have involved an extra syllable.

'Mought' for 'Might' is an odd spelling (occurring in his translation of Dante), as is 'rap'd' for 'rapp'd' in 'A Long Story' – an unfortunate change (as a purist, he might have known that final consonants of one-syllable verbs, except in specially defined cases, must always be doubled when inflected). Similarly he writes 'tip'd', 'pen'd', and 'beg'd'. He spells arbitrarily 'honour' with or without the 'u'; he writes 'manor' and 'manour'; and 'clotter'd for 'clotted', 'cheirful' for 'cheerful'. A list of such misspellings could be continued indefinitely. They are not perhaps in themselves of great importance, but Gray's motivation must everywhere have been the same, namely a desire for singularity.[18]

On the whole, Gray's poetic figures are largely legacies from the past. The numerous abstractions, personifications and other artifices accentuate the remote quality of much of his poetry, keeping it well within the tradition of eighteenth-century versification; only here and there, and mainly through experiments in new forms, are to be seen glimpses of the breaking dawn of pre-romanticism. It seems true to say that few among those who study Gray's English poems, with their strange vocabulary and stranger syntax, their quaint imagery more often designed to express emotions of fear, defiance and violence than rapture and inspiration, can feel, except occasionally,[19] that they are reading 'human sentiments expressed in human language'.[20] The final result of Gray's labours is to drive his poetry beyond the limit of what can be accepted as the 'best words in the best order' (as Coleridge defined poetry).

In conclusion, one is obliged to concede that whatever were his inconsistencies in spelling, in irregular syntax, and in his general handling of the language, he is at least consistent in one respect, that his verse is never 'the language of the age'; nor, perhaps, the common language of any age.

Notes and References

ABBREVIATIONS

Martin   Roger Martin, *Essai sur Thomas Gray*, Paris, 1934.
K.-C.   R. W. Ketton-Cremer, *Thomas Gray; a Biography*, Cambridge, 1955.
G.W.W.A.   *The Correspondence of Gray, Walpole, West and Ashton*, Oxford, 1915.
Corr.   *The Correspondence of Thomas Gray*, Oxford, 1935.

PART ONE

CHAPTER 1

1 References: Horace Walpole, *Memoir of Gray*, reprinted in the *Correspondence of Thomas Gray*, ed. Toynbee and Whibley, Oxford, 1935, III, Appendix Y, pp. 1286–8; Roger Martin, *Essai sur Gray*, Paris, 1934, pp. 8–9, 33–5; R. W. Ketton-Cremer, *Thomas Gray: a Biography*, Cambridge, 1955, pp. 1–9.
2 A. Adler, *Le Tempérament nerveux*, French translation, 1926; A. Hesnard, *La Vie et la Mort des Instincts*, 1926; E. Regis and A. Hesnard, *La Psychanalyse des névroses et des psychoses*, 1929; and others.
3 Dr Hesnard admitted that a diagnosis made after the lapse of over two centuries and on the basis of the data supplied could only be conjectural. It is none the less persuasive. Medical science in the early eighteenth century was very backward. Most ailments were put down to gout or the spleen. Gray's later bouts of real ill health, and also his excessive reserve and 'difficult' character, appear to confirm Martin's and Hesnard's conclusions.
4 K.-C., p. 3.
5 Letter to Wharton, 23 June 1761.
6 K.-C., p. 3.
7 K.-C., pp. 5–6.
8 K.-C., p. 6.
9 K.-C., pp. 17–18.

CHAPTER 2

1 References: *G.W.W.A.*, I, pp. 4–129; K.-C., pp. 10–26.
2 A reference to Horace's Ode 'Sic te Diva . . .' to Virgil whose vessel was on its way to Greece. 'The half of my soul is with thee' (dimidium animae meae).
3 As the editors of the *Correspondence* suggest (I, 13, note 7).
4 In eighteenth-century usage it was correct to write: 'You was', when addressing one person.

5 The date is conjectural. Dr Audley had given his opinion on 9 February, ostensibly in 1736; but it may have been 1735. The English New Year still began officially in March, and contemporary documents are often confusing. The Continent had adopted the new calendar year.

CHAPTER 3

1 References: D. C. Tovey, *Gray and his Friends*, Cambridge, 1890; *G.W.W.A.* vol. I; K.-C., pp. 26-9.

CHAPTER 4

1 References: *G.W.W.A.*, I; K.-C., pp. 30-6.
2 Letter to Mrs Gray, 1 April, from Amiens. All the information up to their leaving Amiens comes from this letter.
3 See Marquis de Rochegude and M. Dumoulin, *Guide pratique à travers le vieux Paris*, 1923, p. 534.
4 Most of the above information was conveyed in two letters to West, dated 15 May and 22 May. These letters were sewn together, after Gray's death, by Mason to form a single letter (No. 62 of the *Gray Correspondence*, I, pp. 106-9) in such a way that it is impossible to be sure where they were joined.
5 *G.W.W.A.*, No. 101, Vol. I, pp. 244-7.

CHAPTER 5

1 References: *G.W.W.A.* I, pp. 254-341; *Corr.* I, pp. 125-82; K.-C., pp. 36-51.
2 'Guilleragues disait hier que Pellisson abusait de la permission qu'ont les hommes d'être laids' (letter to Madame de Grignan, 5 January 1764), noted by Mason.
3 The present 'Mont Cenis' tunnel enters the mountain at Modane, well below Lanslebourg, and passes under the Col de Fréjus.
4 It was probably at Turin that they received an amusing letter from West, dated 24 September, and concluding: 'Signé. Moi R. W. Soussigné. Grimalkin, premier chat.'
5 Noted in his Journal, dated 28 November 1739 (cited in *Corr.* I, p. 132, note 3).
6 Ketton-Cremer (pp. 48-50) has reconstructed these and later circumstances from letters from Mann, belonging to Mr W. S. Lewis.
7 In 'Thomas Gray of Pembroke'.

CHAPTER 6

1 References: Mason's *Memoirs of Gray* (1775); *Corr.*, Vol. I, pp. 184-214; *G.W.W.A.;* Gray's first Commonplace Book; E. Gosse, *Gray*, London, 1882; K.-C., pp. 52-68.
2 Letter of 4 April 1742.
3 Gosse, *Gray*, London, 1882, p. 67.
4 K.-C., pp. 66-7.
5 *Unreformed Cambridge*, Camb. Univ. Press, 1935.

6 Contrary to the usual idea, Cambridge colleges in the main had been started as political, not as monastic, foundations.

CHAPTER 7

1 References: *Corr.*, Vol. I, pp. 215–303; *G.W.W.A.;* D. C. Tovey, *Gray and his Friends;* K.-C., pp. 69–81.
2 Possibly Mrs Chute.
3 A character in Congreve's *The Way of the World.*
4 Note by the editors of the *Correspondence* to Letter No. 123.
5 See his letters of 11 September 1746 to Wharton, and of 15 February 1747.
6 *D.N.B.*
7 *Corr.*, No. 135, pp. 272–79.
8 *Cambridge Past and Present*, London 1926, pp. 123–4.
9 *G.W.W.A.*, No. 168, pp. 98–9.
10 He was studying this in March 1747.
11 *Corr.*, No. 135, pp. 276–7.

CHAPTER 8

1 References: *Corr.*, Vol. I, pp. 303–49; K.-C., pp. 86–115; Tovey, *Gray and his Friends.*
2 This house has been demolished. The site is now 39 Cornhill, and the building is occupied by a discount company (*Corr.*, Vol. I, p. 305, note 6).
3 Ketton-Cremer observes: 'In normal circumstances he [Gray] would undoubtedly have regarded an offer of money, except from so privileged a friend as Wharton, as a deep affront.'
4 Letter to Montagu, 3 September 1748, cited by K.-C., p. 89.
5 cf. K.-C., p. 90.
6 That is, if it circulated in manuscript, because it was not published until 1775. But it is uncertain whether anyone but Wharton and Stonhewer saw it for some years.
7 *Reminiscences of Gray*, reprinted in *Correspondence*, III, Appendix Z, p. 1291.
8 *Corr.*, No. 147, pp. 312–13 and Note 1 to p. 312.
9 *Corr.*, No. 148, pp. 314–17. Walpole, writing to Mann in January 1750, described the *Esprit des lois* as 'the best book that ever was written – at least I never learned half so much from all I ever read. There is as much wit as useful knowledge'.
10 cf. Letter No. 115.
11 No. 149, pp. 317–8.
12 *Corr.*, pp. 322–3. On 25 June Walpole wrote to Mann: 'His cooks have been there these ten days' – headed no doubt by the famous Clouët. A contemporary caricature depicts the Duke in his kitchen supplicating his French chef: 'O Cloe if you leave me, I shall be starv'd, by G–d'; to which Clouët retorts by displaying English broadsheets against Papists.
13 No. 152, pp. 325–6.
14 *G.W.W.A.*, II, No. 170, pp. 101–2.
15 See K.-C., pp. 96–8.
16 K.-C., pp. 95–6.
17 In Gray's letter of 12 June to Walpole (*G.W.W.A.*, II, pp. 101–2), in which he encloses the poem, Gray mentions a book just published by Ashton to

270 *Thomas Gray*

controvert Conyers Middleton. Ashton knew that Middleton was a friend of Walpole's, and yet, although Ashton had owed his advancement to Sir Robert, he did not hesitate to advertise his orthodoxy by attacking works which threw some doubt on established views. Walpole then broke with him.

18 Mason amended the order of words.

19 Lady Brown, who was a Cecil, was the wife of a former British Resident in Venice. Gray appears to have met her in 1746 (*Corr.*, I, p. 253). She was a patroness of Italian and other musicians in London, and lived until 1782.

20 *Corr.*, No. 155, pp. 331-4. The letter was first published by D. C. Tovey in *Gray and his Friends*, Cambridge, 1890.

21 The Elegy is reproduced in this letter without divisions between the stanzas. It begins: 'The Cerfeu tolls the Knell of parting Day . . .'.

22 He was to pay this visit in 1753.

23 From Cambridge. *Corr.*, No. 156, pp. 335-40.

24 *Corr.*, No. 157, pp. 341-2.

25 From Cambridge, 20 February 1751. *Corr.*, No. 158, pp. 342-3.

CHAPTER 9

1 References: *Corr.*, I, pp. 362-76; K.-C., pp. 111-15; Irene Tayler, 'Two Eighteenth-Century Illustrators of Gray', in *Fearful Joy*, Montreal and London, 1974, pp. 119-26.

2 13 June 1751.

3 'The Funeral of the Lioness', which Walpole wrote in 1751.

4 8 September 1751 (*Corr.*, No. 161, pp. 346-8).

5 29 September (Letter to Walpole: *Corr.*, No. 162, p. 350).

6 No. 168 (*Corr.*, pp. 362-3).

7 c. mid July 1752. No. 169 (*Corr.*, pp. 363-5). Gray's letters to Wharton in 1751 and 1752 are concerned with personal matters and college gossip. A long letter to Mason in December 1751, in response to Mason's having sought his advice regarding the five 'Letters' he proposed to prefix to his *Elfrida*, contains a dissertation on how a modern tragedy, as distinct from a Greek, should be composed, a note on the nature of comedy, with a reference to Menander and Terence, and observations on Shakespeare, Otway, Rowe and Maffei (No. 165, *Corr.*, pp. 357-60).

8 When in the end he consented to add explanatory notes, he did so with a bad grace.

9 No. 170 (*Corr.*, pp. 366-7). Incidentally he asked Walpole if he had read Voltaire's *Micromégas*.

10 No. 172 (*Corr.*, p. 371).

11 13 February 1753, No. 173, *Corr.*, p. 372.

12 20 February, No. 174, *Corr.*, pp. 373-4.

13 Seated on a rock under a tree – a laurel, according to Richard Cumberland, Bentley's nephew, in Vol. I, p. 23 of his *Memoirs* (1807).

14 In 'Two Eighteenth-Century Illustrators of Gray' (*Fearful Joy: Papers from the Gray Bicentenary Conference* . . . 1971, Montreal and London, 1974) Dr Irene Tayler compares Bentley's designs with Blake's. Book illustrations had been limited in size prior to Boucher's designs for an edition of Molière in 1734 and Piazzetta's for the *Gerusalemme liberata* in 1745. Bentley's drawings were full-page designs like Piazzetta's, and he interpreted Gray as

Gray liked; Blake represented Gray as Blake liked. One should add that Continental engravers were then more skilful than English.

15 K.-C., p. 115.
16 To Wharton, 9 March 1755 (*Corr.*, p. 420).
17 Fourteen poems appeared in Gray's lifetime, some thirty-two (apart from the Latin verses) after his death. The latter included the 'Stanzas' to Bentley and the 'Ode on Vicissitude'.
18 *Odes*, Book I, 1 and 20; Book II, 12, 17, 20; Book III, 8, 16, 29. *Epodes*, 1, 3, 9, 14; *Satire*, 1; *Epistles*, Book I, 1, 7, 19.

CHAPTER 10

1 References: *Corr.*, I, pp. 376–443; *G.W.W.A.*, II, pp. 131–48; Walpole's *Memoir of Gray*, reprinted in *Corr.*, III, Appendix Y, p. 1287; K.-C., pp. 122–6.
2 And see L. B. Namier, *England in the Age of the American Revolution*, 2nd edn, 1961. On pp. 67ff. Namier cites Chesterfield's and Shelburne's shrewd estimates of Newcastle's character. He was no doubt too anxious to please, and to retain office; he was prone to allow Pitt and others to browbeat him. But he was far from deserving Namier's harsh verdict (p. 68). Namier admitted that no biography of Newcastle had yet been attempted. This need has now been supplied by Reed Browning's equitable study (Yale, 1975).
3 There were also two members for the City. Both were country gentlemen, a fact which probably gave rise to animosity.
4 For part of the above information I am indebted to Dr David Reid; for part, to my wife. See also J. E. Hodgson's *Durham*.
5 Where the poet Swinburne was to spend much of his childhood, until his father's removal to Holmwood, in the Thames Valley (noted by my wife).
6 I owe the above information to Dr C. W. Gibby.
7 The two County members were nominees of the Vane and Bowes families, perhaps by agreement with the Bishop. At the general election of 1761 John Tempest (who lived at Old Durham, a manor house some little way upstream from the City) was returned as a Tory (Namier, op. cit., Appendix A, p. 419). He may have been the sitting member in 1753. For these indications I am indebted to Dr David Reid. Richard Wharton must have been very influential, as well as being a man of property. He became Mayor of Durham in 1760.
8 For a fuller description of this period, see K.-C., pp. 124–5.
9 Recorded in Walpole's *Memoir of Gray*.
10 This outline is recorded in a memorandum-book of 1754; and by Mason in his *Memoirs of Gray*.
11 These subjects will be examined in Part Two, Chapter 5 of the present work.
12 No. 204, *Corr.*, pp. 432–3. The manuscript of the first part of the ode had probably been given to Wharton earlier in the summer.
13 For a study of this ode, see Part II, Chapter 1, Section III (Lyric and Elegiac Poems, continued).
14 One wonders if Mason's French can have been quite so awful. His knowledge of the classics should have told him that *cimetière* from Greek, through ecclesiastical Latin (neuter) would be masculine in French.
15 Noted by the editor of the *Correspondence* as apparently the first use of the word in English.

CHAPTER 11

1 References: *Corr.*, II, pp. 455-545; *G.W.W.A.*, II, pp. 158-74; E. Gosse, *Gray;* K.-C., pp. 136-57; B. W. Downs, *Cambridge Past and Present.*

2 Wharton was also requested to send a 'Canister of Tea', some snuff and a pound of Field's toilet soap.

3 K.-C. relates these in detail on p. 138.

4 Gosse, *Gray*, London, 1885, p. 125.

5 Perceval was a fellow-commoner of Magdalene. The names of the Peterhouse men were Bennet Williams and George Forrester (K.-C., p. 137).

6 Nicholls's *Illustrations*, VI, p. 805, cited by K.-C., pp. 137-8.

7 K.-C., p. 139.

8 He moved into somewhat better rooms in the same building in 1757 (K.-C., pp. 140-1) – the set now known as the Gray Rooms.

9 The reference to Voltaire is explained by the fact that Voltaire, having quarrelled with Frederick of Prussia, had taken a house near Lausanne and then moved to one below Geneva, in 1755, but without making any great fuss.

10 Strictly speaking, it had been preceded by Michaelhouse (1324) and Clare Hall (1326). But Michaelhouse was later absorbed by Trinity, and Clare Hall not definitely founded (by Elizabeth de Burgh, Countess of Clare) until 1359.

11 B. W. Downs, *Cambridge Past and Present*, London, 1926, pp. 119-23.

12 *Cambridge: Painted by W. Matthison and described by M. A. R. Tuker*, London, new edn, 1922, p. 22, and see pp. 18-25.

13 Baron Walpole of Wolterton, with whom Horace was not on good terms.

14 Cited by Gosse, op. cit., pp. 127-8.

15 The remainder of the letter contains details of the food supplied one Christmas for the Duke of Norfolk's household at Framlingham in Suffolk, in the time of Henry VIII – a bewildering assortment of flesh and fowl, with the prices indicated (see *Corr.*, II, pp. 488-90, and the notes).

16 A Huntingdonshire squire who had sometimes entertained Gray and James Brown.

17 cf. K.-C., p. 150.

18 *G.W.W.A.*, II, No. 204, pp. 169-70.

19 K.-C. records that she was the daughter of a Haddingtonshire Laird, and was younger than Gray. It is not known where they had met (K.-C., p. 151).

20 Richard Hurd (1720-1808), later Bishop of Worcester.

21 Cited by K.-C., p. 155. Mrs Garrick, an Austrian, had probably never read Suckling.

22 Johnson in his *Life of Gray*, Algarotti in a letter of December 1762 to W. T. How (*Corr.*, II, p. 532, note 8).

23 Letter to Wharton, 7 October 1757.

24 Reprinted in *The Works of Oliver Goldsmith*, ed. J. W. M. Gibbs. London, 1885, IV, pp. 296-9.

25 See *Corr.*, II, pp. 533-4.

26 13 October; *Corr.*, No. 152, pp. 533-4.

CHAPTER 12

1 References: *Corr.*, II, pp. 550-655; K.-C., pp. 160-77.

2 K.-C., pp. 118-19. Many of these details are recorded in his pocket-book for 1754; others, in a letter to Wharton of October 1753.

3 Recorded by K.-C., p. 164, from a note in an 1821 edition of Gray's *Poems*.
4 This title puzzled me until my wife discovered that *The Guardian* was a play in which Garrick had appeared in the title role.
5 First published by D. C. Tovey in *Gray and his Friends*. 'L.G.S.' is a reference to Lord George Sackville who, being in command of the cavalry at Minden, was said to have failed to 'share in the action'.
6 For an analysis of the various stories about Wolfe's praise of the Elegy, see K.-C., pp. 168–70.
7 Pitt's speech on 20 November, in proposing a monument for Wolfe in the Abbey, was, as Mr Ketton-Cremer indicates, a sort of anticlimax to this tragic affair. Gray called it a 'puerile declamation . . . in the course of it he wiped his eyes with one handkerchief, & Bickford (who seconded him) cried too, & wiped with two handkerchiefs . . ., wch was very moving'.

CHAPTER 13

1 References: *Corr.*, II, pp. 655–768; K.-C., pp. 172–81; W. P. Jones, *Thomas Gray, Scholar*, pp. 93–105.
2 These volumes were to reappear in a collected edition as *The Works of Ossian*, in 1765.
3 See Smart, *James Macpherson*, 1905; P. van Tieghem, *Ossian en France*, 1917, etc.
4 It is doubtful if Bloomsbury was 'pastoral' at this time. North of Southampton Row there were probably market-gardens. My wife noted this passage in Gosse; and elucidated it through the reference in Gray's letter of 1734 to Walpole, below.
5 Gosse, *Gray*, p. 146.
6 '. . . I have an amour carried on almost under my window between a boar and a sow, people of very good fashion, that come to an assignation . . .' (Letter to Walpole, 16 April, 1734).
7 This is in the Harcourt Papers, cited by K.-C.
8 cf. K.-C., p. 174.
9 The figures are not quite accurate. M de la Peyrière was 25, Miss Speed, 34 (*Corr.*, p. 770, note 15).
10 'To be no conjuror' meant to be not very 'bright'. cf. French 'ne pas être sorcier'. But to have obtained the hand of the wealthy Miss Speed, suggests that he was no fool.
11 20 June, *Corr.*, II, p. 681. Gray adds notes on the first leafing and flowering of trees and flowers, and the singing of birds, between 10 April and 3 June.
12 It appeared in full only in 1761. The date of Gray's letter to Walpole (No. 328, *Corr.*, p. 717) is conjectural.
13 Cited by the editors of the *Correspondence* in note 14 to Letter 330. Hurd no doubt did too much honour to Jean-Jacques's virtue, but not to the virtue of the novel, which presents not only sincere love, but the triumph of duty over passion. Gray does not seem to have understood that to a society in which the duties of marriage were ridiculed and the heart was desiccated by wit and cynicism, Rousseau was drawing a picture of what love and marriage ought to be.
14 Noted by W. Powell Jones, *Thomas Gray, Scholar*, Harvard U.P., 1937, p. 99.
15 *Prolegomena in Historiam Norwegicam & Orcadensem*, 1697.
16 Copenhagen, 1689. All this side of Gray's work has been studied in detail by W. P. Jones, op. cit.

17 In the Commonplace Book, cited by Jones, p. 103.
18 As suggested by my wife.
19 cf. the explanatory note by Starr and Hendrickson, on verse 90.
20 See W. P. Jones, op. cit., pp. 94–105.
21 This letter must have been written towards the end of July. See *Corr.*, p. 745, note.
22 Jones, op. cit., pp. 103–4.
23 No. 345, *Corr.*, pp. 752–8.

CHAPTER 14

1 References: *Corr.*, pp. 768–828; K.-C., pp. 189–204; Norton Nicholls, *Reminiscences of Gray*.
2 For his other acquaintances, some noble, some clerical, see K.-C., p. 190.
3 This seems to have been characteristic of Gray, and perhaps one of the reasons why Johnson said that he 'was dull in a new kind of way, and that was why people thought him great'.
4 The letter is quoted in full by K.-C., p. 191.
5 *The Reminiscences* have been reprinted by Toynbee and Whibley in Appendix Z of the *Correspondence* (Vol. III, pp. 1288–1303).
6 Quoted by K.-C., p. 205, from a letter belonging to Mr. W. S. Lewis, which was printed in the *Annual Gazette* of the Pembroke College Society in June, 1938.
7 Cited by K.-C., p. 206.
8 For a fuller account of the relations between Nicholls, Temple, Gray and Boswell, see K.-C., pp. 205–6.
9 These places were mere hamlets at that time.
10 8 October, from Pembroke, *Corr.*, No. 379, pp. 821–3.
11 See Jean Hagstrum, 'Gray's Sensibility', in *Fearful Joy*, p. 13.
12 To Walpole, 18 March, 1764; and cf. to Wharton, 29 April, 1765. See also the letter to Wharton of 21 February, 1764: 'This silly dirty Place has had all its thoughts taken up with chusing a new High-Steward . . .'
13 *Poems*, p. 78, preliminary note to the text.
14 I am indebted to my wife for pointing this out.
15 See *Corr.*, III, Appendix P, pp. 1236–42.
16 See Part Two, Chapter 7.
17 *Transactions of the Royal Society of Literature*, XXXVI, 17 (1918).
18 *Corr.*, p. 855, note 3.

CHAPTER 15

1 References: *Corr.*, II, pp. 857–909; K.-C., pp. 207–18.
2 To Mason, *Corr.*, pp. 858–9, and see Part Two, Chapter 5.
3 Monsieur de St Clouët, as he was called, was a distinguished chef, with the manners and something of the culture of a gentleman. Newcastle was reputedly in dread of losing his services.
4 So Gregory wrote to James Beattie of Aberdeen in the New Year (*Corr.*, p. 896).
5 From a letter from Nicholls to Temple, 3 November 1779. See *Corr.*, p. 888, Note 8. The doings in Edinburgh are narrated from these sources by K.-C., p. 208.

6 30 September. *Corr.*, pp. 889–94.
7 8 November. *Corr.*, p. 899.
8 30 August. *Corr.*, p. 885.
9 The appearance of Paris, except for parts of the Left Bank, has been transformed since the eighteenth century; especially by the work of Baron Haussman during the Second Empire.
10 *Corr.*, pp. 911–19. This is perhaps the most amusing and interesting letter in the whole of the *Correspondence*, full of information about Madame Geoffrin, Mlle de Lespinasse, Madame de Boufflers and J.-J. Rousseau (who was about to leave for England), and the Prince de Conti.
11 Ketton-Cremer refers in this connexion to Charles Eliot Norton's book, *The Poet Gray as Naturalist* (1903). He has discovered that the Linnaeus ultimately came into the hands of Ruskin, and after his death was given to Mr Norton.
12 As recorded in his notebooks. Some entries were published in a limited edition in 1950 by Mr Roger Senhouse (K.-C., p. 299, note 7).
13 28 May 1767. *Corr.*, p. 960.

CHAPTER 16

1 References: *Corr.*, pp. 992–1094 and Appendix S; K.-C., pp. 223–30; Horace Walpole, *Historic Doubts . . .* (1768).
2 Cited by the editors of Gray's *Correspondence*, p. 1007, note 4, from the *Works of Lord Orford*, II, p. 135.
3 *The Sentimental Journey* had just appeared.
4 8 March, *Corr.*, pp. 1025–7.
5 Daughter of the postmistress of Cambridge, as already mentioned.
6 But he accompanied Barrett to Italy four years later.
7 *Corr.*, III, Appendix S, pp. 1253–9.
8 La Butte, a native of Angers, continued to teach French until 1790, the year of his death. Isola, who taught Spanish as well as Italian, had among his pupils the younger Pitt and Wordsworth. His little daughter, adopted by the Lambs, is buried in Little St Mary's Churchyard.
9 *Corr.*, III, Appendix Z, pp. 1300–1.
10 11 guineas would be many times that figure in modern currency.
11 The ceremonies and banquets which celebrated the installation were well organised and brilliantly successful, in spite of a little confusion and the fact that Grafton had to speak extempore.
12 Gray himself must have known that the Earl of Richmond's claim to the throne was illegal, and that he had continued to sustain it only by his marriage with Elizabeth of York.
13 *Corr.*, III, pp. 1078–9.
14 *Corr.*, III, p. 1079, note 8.
15 *Corr.*, pp. 1087–9.

CHAPTER 17

1 References: K.-C., pp. 245–60; *Corr.*, pp. 1110–94; C.-V. de Bonstetten, *Souvenirs écrits en 1831*; M.-L. Herking, *C.-V. de Bonstetten, sa Vie, ses Oeuvres*, Lausanne, 1921.
2 *Corr.*, p. 1085, note 1 cites the passage relating to Nicholls in Marie-L. Herking's book.

3 Probably because in Berne and other north-western cantons Schweizer-
deutsch was spoken; whereas the *literati* of Zürich knew standard German.
Schweizer-deutsch is the spoken language of most German-Swiss today.

4 Vol. II, p. 11, cited by K.-C., p. 247.

5 In French in the original.

6 *Souvenirs . . . écrits en 1831* (Paris, 1831). In the course of sixty years
Bonstetten's recollections may have been distorted or exaggerated, but they
are so distinct that they must be fairly near the truth. He thought that the
secret of Gray's reticence lay in his never having been in love. This aridity
of the heart was in conflict with an ardent imagination; melancholy in Gray
being due to an unsatisfied need of the sensibility.

7 Letter to Michael Lort (*Corr.*, pp. 1112-3).

8 Slightly misquoted from *King John*, Act III, sc. iv.

9 According to Sainte-Beuve, many of Gray's letters to Bonstetten were lost,
with other important correspondence from Madame de Staël, the Comtesse
d'Albany and others, owing to Bonstetten's carelessness in his old age (noted
by I. Lytton Sells).

10 Mason's *Memoir*, pp. 395-9.

11 Reprinted in *Corr.*, III, pp. 1299-1300.

12 From a note made in October 1780 (*Corr.*, p. 1119, Letter 516, note 1).

CHAPTER 18

1 References: K.-C., pp. 260-5; *Corr.*, pp. 1149-94; Letters of Brown, Mason
and Cole in *Corr.*, Appendix W, pp. 1270-82; Gray's will, in Appendix X,
pp. 1283-6.

2 K.-C., p. 261.

3 cf. his letter to Beattie of 2 July 1770, written after he had seen the manuscript
of Book I of *The Minstrel* (see above, p. 137).

4 Brown to Nicholls, 1 August 1771.

5 Roger Martin's theory that Gray's death was caused by arterio-sclerosis,
which would have affected the brain, seems less likely.

PART TWO

CHAPTER 1

1 References: Roger Martin, *Essai sur Gray*, IV, 1, 'Gradus ad Parnassum'.
This is probably the best study yet made of the Latin verses. In the present
work I am indebted for an understanding of the Latin poems and an estimate
of their relative merits to Gavin Townend, Professor of Latin in Durham
University. H. R. Hendrickson in the Oxford edition of the *Poems* has
indicated a large number of the sources.

2 As pointed out by Professor Townend.

3 The usual sense of 'Religio' (which Gray elsewhere spells with two l's) is
superstition; but it also designates a feeling of awe, and so by extension becomes almost synonymous with 'Numen'.

4 *Aeneid*, XII, p. 475, copied by Juvenal, V, pp. 142-3.

5 It will be remembered that West was familiarly known as Favonius, the
mild west wind. Aristius Fuscus was a friend to whom Horace dedicated an
ode.

6 I owe the explanation of this kind of game or 'conceit' to Professor Gavin Townend.

7 By John Sparrow in *Poems in Latin*, Oxford, 1941, xi.

8 cf. also *Odes*, III, p. 29, lines 6, 7.

9 For pointing out this, and many other borrowings, I am indebted to J. R. Hendrickson's explanatory notes in pp. 260–1 of the *Complete Poems*.

10 A line inspired by the *Tristia*, II, p. 520: 'saepe oculos etiam detinuisse tuos'. This and the other borrowings from Ovid have been indicated by Hendrickson, in *Poems*, p. 265.

11 It has been noticed that, while denying the existence of innate concepts, Locke assumed rationality to be innate. In this matter Hobbes had been much nearer the mark in arguing that the generality of mankind are not governed by reason but by the passions – as history has constantly demonstrated. Thus the *practical* effect of Locke's system, in France at least, was to prove disastrous.

12 *The Poems of Thomas Gray, William Collins, Oliver Goldsmith*, ed. R. Lonsdale, Longmans, 1969.

13 cf. the second stanza of 'Ad C: Favonium Aristium':
Dulcius quanto, patulis sub ulmi
Hospitae ramis temere jacentem, etc.

14 Pontus, a word taken straight from Greek, used mostly of the deep sea.

15 As pointed out by my wife.

16 Noted by my wife.

17 Noted, with other sources, by Roger Lonsdale.

18 A reference to Terence's 'Homo sum: humani nihil a me alieno puto' has also been noted; but Terence had probably taken this, as so much else, from Menander.

19 As pointed out to me by my wife.

20 It is strange that the editors of the Oxford *Complete Poems* (1966) overlooked this source. Sir Egerton Brydges was aware of it when he observed that Gray 'had deeply studied the images, the sentiments, the language and the tone of this beautiful Sonnet' (in *Res Literariae*, Naples, 1821, as pointed out by Roger Lonsdale).

21 Preface to the second edition of *Lyrical Ballads*, 1800. This, and Coleridge's commentary, was brought to my attention by my wife.

22 *Biographia Literaria*, 1817.

23 This is apparent from contemporary parodies, and from a recent one: the words and syntax only are imitated, not the sentiments.

24 *Minuet*, London 1935, p. 239. The poem's 'divine truisms' have elsewhere been singled out for praise.

25 Perhaps some of them were?

26 In *Fearful Joy*, p. 95: 'What an ungrateful occupation . . . to write self-pitying epitaphs on oneself!'

27 An echo of Belial's speech in Book I of *Paradise Lost* (as indicated later).

28 Dr Johnson, born at Lichfield in Staffordshire, may have been influenced by the tradition which refers the name to the martyrdom of a thousand Christian converts. The city arms are a field surcharged with dead bodies (cf. lychgate = corpse gate). See Isaac Taylor's *Words and Places*, p. 202 (noted by I. Lytton Sells).

29 K.-C., p. 99.

30 *Caxtoniana*, London, 1875, p. 82, in Essay IX: 'On Style and Diction'. My attention was directed to this essay by my wife.

31 Noted by Roger Lonsdale.

32 Roger Lonsdale observes that 'no definite identification of the churchyard can be made'; but see above.

33 Rowland Parker, *The Common Stream*, Collins, 1975.

34 It was one of Gray's eccentricities to invert subject and object.

35 This probable source has not been indicated by Gray's commentators. It is my suspicion that he, or West, had read Chiabrera. One notices that the metre and rhyme-scheme are the same.

36 As pointed out by M. A. R. Tuker in *Cambridge*, p. 51, note. My attention has been directed to this by my wife. According to Tuker, Tudor Architecture has been called Heraldic Architecture.

37 As indicated by my wife; 'rich with the spoils of nature'.

38 O. Shepard and D. S. Woods, *English Prose and Poetry: 1660–1800* (Boston, 1934).

39 Noted by Roger Lonsdale.

40 In *Les Poètes lyonnais précurseurs de la Pléiade*, ed. J. Aynard. Paris, 1924, p. 109; as noted by my wife.

41 Gray seems to have regarded any attempt at professional advancement as ignoble. cf. his letters to Mason.

42 Noted by I. Lytton Sells.

43 My italics.

44 Indicated by I. Lytton Sells.

45 In the ode 'How sleep the brave, . . .'.

46 They also reminded him of West.

47 Professor Amy L. Reed, in *The Background of Gray's Elegy* (New York, 1924), saw the stanzas as a synthesis of the earlier poetry of melancholy. It can, as she says, be traced back to the ancient world and, in modern times, to Burton's *Anatomy* (1621).

48 They were criticised by Coleridge for their 'rhetorical caprices, and deviations from the language of real life'. Of Gray Coleridge spoke even more contemptuously (see Hazlitt, *My first Acquaintance with Poets*, 1823, indicated by my wife).

49 The expression 'many-twinkling' comes from Book VIII, v. 265 of the *Odyssey*, as Gray indicated in 1768.

50 From Lucretius: 'flammantia moenia mundi'.

51 See Appendix.

52 cf. 'As dear to me as are the ruddy drops that visit my sad heart', *Julius Caesar*.

53 An accusation never proved (see Josephine Tey, *Daughter of Time*).

54 1592. As discovered by Professor Arthur Johnston in *Thomas Gray and the Bard* (Cardiff, 1966), to which I have been indebted in the above analysis.

55 'Cupid himself was steering, seated at the helm'. Pointed out by Roger Lonsdale (p. 92). Matthew Arnold's poem, 'The Future', seems to owe something to this metaphor (I. Lytton Sells).

56 Lonsdale, p. 181. F. R. Green had earlier described the legend as apocryphal.

57 Roger Lonsdale 'Gray and Johnson: The Biographical Problem', in *Fearful Joy*, pp. 72, 78 and *passim*.

58 For an interesting survey of the general question of 'poetic diction' see Donald Greene, 'The Proper Language of Poetry', in *Fearful Joy*, pp. 85–102.

59 Gray's spelling is often irregular and inconsistent.

60 Wordsworth certainly used these lines.

61 For this information and for the sources of Gray's Norse adaptations I am indebted mainly to Roger Lonsdale's commentaries, pp. 210 ff.

62 The Icelandic loom was upright, and the warp and woof were woven from the bottom upwards.

63 By the editors of the *Complete Poems*, p. 212.

64 I am indebted to the notes of the Starr-Hendrickson edition for some of the above information.

65 And not by the 'Saxons', as stated in the Starr-Hendrickson edition, pp. 233-4. The eastern side of the island, from Suffolk to the Firth of Forth was invaded and settled by the Angles.

66 This is No. 308 in Book VII of the *Palatine Anthology*. This, however, became accessible only when Brunck published the *Analecta* in 1772. Planudes' selection, which was made about AD 400, contains a great number that are in the larger *Palatine Anthology*, and four hundred which are unknown elsewhere.

67 *The Reed of Pan*, London, 1902, p. 209.

68 Indicated by I. Lytton Sells.

69 This indicates that the parodist supposed Gray to have been writing his own epitaph in the Elegy; but it has been argued above that the Epitaph is far more likely to have been intended for West.

70 'Conjuror' is here used in the sense of French 'sorcier' = a bright fellow.

71 One of the waitresses at the coffee-house opposite Pembroke Hall had dreamed that Mason had been made a dean. The above was Gray's comment on it.

72 Noted by Roger Lonsdale.

73 As Sandwich was familiarly called.

74 Churchill's satire on the same subject was pointed out to me by my wife. Gray's editors evidently took the title for his verses from Churchill's satire.

CHAPTER 2

1 My italics.

2 As my wife suggests.

CHAPTER 3

1 References: Leslie Stephen, *Hours in a Library*, III, pp. 94-5; Ian Jack, 'Gray in his Letters', in *Fearful Joy*, pp. 20-36.

2 Gray used the word 'sow' as synonymous with 'woman' in his more familiar correspondence.

3 Note by Paget Toynbee in *G.W.W.A.*, I, p. 3.

4 *G.W.W.A.*, pp. 250-4.

5 16 November, 1739, *G.W.W.A.*, pp. 259-60.

6 See below, p. 223.

7 *Corr.*, No. 412, Vol. II, p. 892.

8 Penruddock and Threlkeld.

9 No. 506, *Corr.*, III, p. 1078.

10 As pointed out by my wife, Arnold reproduced Gray's italics in his Essay on Gray, but in his quotation the reader might think that the italics were Arnold's; whereas in fact, it was Gray who used the italics, to indicate the words were borrowed.

11 It is rather too much to suppose, for instance, as does Kenneth Maclean in his paper, 'The Distant Way', in *Fearful Joy*, that Wordsworth was so far

influenced by Gray's description of Grasmere as to be determined by it to make his home there. Wordsworth was Cumbrian-born, and his choice of Dove Cottage would be natural in a lake-lover; add to this the fact that the cost of living there was just about within his means, as Raisley Calvert's legatee.

This presumption of Gray's influence on Wordsworth can be exaggerated also in the literary sphere. The passage in *The Excursion*, often attributed to Gray's influence, describing 'the Poets . . . sown by Nature . . ., endowed with the vision and the faculty divine; yet wanting the accomplishment of verse' seems to imply much more than Gray's 'mute inglorious Milton' of the Elegy – granted that Wordsworth received a hint from it. (His *Ode to Duty* has been discussed elsewhere.)

The grand distinction between them is that Wordsworth was a dedicated poet, Gray an occasional one. For Wordsworth, as for all genuine poets, poetry was 'the pervading principle'. Gray would seem to be, in J. S. Mill's words, one of those poets for whom 'poetry is something out of themselves, foreign to the habitual course of their every day lives and characters.' (This note is contributed by my wife.)

12 Daniel Mornet, *Le Romantisme en France au XVIIIe Siècle*, Paris, 1912.
13 Cited by Arnold Lunn in *Switzerland and the English*, London, 1944, p. 55. See pp. 56-62 for a study of the limitations of this new appreciation of the Alps.
14 *Letters of John Keats*, ed. E. H. Rollins, I, p. 238, cited in 'Gray in his Letters', *op cit.*, p. 29.
15 ibid.
16 See e.g. Gustave Lanson's *Choix de Lettres du XVIIIe siècle*. Paris, 1929.
17 'Gray in his Letters', *op. cit.*, p. 35.

CHAPTER 4

1 References: Austin Dobson, 'Gray's Library', in *Eighteenth-Century Vignettes*, First Series, London, 1829, pp. 129-39 (I am indebted to my wife for referring me to this essay); Norton Nicholls's *Reminiscences of Gray* in *Corr.*, III, pp. 1288-1303; W. Powell Jones, *Thomas Gray, Scholar*. Cambridge, Mass., 1937; G. Whalley, 'A Quiet Hellenist', in *Fearful Joy*, 1974, pp. 146-71.
2 Dobson, p. 132.
3 Dobson, p. 133.
4 Inspired by *The Battle of the Books*, according to Dr Ian Jack.
5 December, 1738, *Corr.*, I, pp. 93-4.
6 See the translation by C. D. Yonge, London, 1854, 3 vols; and E. A. Herbodeau, *Etude et Commentaire . . . d'Athénée*, London, 1933. M. Herbodeau includes attractive verse translations of the verses quoted by Athenaeus.
7 *Corr.*, III, p. 1158 (Letter of 26 January 1771).
8 Garrick's interpretation of 'The Bard' as a call 'to wake slumbering virtue in the Briton's heart', implies a patriotic fervour in Gray difficult to accept.
9 In his review of the odes in the *Monthly Review* for September 1757, Goldsmith thought it a pity that Gray should have addressed only a minority of readers familiar with Greek, and especially Pindaric poetry. 'We must be historians and learned men before we can understand [Gray's odes]', was his private opinion.

10 G. Whalley, 'A Quiet Hellenist', *op. cit.*, p. 51.
11 'Gray in his Letters', in *Fearful Joy*, p. 31.

CHAPTER 5

1 References: The *Correspondence*; Norton Nicholls's *Reminiscences of Gray*; H. W. Starr, *Gray as a Literary Critic*, Philadelphia, 1941.
2 This was exemplified in a recent production at the Edinburgh Festival, where Oedipus comes on to the stage with his eyes painted a horrific red, which was either unpleasant or ludicrous, according to the viewpoint.
3 There is a sarcastic description in one of his letters of an actor overplaying his part.
4 Or so it has been asserted.
5 Letter to West, 1 April 1742.
6 There is even an echo of it in Arnold's 'Stanzas in memory of . . . Obermann':

> . . . that much loved inland sea,
> The ripples of whose blue waves cheer
> Vevey and Meillerie.

7 Rousseau quotes both Petrarch and Metastasio in the *Héloïse*.
8 Chaucer, e.g., could rhyme 'corages' and 'pilgrimages', words which would not rhyme today.
9 See Robert Bridges, *Milton's Prosody*.
10 cf. Longfellow's 'Life is/but an/empty/dream'.

CHAPTER 6

1 References: *The Correspondence*; the Note-Books; Nicholls's *Reminiscences*; C. E. Norton, *The Poet Gray as a Naturalist*, Boston, 1903.
2 *Corr.*, II, p. 725.
3 Letter of 28 December 1767, *Corr.*, III, p. 988.
4 I owe these details to Dr C. W. Gibby.
5 C. E. Norton, op. cit., cited by K.-C., p. 213.
6 Gray's interleaved Linnaeus later came into the possession of Ruskin.
7 C. E. Norton, op. cit., pp. 16–17.
8 Note the last line of the satire on Lord Holland's seat near Ramsgate. Gray liked to have his rooms fragrant with the smell of sweet-scented flowers.

CHAPTER 7

1 'Rien ne vaut dans cette vie-ci que l'occupation et le travail.' This saying of Bonstetten's (caught from Gray) is copied out repeatedly in Matthew Arnold's Diaries. Arnold found it at second hand in Sainte-Beuve's *Causerie* of 1860 (Vol. XIV), where Sainte-Beuve quotes from Bonstetten's then unpublished *Correspondence* (see *Matthew Arnold and France*, by I. Lytton Sells, 1970 edition, p. 324).
2 Beginning with an income of about £400 a year, bequeathed to him by Sarah Gray, he acquired more by the death of his mother and of Mary Antrobus, and a further £400 when he became professor.

3 *Life of Johnson*, ed. G. B. Hill, revised by L. F. Powell, Oxford, 1934, II, p. 327.
4 Leslie Stephen, in *D.N.B.* XXIII, says that he did not dine in Hall. But he was doing so on the day he was taken ill, and had to be helped back to his room. This article (which perpetuates the legend that he climbed down the rope-ladder and fell into a tub of water) is not very reliable factually.
5 Leslie Stephen in *D.N.B.*, XXI, p. 251.
6 The others were Anthony Hamilton and the Abbé Galiani.
7 *D.N.B.*, XXI, p. 253.
8 Reed Browning, *The Duke of Newcastle*, Yale Univ. Press, 1975. Gray is said to have written a satire on 'Newcastle going to Hanover', which has never been published; Mason probably destroyed it. Gray described Newcastle as 'the Owl Phobus'.
9 Letter to Wharton, 5 August 1763, No. 373, *Corr.*, II, p. 806.
10 'Reminiscences', reprinted in *Corr.*, III, Appendix Z, p. 1289. Nicholls adds that Gray thought Hume had been refuted by Beattie. Most people today, including sincere believers, would not agree that Beattie was a match for Hume. There is no evidence that Gray had studied Pascal, whose apologia for Christianity was a source of recurring disquiet to Voltaire.
11 *Memoirs*, p. 186, cited by Ian Jack in 'Gray in his Letters', in *Fearful Joy*, p. 31.
12 See *Corr.*, III, p. 1291.
13 Letter of A. H. Clough to W. Allingham, 25 January 1855.
14 *Boswell's London Journal; 1762–1763*. London, 1950, pp. 282–3.
15 *Edinburgh Review*, XXXI, p. 83.
16 On 'Style', in *Appreciations*, p. 18.
17 London, 1879; 1926 edn, III, pp. 94–129.
18 *A Short History of English Literature*, London, 1898; 1919 edn, pp. 575–7. Gosse and Cazamian both see a fresher lyrical vein in Collins.
19 D. C. Tovey, in *Encyclopaedia Britannica*, X, p. 670.

APPENDIX

1 See above, p. 193.
2 Compare Matthew Arnold's view that it is only an accessory. In the Preface to the 1851 edition of his *Poems* he pointed to the danger of lesser poets imitating Shakespeare's language, whilst failing to attain to his inventiveness and skill in delineation of character. It is probable that Arnold had read Gray's comments, and adapted them to his own use.
3 In his later letter to Beattie, of 8 March 1771.
4 Apart from the use of rhyme, he seems to have felt obliged to write in a classical manner. He was not, of course, alone in this addiction.
   Poetic licence permits unusual word arrangements, but only as a rule for emphasis, or the formal requirements of the verse.
5 *Le Bourgeois Gentilhomme*, Act II, scene i.
6 I owe the above references to Professor Townend, of Durham University, who supplied the specific quotations. Matthew Arnold's use of the term had impressed me first, and led to my notice of its repeated use by Gray. It was obviously a classical allusion.
7 One uses this phrase perforce, as the 'whole tissue of his poetry', according to Leslie Stephen, amounts to little more than an assembling of 'previously manufactured material'.

8 But Wordsworth's imitation of the 'Adversity Ode' is surely in the nature of a parody, even though Russell Lowell describes it (the 'Ode to Duty') as 'incomparable'. Matthew Arnold's 'Progress of Poesy' reads rather like a wry comment (rather than a 'variation', as he calls it). The allusion must be to Gray's poem, as he particularly singles it out for praise in his *Essay*.

9 That is, he objectifies inanimate objects as though they were living, and a metaphor may follow, as 'Fair Science frowned not on his humble birth/And Melancholy mark'd him for her own'; c.f. 'God mark'd him for His own' (I. Walton).

10 By Shelley's definition, 'A Long Story' could not be classified as poetry, as it consists only of a 'certain combination of events which can never occur again', whereas a poem must 'express or imply a universal truth'.

11 There is a three-tiered metonymy in his use of 'shell' for 'lyre', and 'lyre' for the spirit of lyric poetry.

12 Modern tribal harps still use a tortoise-shell.

13 The use of the epithet 'Aeolian' for the wind-stirred harp derives from Aeolus, the wind-god. The epithet in the 'Aeolian lyre' is used by Gray to symbolise lyric poetry, i.e. the poetry of the *Aeolian* Greeks (Sappho, Alcaeus, etc.), as opposed to epic and dramatic verse.

14 Yet Gray himself elsewhere translates Pindar as saying that even the *lyre* is used '*only* to sound the first note of the preludes that precede the dance'. According to the late Professor Jebb, the Aeolian ode was at first not accompanied by any instrument, but was meant to be sung by a single voice; the Dorian lyric was sung by a chorus, executing a movement to the right (in the strophe), to the left (in the anti-strophe), and remaining stationary in the epode. In Pindar's choral dance-songs, the words were accompanied by a lively dance. In his odes, the music was of different characters to suit the occasion. Although he grew up in Aeolian land, he had Dorian blood and the art of flute playing was hereditary in his house. If Gray's quotation is correct, Pindar evidently brought in a flute or pipes, as well as the lyre, for certain odes. The total effect of words, music, dance, and all the scenic accessories of light and colour must have been far removed from Gray's attempted reproduction. The pipe (flute) and tabor are traditional accompaniments of the dance, still used for the English Morris dance and the French *farandole*; as the ancient shawm, an oboe, still leads the band for the charming Catalan *sardane*. The *aulos*, in skilful hands, could provide ingenious rhythmic counterpoint.

15 Another synecdoche, for 'dances'.

16 'Full many a flower', in the next line, is followed correctly by a singular verb, 'is born', etc.; but later, in line 84, Gray is himself confused and uses a plural verb after this construction, writing 'many a holy text . . . *teach* the rustic moralist to die' (how to die?).

   Gray's grammar is not impeccable, as when he makes the turf actively 'heave over many a mould'ring heap'. Johnson considered these expressions the result of affectation and exhibitionism.

17 'Woeful wan' is another instance of alliteration. It is presumably a compound of two adjectives formed on the analogy of 'red hot', 'bright blue', etc. The more usual rule for enlarging the vocabulary in this way is to combine an adjective (or an adverb) with a participle, as 'hard-won'. 'Straw-built', another of Gray's expressions, combines a noun with a participle quite normally. But here the *meaning* is in question; he surely meant 'straw-roof'd' or 'well-thatched'. One fears a need to fill out the verse here.

18 In line with this attitude, one recalls that in his letters he likes to spell the

pronoun 'I' with a small letter (a practice still affected by certain writers).

19 As in the Elegy. This poem is so different from the rest, despite a due sprinkling of oddities, as to provoke the thought that it seems written by another hand.

20 Donald Greene, in *Fearful Joy*, p. 100.

Bibliography

Arnold, Matthew, 'Gray', in *Essays in Criticism*, Second Series, London, 1888.

Attwater, A., *Pembroke College, Cambridge: A Short History*, Cambridge, 1936.

Bonstetten, C.-V. de, *Souvenirs écrits en 1831*, Paris, 1831.

Boswell, J., *The Life of Samuel Johnson* (3 vols) Oxford, 1934–60.

Boswell, J., *Boswell's London Journal, 1762–63*, London, 1950.

Browning, Reed, *The Duke of Newcastle*, New Haven, Yale U.P., 1975.

Cecil, Lord David, *Two Quiet Lives*, London, 1948.

Dobson, Austin, 'Gray's Library', in *Eighteenth Century Vignettes*, London, 1892–4–6.

Downey, J. and Jones, B. (eds), *Fearful Joy*, Montreal, London, 1974.

Downs, B. W., *Cambridge Past and Present*, London, 1926.

Evans, The Rev. Evan, *Some Specimens of the Poetry of the Antient Welsh Bards*, 1764.

Golden, M., *Thomas Gray*, New York, 1964.

Gosse, E., *Gray*, London, 1882.

Herking, M.-L., *Charles-Victor de Bonstetten: sa vie, ses œuvres*, Lausanne, 1921.

Johnson, Samuel, *Lives of the English Poets*, ed. G. B. Hill, 3 vols, Oxford, 1905.

Johnston, H., *Selected Poems of Thomas Gray*, London, 1967.

Jones, W. P., *Thomas Gray, Scholar*, Cambridge, Mass., Harvard U.P., 1937.

Ketton-Cremer, R. W., *Thomas Gray: A Biography*, Cambridge, 1955.

Lonsdale, Roger, 'The Poems of Gray and Johnson', in *Fearful Joy*, 1974.

Macdonald, Alastair, 'Gray and his Critics', in *Fearful Joy*, 1974.

Macpherson, J., 'Fingal' and 'Temora', 'translated from the Gaelic by a poet called Ossian', 1762 and 1763.

Martin, Roger, *Essai sur Thomas Gray*, Paris, 1934.

Martin, Roger, *Chronologie de la vie et de l'œuvre de Thomas Gray*, Paris, 1934.

Mason, William, *Memoirs of the Life and Writings of Mr Gray*, York, 1775.

Nicholls, Norton, *Reminiscences of Gray*, reprinted in the *Correspondence*, Vol III, Appendix.

Norton, Charles Eliot, *The Poet Gray as a Naturalist*, Boston, 1903.

Parker, R., *The Common Stream*, London, 1975.

Roberts, Sir S. C., *Thomas Gray of Pembroke*, Glasgow, 1952.

Sainte-Beuve, C.-A., 'Charles-Victor de Bonstetten', in *Causeries du Lundi*, Vol. XIV, Paris, n.d. first published 1860.

Smart, Christopher, 'Song to David', 1763.

Starr, H. W. and Hendrickson, J. R., *The Complete Poems*, Oxford, 1966.

Taylor, Irene, 'Two Eighteenth Century Illustrators of Gray', in *Fearful Joy*, 1974.

Tovey, Duncan C., *Gray and his Friends*, Cambridge, 1890.

Toynbee, Paget (ed.), *The Letters of Gray, Walpole, West and Ashton*, 2 vols, Oxford, 1915.

Toynbee, Paget, *Supplement to the Letters of Horace Walpole*, 3 vols, Oxford, 1918–25.

Toynbee, Mrs Paget, *The Letters of Horace Walpole*, 16 vols, Oxford, 1903–5.

Toynbee, Paget and Whibley, Leonard (eds), *The Correspondence of Thomas Gray*, 3 vols, Oxford, 1935.

Tuker, M. A. R., *Cambridge*, London, 1907.

Walpole, Horatio, *The Castle of Otranto*, 1764.

Winstanley, D. A., *Unreformed Cambridge*, Cambridge, 1935.

Index

aversion to marriage 5; at Eton 5ff.; education 6, 12, 14; at Cambridge University 7ff.; at Peterhouse College 7, 38, 46, 78; awarded Bible Clerkship and Cosin Scholarship 8; character 9; friendship with Walpole 9, 10; and West 12-37 *passim*; at Inner Temple 12; inherits property 12; on degrees 14, 15; disinclined to academic life 16; reads love studies 16; writes tripos-verses 18; in Europe with Walpole 20-35; quarrels with Walpole 32, 33; reconciliation 32, 33, 44, 220; financial trouble 34; discontented with England 35; death of father 35; opinion of French writers 36, 236; compiles Commonplace Book 37; professorship 41; Bachelor of Civil Law 43; religious views 44; publishes poems 45; at Stoke Poges 46, 55, 60-1, 73, 82, 84, 90, 93; sends poems to Walpole 46, 47; and West's writings 48; opinion of Smart 50; complains of Whalley and Etough 51; satirist 51; studies Greek writings 52; on Aristotle 52; loss of Cornhill house 53; portraits 5, 54, 55, 66, 108; on Walpole's escape from death 58; on publication of 'Elegy' 62-3; 'Six Poems' 64-9; poem to Bentley 68; affected by mother's death 68; recognition of, 68; offered and declines Poet Laureateship 69; professorship 69; assists Walpole with history 69, 74, 220, 221; illhealth of 70, 74, 75, 77, 87, 92, 247; at Durham, 70-3; at York 73, 106, 112; studies Welsh history 24, 75, 95, 97, 100, 241; moves to Pembroke Hall 80; encourages Mason 83; studies Old Norse poetry 83, 95, 100; odes published 84, 85; natural history interest 92, 93, 99, 115; and Henrietta Speed 89ff.; legacy 91; left ring by Lady Cobham 95; on Sterne's work 98; studies Icelandic poetry 100; and Thomas Percy 102; at coronation of George III 102; praises Walpole's book 104; and Algarotti 107; writes Mason on marriage 107-8; tour of, 108; operation 110;

criticises Voltaire and Rousseau 112; at Old Park 113, 114, 117, 118; at Glamis and Holyrood House 113, 222; tours Highlands 114, 222; declines degree 114; in Kent 115, 122, 222; in Suffolk 114, 222; in Norfolk 116; condoles with Mason 116; tour with Brown 117; tour of Lakes 117, 128-30, 222-3; writes burlesque instructions for new edition of poems 119; conception of poetry 120; replies to Walpole's accusation 122; on Lord Holland 123; offered professorship 123-4; attends levée at palace 124; proposals for duties 125-6; installation ode for Grafton 126; affection for Bonstetter 131ff.; helps Temple 139; in North Wales 139f.; ill 141, 142; on Dr Long's burial 142; advises Nicholls 143-4; declines visit to Bonstetter 144; on Voltaire 144-5; death of 145; will of 145; works 147-224

WORKS: *English:*
'Agrippina' 47, 234, 257, 261, 262
'Alliance of Education and Government, The' 182, 203, 204, 249, 263
'Bard, The' 75-87 *passim*, 100, 186-96 *passim*, 239, 249, 253, 262
'Descent of Odin, The' 100, 101, 199, 240, 249
Designs by Mr R. Bentley for Six Poems 183
'Elegy written in a Country Churchyard' 55-69 *passim*, 113, 171-82 *passim*, 187, 218, 238, 246, 249, 250, 251, 259, 261, 262, 280, 284
'Epitaph' for 172, 173, 174, 175, 181
'Hymn to Adversity' 64, 67
'Nature's Darling' 75
'Ode in the Greek Manner' (The Progress of Poesy) 69, 74, 75
'Ode on a distant prospect of Eton College' 166, 253, 259, 262
'Ode on the death of a Cat drowned in a tub of Gold fishes' 165, 170-1, 183, 262, 263
'Ode on the Spring' 59, 156, 164, 165, 241, 258, 263
'Ode to Adversity' 168-9, 239, 258, 283
'Ode to Music', Installation ode 127, 205-7, 261, 264, 265